The Self-Help Myth

POVERTY, INTERRUPTED

EDITORS

*Ananya Roy, Luskin School of Public Affairs,
University of California, Los Angeles*

*Clare Talwalker, International and Area Studies,
University of California, Berkeley*

EDITORIAL BOARD

*Vincanne Adams, Medical Anthropology, University of California,
San Francisco*

*Alain de Janvry, Agricultural and Resource Economics, University of
California, Berkeley*

Victoria Lawson, Geography, University of Washington, Seattle

Bill Maurer, Anthropology, University of California, Irvine

Raka Ray, Sociology, University of California, Berkeley

Eric Sheppard, Geography, University of California, Los Angeles

*Laura Tyson, Business Administration and Economics, University of
California, Berkeley*

Poverty, Interrupted serves as a platform for public scholarship on poverty, inequality, and poverty action. Launched at a historical moment of acute inequalities across and within the global North and global South, the series foregrounds research, analysis, and theory that interrupt mainstream frames of wealth and poverty. In doing so, it presents established and emerging scholars and activists with new pedagogies and practices of inhabiting and transforming an unequal world, while at the same time interrogating how poverty has emerged as the dominant analytic for reflecting on social differences.

The Self-Help Myth

How Philanthropy Fails to
Alleviate Poverty

Erica Kohl-Arenas

UNIVERSITY OF CALIFORNIA PRESS

University of California Press, one of the most distinguished university presses in the United States, enriches lives around the world by advancing scholarship in the humanities, social sciences, and natural sciences. Its activities are supported by the UC Press Foundation and by philanthropic contributions from individuals and institutions. For more information, visit www.ucpress.edu.

University of California Press
Oakland, California

Library of Congress Cataloging-in-Publication Data

Kohl-Arenas, Erica, 1968- author.
   The self-help myth : how philanthropy fails to alleviate poverty / Erica Kohl-Arenas.
      pages cm. — (Poverty, Interrupted ; 1)
   How philanthropy fails to alleviate poverty
   Includes bibliographical references and index.
   ISBN 978-0-520-28343-5 (cloth : alk. paper) — ISBN 0-520-28343-0 (cloth : alk. paper) — ISBN 978-0-520-28344-2 (pbk. : alk. paper) — ISBN 0-520-28344-9 (pbk. : alk. paper) — ISBN 978-0-520-95929-3 (ebook) — ISBN 0-520-95929-9 (ebook)
     1. Farmers—California—Central Valley (Valley) 2. Charities—California—Central Valley (Valley)—Case studies. 3. Poverty—California—Central Valley (Valley) 4. Immigrants—California—Central Valley (Valley) 5. California—Economic conditions—20th century. 6. California—Economic conditions—21st century. I. Title. II. Title: How philanthropy fails to alleviate poverty.
   HD8039.F32U64845 2015
   362.5´57097945—dc23   2015018715

Manufactured in the United States of America

25 24 23 22 21 20 19 18 17 16
10 9 8 7 6 5 4 3 2 1

My father, Herb, has always encouraged me to speak my heart, to write about complex problems plainly, and to chart my own path as a scholar, teacher, and organizer. A lifelong storyteller, intellectual, and provocateur, he is my most valued reader. I dedicate this book to him.

CONTENTS

PREFACE

In the fall of 1989 I moved to Ivanhoe, Virginia, to live and work with Maxine Waller, a charismatic woman caught up in the struggle to save her deindustrializing coal-mining town. Alerted to the proposed sale of Ivanhoe's industrial land, Maxine, the wife of a former coalminer, launched a campaign to prevent the sale. She initially hoped that, if saved, the town might attract new industry. Raised in the culture of a "company town," many miners believed that the land would be sold because they did not work hard enough, that "better" workers elsewhere had induced Big Coal and Union Carbide to move. Despite their original doubts, a cadre of local women joined Maxine, prevented the sale of the land, and embarked on an educational and organizing campaign to plan for the redevelopment of Ivanhoe.

I was changed by this brilliant, rebellious woman and by a community that pulled together to analyze a complex situation, altering a story that told them to be guilty agents in their own demise. As a participant in Ivanhoe's people's economics classes, I saw locals begin to understand the global economy and their place in the world around them, becoming active participants in planning for a future they shared. Coal miners and their wives studied and received high school diplomas, a group of women organized feminist Bible studies classes, micro-enterprises were formed, and a local history book was published. The Ivanhoe Civic League was incorporated to identify future community development problems and plans and to support local families in need. All of these things happened on the townspeople's own terms.

Living and working in Ivanhoe made me passionate about adult education and the potential for organizing that is directed by poor people and not defined by outside agencies, institutions, or industries. Through Ivanhoe, and through their and my mentors Helen Lewis and Myles Horton at the Highlander Research and Education Center in Tennessee, I learned that the most revolutionary and potentially lasting change comes from the people.

Perhaps I already knew this based on my parents' involvement in the social movements of the 1960s and 1970s. I remember participating as a small child in the consumer boycott organized by the California farmworker movement. My mother and father frequently took my brother, sister, and me to the picket lines outside a Berkeley, California, Lucky's grocery store, maybe in 1976. I was about eight, the age my daughter is now, and I remember overwhelming feelings of solidarity as we protested alongside the farmworkers who were hurt by the low wages and chemicals used to produce the grapes that Lucky's sold. I also remember sitting on a bale of hay at a farmworker rally at the Merced County Fairgrounds in Los Banos, in the Central Valley, entranced by the courageous college students who had joined the movement. The songs, chants, and collective energy moved me to believe that anything is possible when people come together with strength and courage.

Alongside the farmworker movement, I grew up around phrases like *freedom, equality, power to the people, feminism, brown power, civil rights,* and *social justice.* I also grew up understanding defeat and the collective realization of the era that ideas alone cannot necessarily change the world—I was born the year that Martin Luther King Jr. and Robert Kennedy were shot. I remember the challenges my parents faced in their struggles to make the public school system more equitable for all children in the 1970s, the tragic losses for progressive school reformers during the 1980s, and the personal and emotional tolls these defeats sometimes took.

Since these formative experiences, with the exception of the Occupy Wall Street and #BlackLivesMatter movements, I have not come across another community development or organizing project so self-directed, so willing to take risks, and most of all, so unconcerned with the constant chase for private foundation funding. Through my own community development and popular education work and subsequent doctoral research at the University of California, Berkeley, I became increasingly critical of programs and initiatives that espouse "grass-roots," "bottom-up," or "empowerment" approaches to social change yet are led by elite institutions fearful of taking on the issues that poor people struggle with, such as industrial abandonment, below-living-wage jobs, vast educational inequalities along race and class lines, racial profiling and police brutality, and the marginalization of poor and immigrant workers.

Throughout the 1990s I observed how the specific facilitation methods, techniques, and terminology of popular education and community organizing I learned through the Highlander Center, and practiced with a variety of grass-roots organizations, were translated into benign "best practices" for forming partnerships with businesses and mainstream stakeholders. As a fellow with the Coro Foundation and the Sustainable Communities Leadership Program, I was trained in "participatory" or "facilitative" leadership using texts written by corporate management gurus including Peter Drucker and Tom Peters. Other examples include Kouzes and Posner's *The Leadership Challenge*,[1] which spells out how to be an effective leader by "challenging the process," "inspiring a shared vision," and "enabling others to act"; Bennis's *Organizing Genius*;[2] and Henton's *Grassroots Leaders for a New Economy*.[3] I was frustrated with these texts because they were popularly presented as "innovative" yet appeared to me as an appropriation and depoliticization of the popular education and organizing approaches that I was familiar with.

At the time, I only partially understood that the trend of engaging communities in a broad array of ill-defined "civic engagement" or "participatory" initiatives represented broader political and economic shifts. During the neoliberal restructuring of the late 1980s and early 1990s, welfare reform and shrinking public budgets placed new responsibilities on volunteers and nonprofit institutions. "Participatory" programs became a popular response to neoliberal reforms at home, and to the structural adjustment programs facilitated by the World Bank and international development agencies in the global South.[4] I clearly remember asking my colleagues, "Civic engagement for what?" and naively pushing the limits of projects not designed to take on the root causes of the problems they claimed to address. I later coached groups to *not* take a participatory approach unless they really wanted to act upon what people had to say.

While working alongside farmworker and immigrant rights organizers in the Central Valley I learned how these trends played out for the California farmworker movement. In keeping with the civil rights struggles across the country, many organizers and leaders were incorporated into the Central Valley's War on Poverty–era Community Action Programs. Others later formed their own 501(c)(3) organizations to qualify for federal funding (per the 1986 Immigration Reform and Control Act) of citizenship adult education services. Today old-time organizers, originally motivated by a movement to gain labor rights and confront the abuses of large agricultural producers, are keenly aware of what has been lost as they develop nonthreatening service or "civic participation" programs in keeping with current funding priorities.

I also came to understand that the struggle over community-based or grass-roots organizing is never fully owned either by those "in the struggle" or those "in power," and that the lines between them are sometimes blurred. The drafters of the War on Poverty did not all have intentions of governmental control when designing and funding the largest pro-poor public program in the United States since the Great Depression. Social movement leaders and community organizers do not always hold unified visions or pure strategies of uncorrupted social change. Foundation staff, inspired by ideas of pluralist civic participation, do not always have agendas of co-optation.

The personal moments touched on in this preface inform my approach as a teacher, researcher, scholar, and practitioner. They provide a context for understanding the central themes of self-help versus self-determination, participatory democracy, social movements, and processes of professionalization and institutionalization that drive this project. Despite the troubling philanthropic relationships described in this book, I remain committed to the liberatory pedagogy that so changed my life in Appalachia, and that I continue to practice. Thus, my scholarship and my teaching at The New School's Milano School of International

Affairs, Management, and Urban Policy sits at the sometimes contradictory intersection of engaging and critiquing the pedagogy of participatory, community-based self-help. I straddle what Ananya Roy has eloquently called the "space between the hubris of benevolence and the paralysis of cynicism."[5]

The case studies featured in this book are based on two years of archival and ethnographic research. The first case study, featured in chapter 2, focuses on the relationship between private funders and the California farmworker movement and is based on archival research and individual interviews. I investigated archived foundation reports and other archives of the United Farm Workers of America in the Walter P. Reuther Library at Wayne State University in Detroit, and at the Dolph Briscoe Center for American History at the University of Texas at Austin. In addition, I benefitted from oral histories and archived materials in the Bancroft Library at the University of California, Berkeley, and I interviewed historic movement leaders, including Dolores Huerta and staff in leadership positions at nonprofit movement institutions.

Research for the case studies featured in chapters 3 and 4 include three primary methods: open-ended individual interviews, participant observation, and analysis of professional program materials. Between 2007 and 2009 I interviewed more than eighty foundation program officers, consultants, and organizational staff currently working on farmworker and immigrant projects in the Central Valley region, and elsewhere in California. I also attended many foundation network gatherings, collaborative meetings, and training sessions associated with the specific projects studied.

The names of all individuals, organizations, and initiatives featured in chapters 3 and 4 are disguised. While most interviewees eagerly discussed their work, many expressed frustration with the inability to talk openly about the politics of funding in their organizations and networks. Many feared losing their favored status in regional funding initiatives, and others worried that speaking out might put their expected individual grant renewals at risk. Therefore, names of individuals and organizations are disguised to ensure that the grants secured by organizations and the jobs held by these generous individuals are not put at risk.

ACKNOWLEDGMENTS

Many generous people and organizations contributed to this project. First, I am grateful to my Social and Cultural Studies doctoral cohort at UC Berkeley, and professors Gillian Hart and Carol Stack, who guided me in the initial stages of shaping this research project. I gained excellent feedback on an early version of the manuscript from Harley Shaiken, John Hurst, and Ananya Roy. My research assistants at The New School, Johanna Taylor and Elizabeth Cuccaro, provided substantial support for which I am also grateful. I would also like to thank Linn Posey-Maddox, Kathryn Moeller, Robin Hayes, and Antina von Schnitzler for reading and providing excellent feedback on chapter drafts. Colleagues at The New School who approved my sabbatical to finish this book are also enormously appreciated. Abigail Kramer, Tracy Connor, and Beth Graham Ingram contributed their copyediting expertise.

If anyone is a better jargon detector than my father, Herb Kohl, whom I also thank, it is Naomi Schneider at UC Press. It has been an honor and a privilege to produce this book with her.

I would also like to thank the editors, Ananya Roy and Clare Tal-walker, and the initially blind peer reviewers, Alyosha Goldstein, Vincanne Adams, and Kathryn Mitchel, of the "Poverty, Inter-rupted" series of University of California Press. I believe that their critical feedback made this a better book. The production team at University of California Press, including Ally Power, Francisco Reinking, and Roy Sablosky, are also greatly appreciated.

Important mentors outside the university include Craig McGarvey, Myrna Martinez-Nateras, and Dr. Helen Lewis. Craig's honest struggle with the power imbalance inherent in philanthropic giving was the window through which I entered this project. Myrna, a long-time popular educator in immigrant communities in the Central Valley, provided significant insight. She also opened her home to my daughter and me as we trav-elled up and down the valley. I am grateful for Myrna and Edu-ardo's generosity, hours of conversation, and continual encour-agement. I found my life role model in Helen Lewis, a skillful popular educator and Appalachian scholar. Helen taught me to embrace the joys and the contradictions that come with working between scholarship and practice.

I would also like to thank the people whom I interviewed, shadowed, or met as a part of this project. Hopefully my writing will help to communicate the inequitable and often tenuous relationship between small community action organizations and private foundations, which many find difficult to publically speak of due to the risk of losing their funding or their jobs. The foundation and nonprofit professionals interviewed are the real narrators of this story, and their combined wisdom is, I hope, found in these pages.

This research was made possible by fellowships from the Spencer Foundation, the Social and Cultural Studies program of the UC Berkeley Graduate School of Education, the Institute for the Study of Social Change, and the Labor and Employment Research Fund at the UC Office of the President. I would also like to thank the helpful archivists at the University of California's Bancroft Library, the United Farm Workers of America archives at the Walter P. Reuther Library at Wayne State University, and the Dolph Briscoe Center for American History at the University of Texas at Austin.

And finally, thank you, Jose and Emilia, for your patience and love. Jose, your understanding of the creative process—of uncovering meaning by getting one's hands dirty—kept me engaged along the way. And thank you for the beautiful book cover artwork.

CHAPTER ONE

Private Philanthropy and the Self-Help Myth

Foundations are bizarre beasts. They are created to
solve societal problems by using inordinate amounts
of wealth—wealth that is inherently contradictory
because it was gleaned out of the inequalities that it
proposes to address.

*Author interview with a foundation program officer, San
Francisco, California, 2009*

At a Hilton Hotel in Chicago, Illinois, dessert and coffee were
served as the opening luncheon plenary of the 2013 annual conference of the Council on Foundations commenced.[1] On a raised
stage in front of a packed room of philanthropy professionals,
Ellen Alberding, president of the Joyce Foundation, introduced
the panel, "A National Dialogue on Healthy and Safe Communities." The lunching crowd chatted over her welcome. Only as
youthful James Anderson, raised in a poor Chicago neighborhood,
stood up to speak was full attention drawn to the stage. Anderson
captivated the room with his story of a triumphant journey out
of poverty, abandonment, and abuse at the hands of his father.
"No one cared about me," he told us. After years of isolation and

loneliness he joined a gang and got hooked on meth. Eventually he found himself in prison. Then, one day, someone from the Wellness Foundation approached him. Being invited to participate in the Anti-Recidivism Coalition was all Anderson needed. He finally found the will to pull it together because someone gave him reason to believe in himself. To rousing applause, and tears in the eyes of the women seated at my table (including me), Anderson concluded: "One person can change a life."

I attended the Council on Foundations conference as an ethnographic researcher interested in the response of private foundations to deepening poverty and inequality in the United States. As I listened to James Anderson's rousing speech, a woman maybe forty-five or fifty years old, with the name Paulina embroidered on her server uniform, carried a large tray to our table. Visibly straining, sweat on her brow, Paulina lowered fifteen plates of grilled chicken, potatoes, and broccoli rabe to her serving stool. I was struck with the contradiction of the buoyant professionals gathered to celebrate their work to alleviate poverty, while being served by some of the poorest people in the United States: food-industry workers. I was also struck by how throughout the course of the three-day conference most panels included a real-life tragedy-turned-victory story of individuals like Anderson who had pulled themselves out of poverty.

These moments provide a window into the philanthropic trend of asking the poor to help themselves, while avoiding the structural causes of poverty and inequality. At the heart of the self-help approach is the enduring belief that entrenched poverty is the result of social and economic isolation that has trapped poor people within a culture of poverty marked by hopelessness and self-harming behaviors. This belief corresponds with the argument that poverty can only be interrupted when individual poor people take responsibility for changing the way they act.[2] Questions of unequal opportunities, histories of exclusion, profiling along the lines of race, gender, class, and legal status, and capitalist economies that produce wealth for a few and poverty for many are most commonly avoided. The mainstream self-help narrative also fails to recognize that success stories are often made possible by an ongoing social infrastructure of aid, including public assistance programs and institutions, family networks, and private charity. James Anderson, for example, did not help himself alone. He was provided with a support system and resources as a youth coordinator with the Wellness Foundation's Anti-Recidivism Coalition.

Over the past thirty years, the self-help approach to poverty alleviation has gained new ground in economically struggling urban centers and rural regions in the United States and the global South.[3] In the United States, the "trickle-down economics" and anti-state policies initiated by Ronald Reagan's administration (1981–1989) included significant cuts to the upper tax brackets and a three-decade trend of trade liberalization, a shrinking public sector, wage stagnation, increase in part-time and low-wage jobs, and expanding inequality.[4] With the conservative attack on the Great Society programs of the War on Poverty, the idea that the individual poor person, not the state, is responsible for helping themselves out of poverty became increasingly popular ideology.[5] During this time the unions, public institutions and programs, and grass-roots groups that organize and advocate for poor people have suffered declining resources and legitimacy. In some cases they have bureaucratized and professionalized in ways that fail to serve the needs of the new working poor.[6] In the same thirty years, these trends allowed private wealth for the top 1 percent of the population and in the philanthropic sector to rapidly expand.[7] In many regions public programs were replaced by privately funded nonprofit organizations that serve poor and marginalized communities.[8]

Yet, have these private investments changed the conditions of poverty or helped the people they claim to serve? This book shows how private foundations maintain systems of inequality by funding individualistic programs that appear to address poverty but that in practice often avoid the root causes of the problems foundations propose to solve. For the people in this book—social movement leaders and nonprofit organizational staff concerned with farmworker and immigrant poverty—the dominant self-help formula ultimately acceptable to foundations is particularly problematic. The poverty in California's Central Valley is not the result of the culture or behaviors of poor people. Instead, just as in resource-rich regions in the global South, poverty is produced through relationships of capital production, often hidden from sight, amidst great wealth. Beyond the main highways and thoroughfares that run up and down the Central Valley of California, many families struggle with food insecurity and poor health, and live in substandard homes, often with no heat or clean running water. This enduring poverty is produced and maintained through large-scale farming that relies on low-wage, labor-intensive seasonal fieldwork, high pesticide use, an entrenched labor contractor system, and unmonitored working conditions for the increasingly undocumented immigrants who produce profit for major agricultural and food retail conglomerates.

Today, poverty rates in the Central Valley are higher than those in postindustrial Appalachia and Detroit.[9] According to the 2012 US Census, three of the region's main metropolitan areas, Fresno, Bakersfield, and Modesto, rank among the poorest in the state and the nation.[10] Fresno County, which produces more than $6 billion per year in agricultural products, ranks as the second-most impoverished area in the nation. Recent journalistic reporting and ethnographic research confirm this seemingly permanent condition, documenting high unemployment, meager wages, widespread food insecurity, health disparities owing to heavy pesticide use and labor-intensive work, substandard housing conditions, and rampant discrimination against immigrants.[11] Indigenous Oaxacan migrants to the valley are the latest to suffer from persistent poverty produced through industrial agriculture.[12]

The case studies featured in this book capture critical historical moments when private foundations attempted to address migrant poverty in the Central Valley region. In each instance philanthropic investments obscured the real stakes involved by asking farmworkers to "help themselves" while silencing stories of the enduring abuses of industrial agriculture. The archival and ethnographic case studies featured in this book, from philanthropic investments in farmworker leadership development leading up to the historic farmworker movement, to the large-scale, foundation-driven initiatives of the 1990s and 2000s, show how foundations fail to address poverty and inequality by setting firm boundaries around definitions of self-help. Limits are most often set on labor organizing, strikes, boycotts, immigrant rights, and advocacy approaches that hold industry accountable for the enduring abuses of farmworkers and immigrants.

However, unlike much of the critical philanthropy literature, which focuses on the successful implementation of straightforward capitalist agendas among major private foundations, the following cases show how foundation investments are actively contested and negotiated. The stories told by social movement leaders, nonprofit organizational professionals, and even foundation staff reveal that the self-help framework dominant in philanthropic circles is not always clear or fully accepted but is rather diversely interpreted and actively negotiated.[13] Sometimes funding frameworks come directly from poor people's movements and are purposefully adopted, changed, and co-opted by foundations. Occasionally, grass-roots groups attempt to co-opt ideas that come from the philanthropic sector. On rare occasions, the interests of funders and social movements align. Self-help can mean consciousness-raising, self-determination, and organizing against dominant power structures, as demonstrated in the people's education, food justice, and community service programs of the historic Black Power movement and the early years of the farmworker movement.[14] The long history of African American self-help in particular, from the industrial education of Booker T. Washington to the more radical politics of the Black Panthers, underscores a more transformative potential.[15] Like the Panthers, Cesar Chavez of the California farmworker movement initially activated the self-help model to build dignity, pride, and ownership in self-directed organizations to replace and challenge mainstream institutions not designed to serve farmworkers and disenfranchised immigrants in rural California.

Most critical scholarship on philanthropy does not show how foundation and nonprofit organizational staff struggle with these alternate understandings and contradictions. Instead of viewing foundations as closed systems adept at implementing clear-cut capitalist agendas, this book focuses on how power is maintained by sometimes well-intended foundation and nonprofit staff who negotiate, translate, and ultimately water down organizing agendas into benign self-help programs acceptable to foundation leadership and networks. When funding grass-roots poor people's movements, philanthropic power runs through the very process of forging agreements between greatly unequal partners such as wealthy funders and social movement leaders. Most frequently, acceptable translations of self-help fall into the spaces between bootstrap capitalism and radical self-determination. From the settlement house movement[16] of the Progressive Era, to the War on Poverty in the United States during the 1960s,[17] to current capitalist approaches to integrate the "bottom billion" into the global marketplace,[18] to recent efforts to train girls to become economic agents in fighting global poverty,[19] local leaders, activists, entrepreneurs, nonprofit professionals, and funders have attempted to reframe self-help agendas. Social movement leaders and community organizers who negotiate philanthropy have achieved important victories. More often, foundations set the terms of debate, attracting attention to the weaknesses, behaviors, and responsibilities of the poor and shifting the focus away from the social, political, and economic relationships of power that produce and maintain poverty.

In the cases featured in this book, foundation and organizational staff struggle to address migrant poverty in California's Central Valley, which is simultaneously one of the wealthiest agricultural production regions in the world and home to the poorest Californians. Compromises between foundation staff and social movement leaders, such as Cesar Chavez of the farmworker movement, and modern-day farmworker and immigrant organizers, in the end produce frameworks of poverty alleviation that exclude questions regarding the structural inequality produced through industrial agriculture. By translating an initially radical stance of "mutual aid" or self-determination elaborated by community organizers into nonthreatening self-help programs, foundations ensure that critique or confrontation of industry is avoided. Within these funding agreements and institutional arrangements a key contradiction of self-help philanthropy is revealed. Private foundation investments in self-help sometimes activate and even politicize the people engaged. Yet that politicization eventually upsets funders who find this politics threatening. When fearful of collective action or uprising, foundations reign in financial commitments and re-inscribe limits around what kind of self-help is acceptable. Eventually, the aspirations of grass-roots organizations are derailed by grant agreements that prescribe firm limits and make demands on the time, energy, and ideology of newly professionalized staff. The historical and ethnographic studies featured in the following pages reveal the contradictory impasses produced through foundation-funded self-help and participatory approaches to reducing poverty. Never completely foreclosed, privately funded movements are, as Piven and Cloward propose in their classic book *Poor People's Movements,* both constituted by and in resistance against bureaucratic institutional structures.[20]

Beyond limiting confrontation of an industry that produces geographic patterns of poverty, the philanthropic approach documented in this book alters the very nature of social change. Distracted and bogged down by professional management and partnership requirements, short-term foundation-funded programs replace the day-to-day engagement required to organize people in movement building.[21] In social movements that aim to create long-haul systemic change, community-based leaders, popular educators, and organizers build spaces where people's lived experiences are shared, analyzed, and crafted in concrete strategies to galvanize alliances against the dominant system and toward creating alternative futures.[22] This process of strategically articulating the concerns and creative visions of those the current system does not serve holds the seeds of fundamental change. Like the dominant self-help approach, it activates people beyond hopelessness, yet replaces competitive and individual mobility approaches with collective dignity, self-determination, and new cooperative ways of working and living. When foundation funding is introduced, resources are shifted away from the daily work of movement building and toward short-term grant deadlines and funding requirements. Inundated with program management, paperwork, and meetings to maintain philanthropic relationships, leaders and organizers become institutional professionals accountable to foundations and not to the people they claim to represent or serve.

The remainder of this chapter provides a framework for understanding the power of philanthropy; the history of American philanthropists' self-help approach in the twentieth century; and the geographical and political context for the archival and ethnographic case studies of philanthropic initiatives to address migrant poverty in California's Central Valley.

THE POWER OF PHILANTHROPY

The key role of private philanthropy in alleviating poverty has long been celebrated in the United States and is gaining popularity around the globe. From Andrew Carnegie's *Gospel of Wealth* (1889) to Bishop and Green's *Philanthrocapitalism: How the Rich Can Save the World* (2008), to the treatises of public figures such as Bill Clinton and Bill Gates, donors maintain that investing private wealth in research, programs, and (more recently) venture capital financing in impoverished regions is the best method for addressing the "poverty problem." But the proponents of philanthropy or "creative capitalism" as the solution to global poverty have a growing collection of critics. In 2007, an organization called INCITE! Women of Color Against Violence published *The Revolution Will Not Be Funded: Beyond the Non-Profit Industrial Complex.* In this book, scholars and activists document how an advanced "non-profit industrial complex"—representing a set of entrenched symbiotic relationships between the state and private funders—maintains relationships of power and fails to address issues of structural inequality. The studies featured in INCITE!'s publication show how the non-profit industrial complex monitors and controls social justice organizations, redirects activist energies into professionalized behaviors, and encourages social movements to model rather than challenge business and corporate practices. At the broad scale, these studies show how private foundations use public money and tax breaks to engage in ameliorative activities that mask exploitative capitalist work that creates poverty and inequality.

The Revolution Will Not Be Funded builds on a tradition of critical "Gramscian" philanthropy scholarship that suggests that the Big Three foundations (Carnegie, Rockefeller, and Ford) are central to maintaining Western capitalist imperialism in educational systems and foreign policy.[23] Drawing on the ideas of Italian cultural theorist Antonio Gramsci, these studies show how capitalist control is maintained not only through direct force but also through "cultural hegemony."[24] Cultural hegemony can be understood as a system of ideological power managed through a set of worldviews, such as the dominant self-help philosophy, imposed on poor and oppressed people. Cultural norms and values promoted by foundations become "hegemonic" when they appear to be natural "common sense," inevitable and even beneficial to everyone, though in reality they only preserve the status quo. In these studies, the focus of analysis is on how the Big Three generate popular consent by claiming to address the causes of systemic marginalization of human populations though, in reality, through ameliorative projects and thinly veiled capitalist ideology, they maintain the systems of power that generate the very problems they claim to address.[25]

A recent study in this tradition shows how the Bill and Melinda Gates Foundation and the Rockefeller Foundation, allegedly concerned with pressing food security problems in Sub-Saharan Africa, are in reality promoting dependency on genetically modified crops and enacting new forms of land privatization through partnerships with Cargill and Monsanto.[26] International activist groups, such as Via Campesina, condemn this trend as a massive land grab from poor farmers and a misappropriation of humanitarian investments for commercial ends.[27] In a similar vein, foundation investments in US public school reform have been shown to almost always advance privatization, choice, and competitive approaches that build market opportunities for private educational service providers while failing to improve outcomes for poor students.[28] Other studies document how in settings such as New Orleans, post-Katrina disaster recovery aid was turned into a for-profit endeavor through partnerships between nonprofit organizations, foundations, and private developers.[29] Even philanthropic insiders join the chorus. Most recently, Peter Buffett, son of billionaire philanthropist Warren Buffett, described the inability of foundations to address the causes of inequality as the curse of "philanthropic colonialism" in which boardrooms in the "charitable industrial complex" are populated by wealthy trustees, "searching for answers with their right hand to problems that others in the room have created with their left."[30]

Like this emerging body of critical scholarship, I found through my own research that seemingly benevolent program frameworks such as self-help, civic participation, and social capital; institutionalization of poor people's organizations; and professionalization of organizing staff weaken and redirect the work of nonprofit organizations that aim to address the structural causes of poverty and inequality. However, unlike much of the literature and popular punditry, I observed that control is not always represented in clear capitalist agendas or unified grand visions. Rather, the power of private philanthropy is a piecemeal process of adapting, negotiating, and eventually incorporating and neutralizing the leadership and strategies of radical social movements at different historical conjunctures.

The relationship between community organizers, movement leaders, and private funders in the Central Valley is akin to the rich historical accounts described by John Arena in his 2012 book, *Driven from New Orleans*. Arena's book, based on his own experiences as an activist and on detailed ethnographic research, shows how leading up to and throughout the neoliberal era of the past twenty years nonprofit organizations in New Orleans played a role in displacing communities and privatizing public housing. Tracing community-based struggles around public housing in New Orleans, from the post-segregation era to resistance around displacement in the 1980s, to the lost opportunities of the HOPE VI housing program, to redevelopment battles after the destruction wrought by Hurricane Katina, Arena shows how grass-roots activists are transformed into nonprofit officials. Although many heated battles arise (and continue), over time the professionalized activists working within nonprofit organizations abandoned direct action organizing in favor of insider negotiations with major institutions, including real estate and the political establishment. In the end, partnerships with nonprofits legitimated the actions of developers and politicians who needed their support but who did not serve the interests of the grass-roots base these nonprofit organizations claimed to represent.

This dynamic is subtler and less straightforward for the investments of foundations in the mostly rural Central Valley region and in a funding area such as agricultural poverty. Both are overshadowed by philanthropic investments in major cities and in sectors experiencing seismic reforms such as education, housing, and health care. For example, the case of the Immigrant Participation Collaborative (IPC)[31], the focus of chapter 3, shows how a diverse range of nonprofit leaders concerned with igniting immigrant rights organizing debated how to achieve their goals through a foundation-funded civic-participation initiative. The IPC's members knew—some, because of years of experience in the farmworker movement—how civic participation and self-help approaches to addressing poverty can either radically challenge or obscure enduring structures of inequality, depending on who sets the limits. They also knew they could "spin" their work to funders, despite what they hoped to achieve on the ground. Rather than being fully duped, appeased, or controlled, the IPC's grantees and the lead foundation program officer strategized around how to attract funding for community organizing projects from what they rightly identified as confrontation-shy "conservative" trustees. Yet, even as the nonprofit grantees attempted to strategically negotiate the grant-making process, participation in the foundation-driven collaborative ultimately distracted IPC members away from an authentic process of organizing immigrant and farmworker communities and constituents.

Another example of these negotiations, featured in chapter 2, examines debates between farmworker movement leader Cesar

Chavez and funders interested in supporting the movement. These parleys contributed to what several recent movement scholars identify as Chavez's move away from farm labor organizing and toward building professionalized staff and nonprofit organizations, which led to the demise of the movement.[32] However, a straightforward story of co-optation and control is insufficient because, although Chavez was angered by the unwillingness of private foundations to fund union organizing, he was conflicted by the union model. Trained in the Community Service Organization tradition of organizing religious congregations and neighborhoods into member-supported civic institutions, Chavez considered himself a unique union leader because he was not a "union man."[33] As recalled by a long-time farmworker organizer I interviewed, Chavez once asked an inner circle of UFW leaders, "Are we the oak tree or are we the mistletoe? Do we want to feed off of a strong and solid industry, like the mistletoe that grows on the oak? Do we want to set our limits around negotiating contracts? Or do we want to build a self-sustaining movement through our own institutions?"[34] Beyond unionization, Chavez was interested in building farmworker-led mutual aid organizations, creating new models of cooperative living, and promoting farm labor as a sustainable and respectable profession. Despite his frustration with foundations, Chavez eventually agreed with the Field Foundation to form private nonprofits, the first being the National Farm Worker Service Center. Yet according to the funders, they could not address issues in the economic sphere. In the end, the agreement to found nonprofit organizations initially met the needs of both funders and movement leaders but required theories of change and professionalized practices that precluded confrontation with industry.

Through my archival and ethnographic research, I observed how professional management requirements and tenuous agreements between funders and community-based institutions are the very mechanism by which strategies are redirected away from addressing the causes of poverty. Asking Central Valley farmworkers and immigrants, the poorest Californians, to agree on poverty action strategies alongside funders and the wealthiest agricultural producers in the world builds consensus around ways in which people can improve their own conditions and preserve the health of the agricultural industry. However, this agreement evades questions about the massive inequality maintained through agricultural production and regional abandonment. Differences, conflicts, and the political and economic stakes of the less powerful are thereby disguised, in the end generating consent. In other words, recalling cultural theorist Ernesto LaClau, "A class is hegemonic not so much to the extent that it is able to impose a uniform conception of the world on the rest of society, but to the extent that it can articulate different visions of the world in such a way that their political antagonism is neutralized."[35]

Beyond California's Central Valley, the power of self-help poverty action gained traction in the nonprofit and philanthropic sectors in the course of the twentieth century, as will be discussed in the following section. I then provide geographic and historical context for the studies featured in this book.

AMERICAN PHILANTHROPY AND THE SELF-HELP MYTH

California farmworkers have been inheritors of the long legacy of self-help poverty programming in American philanthropy.

Combined self-help and civic action (today often termed *civic engagement* or *civic participation*) are commonly conceived of as "good" and necessary elements in approaches to alleviating poverty.[36] One might ask why we would not want poor people to actively participate in, rather than passively receive, poverty programs such as food stamps, housing assistance, earned income tax credits, or cash-based financial assistance. Why would we not want people to help themselves learn new work, parenting, or social skills and gain confidence from their own individual efforts to improve their lives? Yet we seldom ask what these frameworks omit and whom they hold accountable to alleviate poverty. These omissions are key to understanding one of the central dilemmas of self-help philanthropy: when the poor help themselves they may end up taking on the social and economic infrastructure that makes philanthropic wealth possible. As clearly stated in a 1965 Rosenberg Foundation annual report, "Almost everybody approves if farm workers decide to build houses for themselves; not everybody approves if they decide to go on strike."

Constantly present in American poverty programming for more than a century, self-help poverty action has had a powerful influence through what it asks people to do and what it obscures. Recent historical studies have shown that American poverty programs have progressively rejected a correlation between poverty and the relations of production (including market regulation, wages, job creation, structural racism and discrimination, and high costs of housing, food, education, and services) in favor of framing poverty as an expression of the behavioral problems and democratic participation of the poor.[37] By separating questions of production, labor, and institutionalized structural inequality from the moral and behavioral explanations of poverty, the self-help approach has been depoliticized—excluding action that challenges the status quo.[38] Private foundations have played a central role in this transformation, which is evidenced by strategic interventions during specific historical moments of crisis.

Perhaps the original American philanthropist to articulate the self-help approach was Andrew Carnegie. In 1889, more than a decade before the first private foundation was incorporated in the United States,[39] he proposed: "The problem of our age is the proper administration of wealth, that the ties of brotherhood may still bind together the rich and poor in harmonious relationship."[40] Commenting on unprecedented rapid industrialization, Carnegie worried about the growing divide between the rich and poor. However, he was not worried about poor people themselves, as he believed that the growing economic divide was the natural result of progress and the individualistic "survival of the fittest." In other words, he was an early observer and supporter of the vast inequality produced by advanced capitalism. Instead, Carnegie was concerned about the possibility of urban unrest bred from the distrust between people in an increasingly divided society reliant on "thousands of operatives in the factory, or in the mine, of whom the employer can know little or nothing, and to whom he is little better than a myth." For Carnegie, the answer to declining trust between owner and worker was for industrialists to give away their wealth—a process in which "the main consideration should be to help those who help themselves ... to place within reach the ladders upon which the aspiring can rise," so that "the laws of accumulation will be left free, the laws of distribution free."[41] In the spirit of American individualism and bootstrap capitalism, Carnegie proposed that the new rich had a responsibility to help the poor help themselves—in the interest of preventing protest.

Also in 1889, progressive activist and settlement house worker Jane Addams (one of America's first "professional poverty warriors"[42]) founded Hull House with a similar concern about rising inequality in American industrial cities. Initially inspired by London's Toynbee Hall, Hull House was a residential education center that provided opportunities for urban migrants to support their families through cooperative childcare, cooking, savings, and cultural and artistic programs. At the time, this was an innovative approach that encouraged people to improve their own conditions instead of asking traditional charities for assistance. Yet Addams (and the founding cohort of progressive white female settlement house workers) also engaged Hull House residents in action research and eventually community organizing to pressure for corporate and legislative reform of working conditions, wages, and rights for the rapidly expanding population of immigrant factory workers.

By the beginning of the twentieth century, the first three American foundations—the Carnegie Foundation (1905), the Russell Sage Foundation (1907), and the Rockefeller Foundation (1913)—were created to shield substantial industrial earnings from taxation under new federal legislation and to engage in philanthropic activity.[43] All three funded the popular Progressive Era survey research on increasing urban poverty initiated by Addams's settlement house workers.[44] But none would fund the immigrant and labor-related organizing that threatened the circumstances that allowed industrial capital to thrive. For the Rockefeller Foundation in particular, Jane Addams's migrant self-help served two purposes: to alleviate poverty and to protect industrialists from political unrest in the increasingly impoverished American city.[45] Although she refused a full-time faculty appointment at the University of Chicago based on her critique of the Rockefeller-funded research agenda, Addams eventually became a popular lecturer there, and her ideas (and other settlement movement narratives) directly informed a more neutral iteration of self-help poverty action and eventually urban renewal.[46] With a grant from the Laura Spelman Rockefeller Memorial Fund, the Chicago School sociologists, led most prominently by Robert E. Park and Ernest E. Burgess, transformed the structural political economy analysis of Addams's era into a social-psychological "urban ecology" theory of social disorganization and dysfunction in urban neighborhoods.[47] Multiple studies produced by Chicago graduate students followed in Park and Burgess's path, cementing the move toward social disorganization and behavioral deviance.[48]

One graduate student, Saul Alinsky, perhaps the first professional community organizer in the United States and founder of the Industrial Areas Foundation, critiqued the urban-ecology approach of the Chicago School. Through his own work in Back of the Yards, a poor neighborhood centered on the meatpacking industry in Chicago and popularized in Upton Sinclair's 1906 novel *The Jungle*, Alinsky repoliticized self-help poverty action. Alinsky's method focused on neighbor-to-neighbor resident organizing, building individual leadership and institutional power to demand equal resources, opportunities, and political reform. Another set of activist-scholars, Richard Cloward and Lloyd Ohlin, critiqued the dominant theories of the day, proposing that "deviant" behavior (juvenile delinquency in particular) was not the cause but the result of poverty. In proposing that youths' lives are best improved by collectively mobilizing for legitimate opportunities, they brought a structural analysis of unequal opportunity structures back into the self-help framework.[49]

Cloward and Ohlin's opportunity theory was picked up, funded, experimented on, and eventually neutralized by the

Ford Foundation in the 1950s. Founded in 1936, and fully opera-
tional after a gift from the trust of Henry Ford in 1947, the Ford
Foundation entered the philanthropic scene with an intrepid
agenda in foreign policy and urban reform.[50] On the domestic
front in the 1950s, Ford Foundation public affairs director Paul
Ylvisaker hoped to address concerns with the mounting tensions
among Black and Appalachian migrants from the rural South to
the urban centers in the North. During the mid-to-late 1950s,
mass migration of poor southerners to the urban centers of the
North created newly visible geographies of racial inequality and
poverty. Urban poverty was exacerbated by rising unemployment, automation and changing industries, unequal educational
and hiring practices, and declining housing stock. In the wake of
a widely criticized response to these shifts in the form of "slum
clearance" and urban renewal programs, Ylvisaker launched a
series of comprehensive Ford Foundation initiatives. The largest
included the Great Cities School Improvement Project, Richard
Cloward's Mobilization for Youth, and the Gray Areas program,
which became models for the American War on Poverty launched
by President Johnson in 1964.[51] At the center of each of these initiatives was the participation of the poor in self-improvement
and leadership development, theoretically to engage in decision-
making on the matters of most concern in their own lives.

By multiple accounts, each of these Ford Foundation initiatives failed when the foundation's self-help approach reached its
own limits.[52] The 1959 Great Cities School Improvement Project
made one-year grants to ten city school districts. Although the
project initially targeted curricular revisions and teacher training, Ylvisaker had broader urban renewal goals. He was optimis-
tic that a reformulated agenda that incorporated the urban poor
as stakeholders would ease some of the mounting tensions in the

inner city.[53] However, it quickly became clear that the predominantly Black parents brought together in the initiative's programs were most concerned about racial exclusion from the housing and job markets—issues that the project refused to address. Like Great Cities, Mobilization for Youth mandated youth training and participation as a solution to juvenile delinquency in New York's Lower East Side neighborhood. However, their efforts were defunded when the radical program staff organized to challenge local bureaucracies and school officials. In these instances, one of the main contradictions of self-help philanthropy is revealed: the goals of activating the poor end up threatening the social and economic infrastructure that foundations rely on to make profits.

In the early 1960s, when tensions in urban areas across the country were rising (including protests against slum clearance, calls for community control, heightened mobilizations by the Black and Latino self-determination movements, and the general mood of social unrest inspired by national-independence movements around the globe), Ylvisaker was aware that critiques of racial discrimination and unequal opportunity structures were at the heart of the growing turbulence. He also knew that at this time his board of trustees would not be comfortable framing any Ford Foundation project around race.[54] In an effort to present (to the emerging social movement organizations) and obscure (to his board and to other philanthropic interests) the central issues of the time, Ylvisaker framed the Gray Areas program with behavioral barriers that prevented southern Black and Appalachian migrants from assimilating and integrating in the northern city. This time, the foundation required the formation of networks of new and existing nonprofit organizations to collectively form migrant education, community development, and neighborhood safety programs funded and managed by the foundation. Again, the aim was to help people improve their own conditions by becoming active, responsible citizens and partners in an experiment in multi-stakeholder community development.

The Gray Areas program cooled tensions by redirecting local organizations and leaders toward improving their own individual behaviors and away from racial protest as in the previous initiatives. Programs were quickly defunded when partners from the Black Panthers took their self-help to the political bargaining table and demanded control.[55] In this instance, the limits presented by the Gray Areas program reflect the historical and enduring tension between "racial uplift" and "Black Power."[56] Whereas Black Panther leaders in Oakland connected Black self-help with collective resistance to social, economic, and political oppression of a colonized ghetto under global Western imperialism, the framers of the Gray Areas program played on the middle-class Black tradition of "racial uplift." The project's migrant education and neighborhood safety programming echoed an assimilationist ideology historically articulated by Black elites in concert with white liberals during the Reconstruction Era that promoted discipline and educational achievement as a means of mobility into the middle class. This approach is in tension with the more radical anti-imperialist and economic justice project promoted by both Malcolm X and Martin Luther King, which called for group empowerment toward universal and international human rights. These ideological and tactical debates continue today as conservative politicians evoke a "color-blind" self-help ideology that pejoratively pathologizes poor Black families, while a racial justice movement calls individuals to action to end racial profiling, police brutality, and a "prison–industrial complex" designed to control Black populations.

Instead of retreating from Black activism during the late 1960s to 1970s, under the leadership of foundation president McGeorge Bundy, the Ford Foundation continued to support, negotiate, and forge agreements with Black leaders in key organizations such as the Congress of Racial Equality (CORE). Karen Ferguson's recent book *Top Down: The Ford Foundation, Black Power, and the Reinvention of Racial Liberalism* shows how Ford made significant contributions to watering down Black Power ideology toward the new "color-blind" racial liberalism seen today, through the establishment of foundation-funded programs and the training of Black leadership.[57]

This era of Ford Foundation funding also had international implications. The community-participation-plus-policing elements of its juvenile delinquency experiment dovetailed directly with international Cold War counterinsurgency and security programs abroad.[58] Alongside Ford, the Rockefeller Foundation, in partnership with the World Bank, implemented self-help poverty action programming in international contexts where national independence battles were being fought and in which the "communist threat" was presented by indigenous poor people's movements in the late 1950s and early 1960s.[59] Scholars have documented the ways in which Rockefeller's global development and "Green Revolution" funding was an attempt to contain peasant uprising in the face of resource scarcity and growing populations in the global South.[60] In these contexts, poverty action was negotiated from the top by foundations, governments, and major development institutions and from the bottom by grass-roots organizations and leaders. In the United States and Latin American contexts, those on the right and the left of the political spectrum appeared to agree that community action among the poor should be encouraged. Yet they understood very different things: was self-help designed to engage diverse stakeholders in maintaining the status quo, or to encourage consciousness-raising and revolutionary action?[61]

Only a few years after the Gray Areas program folded, the self-help framework was rearticulated through the increasingly accepted "culture of poverty" theory developed by Oscar Lewis and popularized by Harrington's widely read *The Other America*.[62] In step with the civil rights movement, self-help was rearticulated in the War on Poverty's call to enlist the "maximum feasible participation" of the poor. Through the War on Poverty, the poor were encouraged to join federally funded Community Action Projects (CAPs) through local stakeholder committees, infrastructure development projects, and leadership training. Furthermore, the poor—at least at the start of the War on Poverty—were encouraged to mobilize grass-roots collective action to challenge responsible institutions and societal structures.[63] However, like the Ford Foundation projects, the War on Poverty is widely criticized for curtailing and defunding the activities of CAPs whose definitions of self-help were deemed too confrontational.[64]

During the neoliberal shift of the 1980s, the idea of self-help took yet another turn as conservative politicians and public intellectuals put forth the now well-worn argument that a bloated welfare state (as a result of the public programming and legislation from the New Deal era to the War on Poverty) has created dependency among the poor.[65] With the election of Ronald Reagan in 1980 and the defunding of many public programs for the poor, the new self-help emphasized individual reliance, entrepreneurialism, and market strategies, replacing the social-action tone of the 1960s. Critiquing the era from 1980 through the early 2000s, a rapidly expanding body of scholarship on the "Shadow State,"[66] non-profit industrial complex,[67] and international "NGO-ization"[68] of global social movements maps the rapid expansion, institutionalization, professionalization, and continued depoliticization of nonprofit organizations increasingly contracted to do the work of a hollowed-out welfare state. The neoliberal ideology that promotes privatization, deregulation, liberalization of the market, and a hyper-focus on entrepreneurship further separates questions of the relations of production from the moral, behavioral, and now entrepreneurial responsibilities of the poor.[69] Recent critical global development scholarship describes the participation of the poor in programs such as microcredit and conditional cash transfer programs as representing a new neoliberal rationality that structures the lives of the poor around solving their own problems while obscuring the capitalist relationships that maintain poverty in the global South.[70]

Yet, as this brief history has shown, self-help is not a new or unified approach to poverty alleviation unique to the global South. In the course of the twentieth century, the self-help framework has served to depoliticize the collective struggles of the poor through wielding public consensus on nonthreatening understandings of antipoverty work. These worldviews and conceptual frameworks are negotiated and spread through professionalized institutional relationships that incorporate and replace other forms of organization such as collective action, unionization, and cooperative or syndicalist approaches to organizing social change.[71] By tracing the history of self-help poverty action, we see how real and identifiable state and private actors promote programs that attract attention to the weaknesses and responsibilities of the poor and divert attention away from the capitalist processes that create poverty.[72]

In the wake of the recent financial crash and after the fifty-year anniversary of the War on Poverty, more people understand and acknowledge the structural causes of growing inequality. Research on industrial abandonment, histories of redlining and racial exclusion in the banking and housing sectors, jobs paying less than a living wage, unaccountable financial institutions, rising housing costs, disparities in educational opportunity, the racial wealth gap, food insecurity, and systemic racial profiling and violence in neighborhood policing have recently been popularized by public scholars such as Thomas Picketty,[73] Robert Reich,[74] Joseph Stiglitz,[75] Darrick Hamilton,[76] and movements such as Occupy Wall Street, #BlackLivesMatter, and Communities United Against Police Brutality.[77] Yet the enduring self-help poverty action framework has been cemented as "common sense"—a body of unexplored ideas, taken for granted, that maintains the status quo.[78] New radical movements are reclaiming self-help poverty action to address regional abandonment and structural racism in places such as Detroit, exemplified in Grace Lee Boggs's *The Next American Revolution*.[79] Yet even Boggs proposes that the antagonistic organizing of the 1960s is no longer viable and that people must instead build a new culture from within. In this context, foundations interested in supporting nonprofits doing antipoverty work have less negotiating and translating work.

THE OTHER CALIFORNIA:
POVERTY IN THE CENTRAL VALLEY

Today, many of the towns dotting California's main agricultural valley still resemble the migrant "Okie" settlements of the Great Depression.[80] Characterized by seasonal labor and substandard housing, conditions for the mostly Mexican, and increasingly indigenous Oaxacan, migrant field workers have hardly improved since the farmworker movement.[81] Drought and financial crisis have worsened an already dire situation. In towns and nearby urban hubs such as Modesto, Merced, Fresno, and Bakersfield, migrant families rely on food banks and donation centers to feed and clothe their children. Many agricultural field workers who decided to stay and establish a community, and who had maintained a meager sense of security by the 1990s, are now hitting the road and reinventing the migrant harvest trail from California to Oregon, Washington, Texas, and Arizona. Few return to Mexico, fearing tightened border security, increasingly dangerous conditions along migrant crossings, and permanent separation from their American-born children. The current drought has made farm labor jobs even more irregular, putting farms, field workers, and their families in an increasingly precarious position.

Produced and maintained through geographies of industrial agricultural production—including seasonal low-wage migrant employment, excessive land and water use, competition in global agricultural markets, and immigration policing—Central Valley farmworker and immigrant communities are among what Ruth Wilson Gilmore describes as advanced capitalism's forgotten places, "exhausted by the daily violence of environmental degradation, racism, underemployment, overwork, shrinking social wages, and the disappearance of whole ways of life."[82] Yet poverty in California's Central Valley is not new, and the people who struggle financially in this region are not silent, destitute, hopeless, or without agency. Periodic outrage at and organizing against California's industrial agricultural system has cast national attention on the region, from John Steinbeck's *Grapes of Wrath* (1939) and Carey McWilliams's *Factories in the Field*

(1939), to Dorothea Lange's Works Progress Administration photographs of dustbowl migrants, to Edward R. Murrow's nationally televised 1960 exposé, *Harvest of Shame,* to multiple waves of farm labor organizing.

As these historic moments and more recent studies have established, much of the region's poverty is produced through a fragmented farm industry organized around what Philip Martin calls the "three *c*'s" of farm labor."[83] The first C stands for *concentration.* Since the turn of the twentieth century, the vast majority of farmworkers have been employed on the largest farms that rely on labor-intensive seasonal work. On these farms a majority of field workers are without wages for significant portions of the farm cycle. Higher up in the food chain, concentration also concerns the food buyers, including supermarket conglomerates and food retailers like Walmart and McDonalds. Most large buyers have codes of conduct for fair treatment of workers along the supply chain of the food they purchase. However, local conditions are seldom monitored on either domestic or foreign farms. A recent journalistic series in the *Los Angeles Times* reveals the inhumane treatment, including withholding of wages, squalid living conditions, lack of water, and forced debt structures, suffered by farmworkers on the "mega-farms" in Mexico that many US food retailers buy from.[84] As is the case in the Central Valley, large chains such as WalMart, Safeway, and Whole Foods profit from produce from large farms that are seldom held accountable for the fair-treatment principles they all claim to embrace.

The second C stands for *contractors.* Farm labor is managed by contractors who negotiate, and profit from, the difference between what the farmer will pay to have a job done and what the workers are paid. Farmers benefit from this arrangement because it streamlines the hiring process and also makes it difficult for worker advocates to directly negotiate and enforce wage standards and farm labor health, safety, and fair-treatment regulations. To this day, large growers find it easier to pay fines for labor and environmental abuses than to follow the regulations established by the farmworker movement and its allies.

The third C of California farm labor stands for *conflict*, a history of protest that continues but that has been unable to significantly change the industry. In the course of the twentieth century, this previously alluvial valley basin was made and remade by sometimes violent struggles over minerals, water, farmable land, and multiple socioeconomic, cultural, and political stakes—including the farmworker movement at its height during the 1960s and 1970s.[85] Through an innovative combination of place-based community organizing, mutual aid associations, culturally inspired leadership, and strikes and international boycotts, Chavez and the farmworker movement showed how people in a forgotten place can build pride, form powerful worker-led institutions, and connect local struggles beyond regional landscapes—breaking patterns of dependency in favor of self-determination and multifaceted social movements.

But despite the struggles and victories of the farmworker movement, migrant poverty endures. Throughout the 1980s and 1990s, the rapid expansion of low-wage, labor-intensive production systems and the active recruitment of undocumented workers from poor regions in Mexico—with increasingly fewer services and rights in the United States—further jeopardized an already impoverished farmworker population.[86] Between 1994 and today, trade liberalization under the North American Free Trade Agreement has decimated a large number of farms in rural Mexico unable to compete with the flood of genetically modified and tax-subsidized farm products from the

United States. Additional agricultural migrants, many of them indigenous people from Oaxaca, have traveled north in search of new ways to feed their families. Within this context, the Central Valley has attracted multiple antipoverty initiatives. Through my research on philanthropic investments in addressing migrant and immigrant poverty in the region, I observed how nonprofit organizations negotiate new articulations of self-help poverty action. At certain conjunctures, grass-roots leaders and private funders embraced the same articulation of empowering the poor to address questions of poverty, isolation, and marginalization, opening up a productive middle ground from which to organize. More often, they prescribed clear and certain limits. Although philanthropic investments have not alone altered the terrain of farmworker organizing, they have promoted theoretical frameworks and professionalized management practices that constrain the work of regional advocacy and organizing institutions around developing and integrating immigrants—but they do not organize, strike, or challenge any aspect of farm production or unequal opportunity structures.

Most recently, the explicitly "win-win" or "double bottom line" model of addressing poverty while also producing a return on investments for private partners and the industry has been taken up by funders inspired by the union–grower alliance for immigration reform—as represented in the AgJOBS legislation designed in an unprecedented compromise between farmworker advocates and major agricultural employers to address labor supply and the current immigration crisis. Despite worsening conditions for migrant field workers, many advocates believe that given the current climate of global financial crisis and competition, and the increasingly threatened status of undocumented workers, partnerships with growers to improve agricultural productivity are the only viable strategy for improving the lives of farmworkers. The rhetoric of farmworker advocates now includes saving California agriculture from the dangers of global competition and the need to ensure a sustainable workforce through new guest-worker programs.

Part of the new worker–industry alliance includes historic movement nonprofit organizations working with growers to improve production strategies and industrial efficiency, thereby increasing the profit and competitiveness of farmers while increasing the output (and theoretically the wages) and sustainability of workers. Growers and farmworker advocates alike argue that in the context of the rapid globalization of agriculture, in which the cost of doing business is higher (e.g. for land, water, equipment, labor, and regulation costs) in California than in the global South, the human worker is the most malleable input to increase competitiveness. The grower needs to stay competitive, so it cannot risk changing, and the workers needs to learn new skills to boost production. Theoretically, this approach is a win-win situation, raising farm profits and workers' wages at the same time. Yet in this turn of events, self-help has taken a strange twist, with the poor responsible not only for themselves but for saving the industry.

Although the tools used in the win-win model may be promising in some respects, such as immigration reform, the negative effects are significant. Beyond the considerable limits to changing the agricultural industry, the win-win approach to self-help, when used among participants with such divergent power, denies central elements of politics and social change: building collective consciousness, conflict, and the identification of difference. The farmworker movement's self-help originally meant contesting an industry and society which refuse to acknowledge the dignity of the poor and marginalized, and in the process conferring dignity on oneself. Radical self-help proposes that without this consciousness, created through the identification of relationships of power and oppression, the self is not helped. Part of the great success of the farmworker movement was its ability to dramatize the stark differences in life experience, privilege, and power between the farmworker (*la campesina/el campesino*) and the grower (*el mayordomo*) based on the lived experiences of farmworking families. Through their stark and simplified plays of *campesino* versus *mayordomo*, friend versus enemy, and good versus evil, *El Teatro Campesino*, a roving theater troupe that toured the fields, picket lines, nation, and globe, showed workers that every identity is relational and that the conditions and the very existence and suffering of the *campesino/a* was determined by opposition to the wealthy grower, or his or her "constitutive outside."[87]

Wielding new understandings of power and change, these images were spread through Radio Campesino and the pages of the movement's paper, *El Malcreado* (which means "the mischievous," or those who talk back to their parents; it was named after the paper of the Mexican Revolution). Despite the complexity and diversity within the farmworker population, these relational representations of the difference between "us" and "them" prompted anger, action, and a sense of collective struggle—the seeds of a movement. As in the more radical self-determination movements of the era, through diverse representations and actions, a generation of farmworkers, college student volunteers, legal aid workers, Catholic priests, and movement leaders learned from critical praxis that, as articulated by Paulo Freire, "Washing one's hands of the conflict between the powerful and the powerless means to side with the powerful, not to be neutral."[88]

When funders, movement leaders, and advocacy institutions speak only of the kind of self-help they can agree on, what, then, is erased from regional organizing agendas? In our current moment, after agreement on immigration reform or how farmworkers can help save agriculture, growers will still find it easier to operate above the law. Only a few migrant field workers will have political power, human rights, healthy living conditions, fair wages, or children who believe that the world is full of opportunities. Thousands of California farmworkers will still sleep under the trees and in the drainage ditches of the fields they work in the hot sun of daylight.

PLAN OF THE BOOK

For two years, I immersed myself in the lives of community organizers, policymakers, and foundation staff to understand the ideas, cultures, and politics of their daily lives. I did not study the lives of Central Valley farmworkers and immigrants. There are several beautiful, moving, and politically important accounts of the lives of farmworkers,[89] yet few studies address the institutional structures that aid or hinder improving the conditions in agricultural communities. This book provides a new lens for examining the institutions and professionals who manage poverty programming, not "the poor"—or farmworkers—themselves. This is also not a comprehensive account of the farmworker movement or even farmworker organizing; rather, the three case studies provide a window into the relationship between private foundations; social movements; and the ideas, institutional structures, professional processes, and relationships negotiated through attempts to address entrenched poverty in a region.

The book begins with the social movements of the 1960s and the heated conversations and compromises between Chavez and the philanthropic investors in the farmworker movement. The first case study shows how the negotiations between Chavez and philanthropic allies resulted in the incorporation of nonprofit "movement institutions." Chavez eventually retreated from union organizing to these institutions when the movement faced its most severe challenges. The ostensibly unified organizing message of building social, economic, and cultural power among migrant farmworkers was fractured when meeting its most threatening external and internal leadership challenges, including negotiations with private funders. Eventually, specific frameworks and exclusions separated the social movement from the union—and social justice from economic justice. Consumed by funding his new organizations, Chavez ultimately accepted a translation of farmworker self-help that featured poor field hands in need of philanthropic charity—but not a movement in struggle for self-determination and ownership among workers.

The second case study features the post–welfare reform era of the late 1990s and early 2000s, when foundations first experimented with designing and managing large-scale philanthropic "collaborative initiatives" in regions suffering from shrinking public resources. This chapter shows how nonprofit leaders working under the umbrella of a foundation-driven "immigrant civic participation collaborative" negotiated the foundation-prescribed limits as they struggled to address migrant poverty, marginalization, and an emerging immigrant rights movement. Through an ethnographic case study of the Stewart Kinney Foundation's Immigrant Participation Collaborative,[90] which received more than $5 million per year from 1996 through 2003, I show how the popular funding frameworks of the era—

including civic participation and social capital—diluted the organizing agendas of member partners, introduced new professional institutional practices, and fractured coalition-building in the region. While the collaborative structure proved cumbersome and distracting to member organizations, the civic-participation framework was strategically negotiated and created openings from which to launch new organizing campaigns.

The final case study is an ethnographic investigation of a $50 million foundation initiative that reflects the recent entrepreneurial and market-based trend in philanthropic giving. The "win-win" model of the Western Foundation's Farm Worker Community Building Initiative sought to facilitate processes that identify where growers and workers can collaborate. It would not allow any issues to be aired that challenge the economic interests of growers. I argue that advocates operating with this model, at a time when growers and workers alike suffer from financial insecurity, do not address the structural issues inherent in a labor system that requires a constant influx of migrants from poverty-stricken areas of Mexico. Through the story of the Western Foundation's initiative and its strictly enforced "asset-based" model, this chapter shows how the neoliberal framework is not always presented through conspiratorial agendas but is solidified by reworking movement strategies into programs that claim to guarantee mutual prosperity.

The combined chapters show how professional foundation staff, working in the interest of their philanthropic institutions, negotiate the inherent political limits of mainstream philanthropy. From the establishment of the Rockefeller, Carnegie, and Ford Foundations to the multiple general-purpose foundations making grants to nonprofit organizations today, philanthropic giving has clearly defined boundaries.[91] Created and maintained by wealth generated from the surplus of capitalist production, foundations interested in poverty alleviation will generally not fund labor organizing. Foundations interested in environmental degradation generally do not fund organizations fighting global corporate abuses of land, nature, and people. Foundations interested in immigrants prefer to fund citizenship education, not immigrant rights. In other words, foundation priorities reveal the grand paradox of funding working-class organizing through the surplus of capital. Can the surplus of capitalist exploitation be used to aid those on whose backs this surplus is generated? Can these surplus dollars contribute to addressing entrenched poverty while refusing to address systemic questions of labor, migration, and human rights? The stories told in this book highlight how professionals—social movement leaders, organizational staff, consultants, and foundation program officers—struggle with these questions.

CHAPTER TWO

The Hustling Arm
of the Union

*Nonprofit Institutionalization and the
Compromises of Cesar Chavez*

On March 10, 1968, in the Central Valley town of Delano, a weak
Cesar Chavez, held up by two elder farmworkers in faded som-
breros, walks slowly through crowds of supporters waving black-
and-red flags. With the word *huelga* (strike) boldly emblazoned
above an Aztec eagle, the flag inspires dignity among the Chicano people and hope for change on behalf of the state's agricultural field workers. Flanked by his mother and Robert F.
Kennedy—and under the watchful eyes of Dolores Huerta and
his wife Helen—Chavez feebly sits to receive a morsel of bread
from a Catholic priest. The priest speaks: "And he took bread in
his hands, blessed it, and gave it to his disciples saying, 'Eat all of
it. For this is my body, the body of Christ. Amen.'" On this day,
Cesar Chavez emerges from a twenty-five-day fast to call for
nonviolence during one of the most heated moments on the
picket lines of the historic California farmworker movement.

This scene comes from the 2014 film, *Cesar Chavez,* directed by
Mexican actor Diego Luna and performed by Latino Hollywood

stars. The film's release, nearly fifty years after the Delano grape strike that launched the movement, follows the publication of several new books that complicate a story most commonly told, as in the film, through the singular heroic efforts of Cesar Chavez. In *Trampling Out the Vintage: Cesar Chavez and the Two Souls of the United Farm Workers*, Frank Bardacke, a former antiwar student activist who became a seasonal farmworker, reveals the success and the undoing of the movement through the tensions between its "two souls."[1] The first soul was the union built by fieldworkers and an army of volunteers fighting growers through organizing, strikes, and public actions across California's Central Valley. The second soul was composed of progressive middle-class allies throughout the country motivated by the consumer grape boycotts and alignment with the civil rights and student movements of the time. Bardacke shows that when the two souls of the movement worked together, they had great force. However, when Chavez failed to grant legitimate power to the grass-roots farmworker soul, he faltered, thus breeding discontent, distrust, and eventual retreat from union and community organizing. In many ways, Matt Garcia's book, *From the Jaws of Victory*,[2] and Miriam Pawel's recent biography, *The Crusades of Cesar Chavez*,[3] confirm Bardacke's analysis. They also show how troubled relationships within the leadership of the movement, Chavez's ego, and priorities to focus on institutional management (or mismanagement) rather than strikes and the grass-roots volunteers led to the movement's eventual demise.

This chapter joins the conversation about the reappraisal of Cesar Chavez and the farmworker movement by focusing on relationships with regional philanthropic efforts to address migrant poverty in the Central Valley. Bardacke, Garcia, and Pawel add internal complexity and a broader array of actors involved during the middle of the twentieth century, yet they touch only briefly on the role of foundations. The historical accounts featured in the following pages expose how Chavez's turn away from the farmworker soul of the movement was directly aided by the political and professional requirements of both public and private funders. However, unlike in much of the critical literature, a straightforward interpretation of philanthropic co-optation of a grass-roots union is an insufficient explanation for the failure of the movement. Instead, the incorporation of privately funded nonprofit organizations reveals both a retreat from union organizing, and Chavez's attempt to return to his original vision. In tune with the civil rights and liberation movements of his era, Chavez was never sure that traditional unionization was the best strategy to address the fundamental questions of pride, self-determination, and self-organization that he originally hoped to address.[4] Initially he proposed building a new society through a revolution in values to inspire dignity in farm labor through mutual-aid institutions, self-help volunteerism among workers, and cooperative work and living.

In the early 1970s, worn down by hunger strikes, death threats, surveillance by the FBI, and unfounded fears of disloyalty among his field organizers, Chavez retreated from the union to the nonprofit "movement institutions" as a space to experiment with his original notions of self-determination, communal living, and mutual aid. Recent scholars of the movement claim, perhaps accurately, that during this time Chavez was distracted away from union organizing by his own ego and fascination with organizational management. Yet his retreat to the nonprofit organizations also resonated with his original vision to create a diversity of self-sustaining farmworker organizations. Nonetheless, divorced from the action in the fields and working under a professionalized and privately funded model, the staff of the new nonprofits became preoccupied with fund development and administration. Consumed with developing his new organizations, Chavez ultimately accepted a translation of farmworker self-help that featured poor field hands in need of philanthropic charity—but not a movement in struggle for self-determination, community control, and collective ownership among workers.

In this instance the power of philanthropy was wielded not through explicit agendas of control but through negotiation, compromise, and increased professional administrative demands. Radical social movement ideas are translated into nonthreatening understandings of self-help acceptable to funders, and movement leaders are incorporated within professional approaches to service delivery.

The movement's relationship to private funders featured in this study begins with the Rosenberg Foundation's "self-help housing" programs in Tulare County, which trained farmworker leaders who eventually became involved in the first strikes led by Larry Itliong, Cesar Chavez, and Dolores Huerta. The radical "mutual aid" approach of the early movement years was unexpectedly transformed through relationships with the Rosenberg Foundation, formal unionization, associations with the War on Poverty, and investments from the Ford and Field Foundations. Instead of a black-and-white picture of grass-roots organizers co-opted by imperialist foundations, the complexly intertwined and often conflicted relationships between grassroots political organizing and self-help philanthropy are negotiated at pivotal moments of the movement. Originally inspired by the alignment between the civil rights movement and the struggle for farmworker justice, public and private funders set up untenable institutional structures. Representing the central contradiction of self-help philanthropy, their programs trained and activated farmworker leaders to improve their own living conditions and in the process inspired them to engage in labor and protest politics deemed unacceptable and threatening to foundations. Inundated with managing benign service programs eventually reigned in and approved by foundations, and the required reporting and paperwork, Chavez retreated to what he once called "the hustling arm of the union,"[5] away from organizing in the fields.

MIGRANT SELF-HELP AND THE ROSENBERG FOUNDATION: FARMWORKER LEADERSHIP AND THE SEEDS OF THE MOVEMENT

The historical convergence of resources provided by the Rosenberg Foundation, the US War on Poverty, and the Ford and Field Foundations contributed to the initial momentum of the farmworker movement and to its institutional incorporation and professionalization. The Rosenberg Foundation, in particular, invested in valley farmworker communities for more than three decades leading up to the movement.[6] The first wave included Depression-era grants to support migrant community and child-care centers incubated through the WPA. The second funding era was characterized by investments in "self-help" projects during the late 1950s and early 1960s. These programs aimed at assisting farmworkers in developing community infrastructure and leadership through the construction of their own homes. The third wave included the foundation's support for early movement organizations such as Migrant Ministry and the American Friends Service Committee's Proyecto Campesino, which organized with Chavez and Huerta during and beyond the 1965 Delano strike by the National Farm Workers Association (NFWA, later renamed the United Farm Workers, or UFW).

Appointed trustees of Max L. Rosenberg established the foundation in 1935. Rosenberg was the president of Rosenberg Brothers & Company, the California fruit packing and shipping firm he and his brothers founded in 1893. In his will, Rosenberg "left the bulk of his estate to establish a foundation with broad charitable purposes and wide latitude in how the foundation might be operated."[7] In 1936, the Rosenberg Foundation opened an office in San Francisco, hired staff, and began making grants. The "first foundation program officer west of the Rockies"[8] was Leslie Gaynard, followed by Florence Wycoff, and then Ruth Chance. All three women were concerned about migrant poverty in California and were advocates of the self-help approach.[9]

Rosenberg had a history of building relationships with regional leaders to support work emerging from the needs of local people, such as their partnership with the WPA during the Depression era. One such relationship in the late 1950s was with the Quaker Friends. Members of the California Quakers wanted to develop a farmworker project to address the increasing poverty and insecurity in Central Valley migrant communities. In 1955, Rosenberg Foundation program officer Leslie Gaynard convened the Bay Area Friends with a man named Bard McAllister, who directed the Central Valley's American Friends Service Committee office in Visalia, a small town in Tulare County with a large farmworker population. Together, they asked McAllister to look for a Central Valley location in which to fund a farmworker poverty program.[10] That year, many migrant communities in the region's southern San Joaquin Valley were in need because a major flood had disrupted their work in the fields.

One project that McAllister helped establish was SCICON (Tulare County Science and Conservation School Project), an outdoor education program partially designed to address tensions between the Anglo growers' children and the Latino workers' children. The Latino child population was increasing because Mexicans brought to the valley under the US–Mexican bracero program had begun to have children and settle. The idea behind SCICON was to build institutional relationships and leadership skills for local migrant youth through intercultural exchange. Trainers for the programs came primarily from farmworker families and built leadership skills and relationships with local schoolteachers, principals, and Anglo families. Though seldom mentioned in histories of the farmworker movement, program staff trained through SCICON in the 1950s played an active role in the movement of the 1960s. These included farmworker leaders such as Pablo Espinoza. He was one of the first SCICON trainers; he became a UFW volunteer organizer, then an Office of Economic Opportunity (OEO) staff person. Eventually, he was appointed director of Proyecto Campesino in Visalia.[11]

Rosenberg later worked with McAllister to form Self Help Enterprise (also funded through the War on Poverty). Rosenberg described the work of Self-Help Enterprise as an innovative community development tool. The goal of Self-Help Enterprise began but did not end with the financing and construction of homes. After more than twenty homes were built by local farmworker families in the first few years of the project, "the children from these homes seemed to have better 'self-images' than many other farm labor children, their motivation for education was higher … and their parents became more involved in community activities."[12] Rosenberg describes their work in Tulare County as a part of a new community development approach that engages poor people in building a sense of self-worth, leadership, opportunity, and access to mainstream institutions through their own participation in the project.

Self-Help Enterprise's facilitative community development model directly aligned with the poverty action programs taking shape in the early 1960s. Building on Oscar Lewis's (1959) "culture of poverty" theory, Michael Harrington's widely read *The Other America: Poverty in the United States* (1962, 1968) was one of the central treatises that informed the "maximum feasible participation" design of the War on Poverty. Harrington argued that the "new poor" were not at fault for their poverty; rather, they had been "left behind" in the face of industrial change, essentially "in the wrong place [wrong industry, wrong neighborhood, wrong ethnic group] at the wrong time." Once this historical act of dislocation takes place, the conditions of the poor transform from social into cultural circumstance through an entrenched cycle of poor behaviors, isolation, and hopelessness. According to Harrington and the poverty policy of the time, the best hope for saving the new American poor from the fate of invisibility and untold suffering was public programs to motivate and inspire the poor to become civically engaged and build mainstream institutional connections. Unlike the ethnic organizing and union organizing attempted in Central Valley farmworker communities in the nineteenth and early twentieth centuries,[13] Rosenberg's Central Valley migrant programs created a new farmworker leader more concerned with empowerment through education, relationships with mainstream institutions, and migrant-led infrastructure development. Because of its educational and relational, as opposed to confrontational and systemic, approach to self-help, the model garnered mainstream institutional support in local communities.

However, a 1965 grant to Migrant Ministry revealed the limits of Rosenberg's commitment to farmworker self-help. During this time, tensions were building and leading to the early rent and grape strikes of the movement. Rosenberg Foundation program officer Ruth Chance decided to increase the foundation's funding levels for Central Valley farm labor programming. In the context of intensifying resistance from growers, a risk-taking Chance believed that concentrating farmworker funding through the church might be the most strategic and safest approach. Migrant Ministry, an ecumenical farmworker support organization working closely alongside the NFWA, became an obvious organization to fund. According to the foundation, the aims of the Migrant Ministry grant were to develop farmworker leadership and institutional connections, and to further concretize the new self-help community development model through a series of regional conferences.[14]

That summer, the Tulare County Housing Authority radically increased rents on the tiny metal-roofed shacks in which many farmworkers lived. NFWA leaders asked Migrant Ministry to assist in a rent strike. By fall, when Migrant Ministry staff officially joined the rent strike, and eventually grape picket lines, Rosenberg told the organization that the foundation's grant was not to be used for organizing unions. Chance emphasized that the grants were meant to train leaders and to strengthen farmworker communities; strikes and union organizing were not to be associated with the foundation. Written the same year as the first NFWA strike, the 1965 Rosenberg Foundation annual report highlighted the success of the foundation's self-help model while warning, "Almost everybody approves if farm workers decide to build houses for themselves; not everybody approves if they decide to go on strike." Chance discontinued funding to the

Migrant Ministry leadership training that had led to worker organizing but continued to fund institutions that asked migrant families to solve their own problems through education and boot-strap infrastructure development. As we will see in the following section, it was partially the popularity of these projects that inspired Chavez to seek philanthropic support for the movement in the interest of preventing resources, volunteers, and allies from reinforcing more moderate forms of farmworker action.

THE COMMUNITY UNION: ORGANIZING FARMWORKERS FOR MUTUAL AID

Cesar Chavez was trained as an organizer by the Community Service Organization (CSO), which was founded in 1948 by Fred Ross. The CSO was established on the organizing model of and with support from Saul Alinsky's Industrial Areas Foundation, introduced in the previous chapter. By the 1950s, Alinsky had become one of the premier thinkers and practitioners of neighborhood-based community organizing. Despite Alinsky's popularity in the 1950s, he was refused funding by both the Ford and Rockefeller Foundations based on the "political nature" of his approach to building power among local residents to confront unequal opportunity structures. However, through Alinsky's connections at the University of Chicago, the Emil Schwarzhaupt Foundation generously funded him and the CSO. Successful alcohol distiller Emil Schwarzhaupt had created a trust to be spent in twenty-five years on groups addressing the social and political issues of the time. When Schwarzhaupt died in 1950, the executive secretary of his foundation, Carl Tjerandsen, a friend of Alinsky, gave most of the money away to progressive organizing institutions, including the Industrial Areas Foundation, the

Highlander Folk School, the Southern Christian Leadership Conference, and Migrant Ministry.[15]

The Schwarzhaupt funds and the connections made with fellow grantees such as close movement ally Migrant Ministry were instrumental in the training of Chavez, who spent the early 1960s translating his CSO training to the context of farmworker towns in the Central Valley. By organizing religious congregations and neighborhoods into civic institutions, the CSO model aimed to build independent democratic leadership in poor and underrepresented communities. In contrast to a union, which is organized around a workforce in relationship to a specific industry, the CSO used door-to-door "one on one" and "house meeting" organizing techniques to solicit the interests and concerns of entire geographic communities, not only workers. In this sense, the goal was to become a strong self-sustaining institution operated by and for those it aims to serve.

In 1962, the CSO denied Chavez's proposal to specifically organize farmworkers and the agricultural industry, primarily because organizing workers around one industry veered from the CSO approach and was not deemed feasible. On his own, Chavez brought his family to the Central Valley to begin building what would become the most successful farmworker movement in US history.[16] Having studied the failures of past attempts to organize migrant farm labor, Chavez believed that organizing workers in a traditional union would never work. Instead, in keeping with his CSO training and his Catholic upbringing, and inspired by his contemporaries Dr. Martin Luther King Jr. and Mahatma Gandhi, Chavez sought to organize farmworkers as a cultural and religious people, situated in their geographic communities, into a social movement. Central to the early philosophy of the movement was the spirit of volunteerism, community service, and collective ownership. According to Dolores Huerta, the main organizing principle emphasized the importance of an all-volunteer, dues-paying membership: "There was a strong belief in not taking money from the outside and in insisting that farmworkers pay and volunteer for the movement.... With the dues from our early members that Cesar and I got from organizing house meetings for a year, we organized farmworker leadership conventions in each town."[17]

From 1962 to 1964 Chavez, Huerta, and a small group of volunteer organizers traveled door to door, organizing house meetings night and day, recruiting field workers, and asking new members to pay dues. According to early advocate Don Villarejo, the NFWA would not take a dime of money from outside their own pockets—if there was any money or meaning in the movement it had to be based in workers.[18] By 1964 the NFWA had a thousand members. Throughout the early 1960s, members and volunteers were engaged in service to the movement, alongside organizers who were paid as little as $5 a day. Activities included efforts to build labor cooperatives that set hiring and wage practices; service centers that provided health, legal, and educational opportunities for workers; public communications campaigns that used arts and media to convey pride and dignity in farm labor; business cooperatives in car repair; organic gardens; and leadership and job training programs for workers.

In the earliest days, Chavez did not imagine that union organizing would become the focus of the movement. As recalled by movement ally and Migrant Ministry director, James Drake: "We always thought it would be different from a union.... If somebody died, the family was going to be helped. If somebody needed tires, the association could help. If they were having trouble with immigration or welfare, the association would help. We would have a radio program. *El Malcriado* would be a community paper, not a union paper."[19]

Drake and a cadre of volunteer organizers inspired the blending of Chavez's CSO approach with the tradition of *mutualistas,* a community self-help model popular in the 1920s and 1930s in Mexico. Gilbert Padilla, a leader in the movement, was a member of one of the oldest *mutualista* groups, which started in the nineteenth century in Mexico and helped migrant families across the Central Valley well into the early 1930s. According to the founding organizers, "the entire approach of the new association was based on the old mutualista idea of building community and power through mutual self-help."[20] However, the union model was quickly thrust on the NFWA in 1965 when the mostly Filipino-American members of the AFL-CIO–supported Agricultural Workers Organizing Committee (AWOC), led by Larry Itliong, walked out on strike against grape growers in the Delano area. Under pressure from AWOC and their own members, Chavez's mostly Latino NFWA decided to join AWOC and was unexpectedly thrown into a five-year grape strike. In the course of only a few months, the dogged door-to-door community organizing and mutual aid approach quickly transformed into the largest union movement of its time.

Chavez rose to the occasion and became a spokesperson for the strike, both in the fields and nationally. He was a strategic leader and did not advocate (as many past union leaders had) for farmworkers to be included in the National Labor Relations Board (NLRB), because consumer boycotts were excluded under the NLRB. As a result, Chavez was able to successfully launch a boycott of grapes, which became a central strategy of the movement. As Chavez's public statements of social justice, nonviolence, and ethnic pride attracted support from a diversity of union, student, church, and civil rights activists from around the country, the consumer boycott became international and lasted for five years. Soon Chavez's ally, Walter Reuther, president of the United Auto Workers (UAW), came to Delano and decided to financially back the strike. With support from the UAW, the NFWA began a boycott of a major wine grape grower, Schenley Industries.

In the spring of 1966, the grape boycott gained support around the country. Senator Robert F. Kennedy, a fellow Catholic, joined the picket lines. Striking farmworkers embarked on a highly publicized "pilgrimage" from the grape fields of Delano to the state Capitol in Sacramento. The union soon expanded its efforts by striking and boycotting additional grape growers, including DiGiorgio Fruit Co. and Giumarra Vineyards Corporation. After DiGiorgio brought in the more industry-friendly Teamsters to oppose Chavez's NFWA, the AWOC and the UFW merged to form the United Farm Workers of America as an affiliate of the AFL-CIO. After the merger, the DiGiorgio workers voted in the UFW.

The move toward formal incorporation as a union affiliated with the AFL-CIO was far from unanimous. Dolores Huerta was wary. James Drake was initially protective of the idea of the NFWA serving as a self-help association owned by farmworker families and feared that this approach would be discarded once the movement formalized into a union.[21] This moment of transition toward incorporation as a union, and the eventual decision to found nonprofit organizations, was critical for the movement's articulation of self-help. Would resources be devoted to building a farmworker-led membership base and self-sustaining mutual aid organizations to transform the industry from the bottom up, or would they direct resources toward formal institutions that required paid staff and outside resources?

Between 1965 and 1967, philanthropic allies were also uncomfortable with the approach of the farmworker movement, one of the most uniquely multifaceted, diversely resourced and brilliantly strategized movements of the 1960s.[22] Was it a regional farmworker self-help poverty program? Was it a Chicano wing of the civil rights movement? Was it a union? Some public and private funders were attracted to the mutual aid and community service philosophy, which aligned with the self-help orientations of the federal War on Poverty. Others were attracted to the cultural pride and social justice spirit, which worked alongside the ideals of the civil rights movement. Yet most funders were wary of the movement's growing union organizing capacity and affiliations.

Initially, key leaders of the farmworker movement were equally wary of outside funders. Some even promised to never seek grants from public or private agencies, which they believed might co-opt a more radical worker-owned movement. Despite its own funding from the National Council of Churches and the Max L. Rosenberg Foundation, Migrant Ministry argued that publicly and privately funded self-help housing and infrastructure programs risked co-opting the advocacy and organizing potential of the movement.[23] Regardless of the moral and political stance against outside funds, movement leaders changed their minds when they found out that multiple farmworker-serving organizations were receiving large grants from the OEO's War on Poverty. According to lead organizer Gilbert Padilla in an interview with Marshall Ganz, Chavez feared that if "the NFWA did not get the OEO funds, others would who might not share the NFWA's organizing agenda ... and by reversing itself on rejection of outside money, the NFWA tried to preempt claims of others who might use funds in less productive ways."[24]

Thus, competition with other farmworker-serving organizations in the Central Valley, such as the programs supported by Rosenberg Foundation and the unprecedented financial investment in fighting rural poverty by the newly established OEO, influenced the decision of NFWA leaders to seek significant amounts of public and private funds. In 1965, only a year after claiming that public funds would corrupt a volunteer-led farmworker movement, the NFWA applied for an OEO grant of $500,000. The NFWA was forced to return these funds amid protest among growers and mainstream stakeholders who were upset that the OEO was supporting strikes and unionization. However, by 1966, the movement was seeking support from private funders, resulting in a heated debate on the limits to farmworker self-help and the incorporation of the private, nonprofit movement institutions to which Chavez eventually retreated.

THE WAR ON POVERTY: COORDINATION, COMPETITION, AND CO-OPTATION IN THE FIELDS

Between 1965 and 1967, the OEO attracted farmworker leaders to work with federally funded poverty organizations in the Central Valley. The new organizations presented a dilemma for the growing union movement, which relied on a limited pool of volunteers and resources. Would these federally funded programs distract leadership from and corrupt the worker-owned movement, as originally hypothesized by Chavez and Migrant Ministry? Or might they bring new talent, energy, and funds to the region? Chavez attempted to capitalize on the assets of the new poverty programs. But the young and energetic staff employed by OEO projects quickly learned that they were prohibited from having any relations with the union. Eventually, the War on Poverty brought resources to the valley but also introduced institutional barriers, organizational turf battles, and limited definitions of farmworker self-help.

The War on Poverty's Community Action Projects (CAPs) in the Central Valley were dominated by the Quaker American Friends Service Committee (AFSC) affiliates in Tulare County, introduced in the previous section.[25] According to the OEO's requirement of "maximum feasible participation" of the poor, local committees with an even one-third split among officials, people from city organizations, and the poor shaped the agenda for each CAP. The CAP programs, ranging from youth services to daycare to migrant health and legal services, were managed by local volunteers, farmworker leaders, and paid poverty staff. With a long history of serving migrant populations in the self-help poverty action model popular with the OEO, AFSC leaders were logical contacts for federal officials looking to establish CAPs. According to Kirke Wilson, president of the Rosenberg Foundation from 1976 to 2002 and a former farmworker organizer, the OEO was impressed by the Tulare CAPs (because of the trail-blazing work of the AFSC in Tulare) and hoped to replicate their active engagement of the poor in other counties and states. What they found out later was that the Tulare CAPs were particularly successful because a large pool of talented people, including an array of college students and young idealists, were attracted to Visalia (a hub city in the agricultural Tulare County) to get involved in the emerging UFW movement. Many of these young activists, students, and volunteers could not find access to the movement, as Chavez tightened the ranks (described below), and turned to the CAPs as a way to get involved. As the strike intensified in 1965, local growers became suspicious of the involvement of the US government (specifically the OEO) in fueling strikes. Under pressure from growers and their political allies, the OEO began to reign in CAP staff eager to join the strikes and vetoed poverty funding that had anything to do with organizing farmworkers.

The OEO-founded California Rural Legal Assistance (CRLA) was a key example of the growing conflicts between the UFW and the War on Poverty projects. Founded in 1966 with an OEO grant to provide legal services to California's rural poor, CRLA was an immediate ally to the farmworker movement. However, although many of the original CRLA staff were eager to help build the movement, the OEO made it clear that CRLA must separate their own work on behalf of farmworkers from union negotiations with growers or support of members involved in union cases. As the strikes intensified and contracts were gained, the union needed additional legal assistance, and some CLRA staff's involvement blurred the lines between the poverty organization and the union. As a result, leaders of the poverty programs required staff to pull back from supporting the union. In February 1967, James D. Lorenz, the director of CRLA, wrote to Chavez to clarify the lines between the work of an OEO organization and the union:

> Dear Cesar, Despite our meeting on February 8, when, for the first time we talked about what CRLA could and could not do for farmworkers in California, I have the feeling that there have been a number of problems which are likely to persist between you and ourselves, unless we bring them out on the table. The main problem is a lack of clarification about the things we can and can't do....

Several days ago, one of your people said to me that CRLA is no better than any other poverty organization. I don't think that's true but at the same time, I know that he feels cheated because we are not representing you in negotiations with growers, and we are not bringing lawsuits on the Union's behalf. That's correct and must continue that way, much as I personally sympathize with what you are doing. That was a part of the original understanding with the OEO, an understanding that you were willing to go along with.[26]

Though Chavez rejected the federal poverty program model, which asked the poor to join time-consuming stakeholder processes that prohibited talk of union organizing and strikes, he wanted to use the new legal talent brought to the region through poverty programming. Although the OEO tied poverty program directors' hands so they could not directly support the movement, the OEO could not control individual leaders such as Pablo Espinoza and Jerry Cohen (a lawyer and central figure in the movement) who worked with both and refused to recognize the lines between movement organizing and poverty services, or between a legal service agency and a union.[27] Frustrated with the limits drawn by the OEO yet cognizant of the value the poverty programs staff brought to the movement, Chavez continued to lobby for federal funding for CRLA with the hope of keeping the young legal talent in the Central Valley.[28] Although the lines were drawn between the organizations in terms of staff time, CRLA and the UFW became close allies in the battles against growers.

While the UFW was able to successfully partner with War on Poverty–funded organizations such as CRLA, the growing need to staff official union organizing and contract negotiation made the UFW protective of its own leadership and competitive for funds and human resources. For example, in a 1967 letter to the director of the Central California Action Associates, another War on Poverty program, Chavez wrote:

> It has come to my attention on several occasions that your staff people have been soliciting assistance from our staff and permission to attend our meetings in the San Joaquin Valley. I would like to advise you that the policy of our union is that no other local group is permitted to make any arrangements, financial or otherwise, without consulting the head office first.... I would greatly appreciate it if your staff would not infringe on the time of our farmworkers.[29]

It makes strategic sense that Chavez would attempt to keep volunteer leaders focused on the strike, the boycott, and the union—away from organizational "poverty program" activities that risked draining the limited resources available to farmworkers. However, some of the poverty agencies and poverty staff were fighting *against* OEO vetoes to *join* the movement for farmworkers and were dismayed when Chavez began to tighten control and ownership over members. According to my interviews with movement leaders (and validated in the recent studies by Bardacke, Garcia, and Pawel), although the pre-strike days were organized around a loose member-owned model with a broad social movement base, Chavez and a small group of preacher activists from Migrant Ministry redirected decision-making away from workers toward a centralized leadership after the strike went public. Within the context of institutional competition, divergent definitions of farmworker participation, and the development of a formal union, it was not only the OEO but also Chavez himself who began to disarticulate the broad-based mutual aid and community control element of self-help from the formal union model.

Eventually, under pressure from farmers, school boards, welfare departments, and citizen groups fearful of the activities of the CAPs, the OEO vetoed the most radical and poor-people-run poverty programs in the Central Valley and the nation. As early as 1966, a small group of poor-people advocates, including UFW allies Walter Reuther (president of the UAW), senator Robert Kennedy, and disillusioned OEO director Richard Boone, convened a large number of religious, civil rights, labor, academic, and philanthropic organizations to build a new poverty organization. The idea was to support the kind of poor people's movement the OEO was increasingly dropping. With a start-up grant from the Ford Foundation, Reuther and Boone founded the Citizens' Crusade Against Poverty (CCAP) and recruited movement leaders including Huerta, Martin Luther King Jr., and Bayard Rustin to sit on the board.[30] CCAP advocates were particularly angered that under President Johnson millions of War on Poverty dollars were being transferred from neighborhood legal, health, and migrant services to Department of Labor job training programs (particularly when no jobs existed). According to one CCAP official, "OEO is the only agency which has the authorizing legislation and the desire on the part of its officials to diffuse power—place it in the hands of the people.... Now the programs are being placed in the hands of an apparatus which places a premium on centralizing the power within the government."[31] In this context, the CCAP turned away from the government and toward private foundations. With a $4 million four-year commitment from the Ford Foundation, the CCAP sought to provide funds to train community workers to help the poor organize for sustained funds from the OEO and participate more effectively in the War on Poverty. A grant from the CCAP was the first introduction to private foundations for many movement organizations, including the UFW.

A CCAP grant to the UFW in 1967 introduced the farmworker movement to program staff at both the Ford Foundation and the Field Foundation, both major funders from 1967 through the early 1970s. Headed up by Reuther, CCAP granted the UFW $200,000 to train emerging farmworker leaders in the Central Valley through the UFW's then unincorporated National Farm Worker Service Center (NFWSC). The UFW hired Fred Ross (CSO founder and longtime ally) to develop and implement a training program in which farmworker leaders would learn how to organize and represent farmworkers to local agencies. Ross was also charged with establishing the NFWSC as a viable institution to serve the needs of local farmworkers.[32] After only one year of the UFW/NFWSC/Fred Ross training program, the CCAP informed the UFW that the Ford Foundation was ending funding to CCAP. With additional funds from the Ford Foundation, a new organization called the Center for Community Change (CCC) was founded to absorb OEO- and CCAP-related projects.[33] By 1968 the CCAP was in battle to keep alive the remaining CAPs around the country that were truly poor-led, including the highly contested Child Development Group of Mississippi.[34]

In 1968, the year that the poverty programs were handed to other federal departments or the Ford Foundation's CCC, violence and tragedy struck. With the assassination of Dr. Martin Luther King Jr. and senator Robert Kennedy, an escalating war in Vietnam, and violent uprisings around the country, leaders of the civil rights and farmworker causes believed that the movement was cresting. The farmworkers in particular lost two key allies and friends, King and Kennedy, when they needed them most. Between 1967 and 1970, hundreds of UFW strikers, volunteers, and allies toured the country advocating for farmworkers and the growing movement. In the violent year of 1968, grape strikers in the Central Valley threatened to turn to violence. In response, Chavez fasted for twenty-five days to redirect the movement toward peace. Only months before he was shot, King had sent Chavez a message of solidarity. Chavez remained weak after his fast but continued to promote the boycott internationally and in this same year dedicated most of his staff to Robert Kennedy's Democratic primary campaign for president—until the day he was also shot. Kennedy was an important ally to the farmworker movement in introducing their cause to both the civil rights movement and mainstream politicians. His assassination was very difficult for Chavez. These major blows were compounded by Chavez's growing paranoia, which was fueled by death threats, FBI surveillance of the movement, and his unfounded suspicion of disloyalty among his closest allies and organizers.[35]

During this time, the Teamsters union returned as a major rival in winning contracts with farms in the fields of California. The Teamsters were known to negotiate more relaxed contracts with no housing or pesticide clauses and a lower minimum wage, and they were moving in on expiring UFW contracts. Within this context, and a weakened Chavez with increasing distrust of the farmworker and volunteer leaders within his own movement, the UFW became more distant from the fields. In 1971, Chavez relocated from Delano to a retreat outside of Bakersfield called La Paz.[36] There, Chavez and a central group of movement leaders and family members formally incorporated the National Farm Worker Service Center as a 501(c)(3) nonprofit organization, once called by Chavez "the hustling arm of the union," alluding to its ability to attract tax-deductible philanthropic donations. The forming of the NFWSC and subsequent non-profit institutions further distanced an already separated movement from the fields.

THE HUSTLING ARM OF THE UNION:
FUNDING THE NATIONAL FARM
WORKER SERVICE CENTER

In 1966 a central group of movement leaders established the NFWSC to provide services and engage farmworker families in educational programs. The NFWSC's first large grant was through the Ford Foundation for the CCAP organizer-training program. When the CCAP folded into the CCC, the UFW's still unincorporated NFWSC was required to report to the Ford Foundation with the CCC as an evaluator and grant monitor. It was not until the incorporation of the service center as a nonprofit organization in late 1969, under the leadership of LeRoy Chatfield, that the NFWSC was able to receive funds directly from a private foundation without an intermediary such as the CCC. While the NFWSC was officially incorporated to receive foundation funds, movement leadership did not anticipate the way this process would limit the kind of farmworker self-help that was possible. Strict lines were quickly drawn between the social service work and economic justice organizing. The UFW's relationship with private funders, particularly the Field Foundation, paved the way for the retreat from organizing to a nonprofit institutional model—a space that became all too comfortable when crisis intensified within movement leadership and in the fields.[37]

The Field and Ford Foundations were attracted to the "community union" mutual aid philosophy of the farmworker movement, which fit the mainstream approaches to self-help poverty action of the day. The first UFW appeal to the Field Foundation was in 1966 in a pitch from Richard Boone's ally in poverty programming, Edgar Cahn. Cahn had drafted legislation for Johnson's War on Poverty and was particularly influential in encouraging the participation of the poor in the programs that serve them. Cahn's letter to Field Foundation director Leslie Dunbar shows that he believed that private funders might assist the farmworker movement.[38] In the letter, Cahn lists the characteristics of a farmworker community union within the context of the then innovative self-help poverty action framework, including that it would (1) focus on a defined geographical area experiencing entrenched poverty, (2) be governed by local residents and stakeholders, (3) mesh trade union functions with community service and programming, (4) mobilize outside resources, including governmental and private funding, and (5) set up diverse citizen review committees to evaluate and monitor the union activity.

According to Cahn, the community union would, like the early Community Development Corporations of the inner city and the rural South (another product of Ford Foundation intervention in inner-city conflict), "attempt to stabilize the fluid labor market picture of the migrant workers by adaptation of the 'community corporation' concept that Milt Kotler, Robert Kennedy and others have been exploring." In other words, building on the earlier projects of the Ford Foundation, the community union model would provide an institutional basis for organizing disenfranchised groups of people through their own participation, monitored by a diverse array of regional stakeholders. Cahn's plea to Dunbar included a discussion of how he hoped that Field and other private funders might be able to help the union out of the legal bind it found itself in, with the OEO restricting the legal work of CRLA. The ensuing three-year conversation between Chavez and Dunbar exposed the lines that funders drew around the movement's approach to farmworker participation and the effect these constraints had on the future direction of the UFW.

On January 30, 1967, one month after the original pitch from Edgar Cahn, Dunbar responded to a January 19 letter from Chavez, with a copy sent to Cahn, explaining:

> Dear Mr. Chavez: We have your letter of January 19. As I told you when we talked, I do not know what we can do with this, but I shall do the best I can to get you an early answer. I suppose I did not truly realize until I saw your letterhead that you were fully affiliated with the AFL-CIO. I wonder what success you have had or could reasonably anticipate in securing the necessary assistance from the AFL-CIO. I enjoyed very much talking with you and hope that we may have an opportunity to meet some day. Sincerely yours, Leslie Dunbar.[39]

Dunbar's letter to Chavez shows that the movement's resemblance, connections, and work to support unionization initially made it "unfundable" to private foundations. At the risk of quoting at great length, below is a response from Chavez that makes a compelling case for why the farmworker movement, like the civil rights movement, desired private foundation assistance for legal representation. Chavez addressed Dunbar in a letter dated January 30, 1967:

> Dear Mr. Dunbar: It has come to my attention that the Field Foundation would like more comprehensive information regarding our request for assistance in financing a full-time attorney to work with the [United Farm Workers] Organizing Committee, AFL-CIO.... Let me point out that the problems involved in organizing farm-

workers are unique. Excluded as we are from the basic protective legislation of the National Labor Relations Act, we have had to improvise means of organizing other than those usually used in industrial cases. Our approach has been to offer a broad program of services, which build a base of membership cooperation from which to launch out in the direction of strikes for union recognition.... In every action we take we face tremendous opposition. On a local level this comes from the growers themselves in concert with the power structures they control, i.e., city council, police department, school board, and country officialdom. On higher levels we run into political opposition (such as that of Mr. Reagan in California and Mr. Connolly in Texas) and unified opposition from state organizations of growers and their institutions.... Most of our needs are those of workers either "outside of the law" or discriminated against by the law. Consistently our pickets have been arrested as a means of harassment. Our civil rights are disregarded daily....

The key point I wish to make is that even though the AFL-CIO and the IUD and the UAW have been of tremendous help we cannot come close to affording the costs of the strike, much less the luxury of legal defense.... In many ways the need of attorneys is similar to those who aided in the civil rights workers in the South. We need attorneys who fight in this jungle, where we are. We need attorneys who can help us organize, using the law as a weapon, rather than standing by as we now do, seeing the law used against us. We operate in an area of grayness, where few laws apply, and where many of those used against us are of questionable constitutionality. I hope this helps to explain our dire need of a grant for legal assistance.

Sincerely, Cesar E. Chavez[40]

When this letter was written, Chavez and the organizers of the UFW were in the middle of heated strikes with the major grape growers in the Central Valley and were expanding their operation to Texas. Movement volunteers and members were traveling around the state and country spreading the word about La Causa and the California table grape boycott. Chavez himself was preparing for a national boycott, and the strike lines were becoming violent. The union was under pressure from angry grower associations, status quo citizen organizations, local and state representatives, and an increasingly embattled War on Poverty. In this context, and despite the movement's initial resistance to outside public and private funds, Chavez made a compelling case for private funding in his letter to Dunbar: only private funding could support organizing work outside of the current, and potentially unconstitutional, interpretation of the law, and only private funding could support the rights of migrant agricultural workers. However, Chavez would soon discover that although private foundations were willing to fund community service and even unprecedented change in civil law during the social movements of the 1960s, questions of labor relations remained outside their grant guidelines.

It became very clear that funders of the movement drew the line around their support not at community service or even at legal action but directly at labor organizing. Dunbar responded to Chavez's letter, citing the AFL-CIO affiliation as of primary concern: "I am afraid the answer is that we shall not be able to assist you at this time in employing legal counsel.... I think the problem is, quite frankly, that we do not wish to make a grant for the direct support of a unit of the AFL-CIO."[41] Dunbar understood that his board would not approve of a grant to a major union and attempted to redirect Chavez to the legal institutions that charted the way for and flourished after the Civil Rights Act of 1964. Unfamiliar with the logic of private foundations, Chavez did not take this news lightly.

> Dear Mr. Dunbar: I am quite disappointed to receive your letter of March 14 describing the decision of the Field Foundation not to make a grant to the U.F.W.O.C. The disappointment is all the

greater considering the reasoning behind turning down our request.... Your letter implies that our organization does not come within the area of your interests, which are civil rights, human relations, and child welfare. Somehow we are not able to draw the same conclusion that you draw, that concern for labor relations puts us in another "area of interest" outside that of civil rights, human relations, and child welfare.... I ask that the decision taken be re-examined. It is not just that the farmworkers choosing to join our organization should be discriminated against because of our affiliation with the AFL-CIO. Sincerely yours, Cesar E. Chavez[42]

Almost two months later, Dunbar responded to Chavez's angry reply by reminding him of his suggestion that the Field Foundation might be able to fund legal counsel for the farmworker movement if formally channeled through a legal agency such as the ACLU. Subsequent correspondence between Leslie Dunbar, Edgar Cahn, Jack Pemberton of the ACLU, and Martin Garbus of the Roger Baldwin Foundation of the ACLU alludes to a series of phone calls meant to persuade Chavez to go the way of a partnership with a legal agency. In June 1967, Dunbar informed Garbus that the Field Foundation board had approved a grant of $25,000 (the amount requested) to protect the civil liberties of the migrant farmworkers (that is, the legal staff of the United Farm Workers Organizing Committee, or UFWOC, later renamed the UFW), expressed his admiration for the UFW, and enclosed a check to the Roger Baldwin Foundation.[43] In a similar model as civil rights movement organizations partnering with legal aid agencies, the Field-funded relationship with the Baldwin Foundation worked out well, according to a series of cordial and satisfied letters from Chavez, Garbus, and Dunbar in 1967 and early 1968.

However, Field's concerns about funding organizing in the economic field soon re-emerged. In the spring of 1968, Garbus wrote to Dunbar asking for more funds to enlarge the legal team in the face of serious challenges by the industry and the threats to CRLA, which had been covertly providing legal services to the movement. "The migrant organization is at a critical point and may not last unless additional help is provided," Garbus wrote.[44] The crisis facing the movement included the CRLA Central Valley offices being restricted from working on any case related to the strikes (under pressure from the OEO), grape growers actively recruiting undocumented immigrants to break the strikes, violence against strikers at the hand of local police, capricious firing of union members, general discrimination against migrant families by local officials and service providers, and emerging pesticide poisoning cases—all situations that called for legal assistance. Jerry Cohen, working with a volunteer legal team, was struggling to keep up as the cases mounted.

Instead of continuing support to the legal program at this critical juncture in the movement, a conflict arose that yet again reignited the Field Foundation's resistance to funding a union. A four-month correspondence between Leslie Dunbar and Jerry Cohen raised questions for Dunbar that proved fatal for the movement's legal services funding from the Field Foundation. Cohen was known as a fiery and (successfully) antagonistic person who never shied away from speaking his mind. After he was reprimanded by Dunbar for a fiery speech to the press, which included evidence of the US government's buying table grapes to sabotage the boycott, Cohen asked Dunbar if he might resume speaking to the press about a $75 million antitrust suit growers were attempting to file, designed to frighten chain stores out of boycotting grapes. Cohen argued that his speaking out on this case would not jeopardize the tax-exempt status of the Field Foundation funds because "the AFL-CIO contributes $9,000 which is used exclusively for my salary. Therefore I alone would be spokesman to the press on union related suits. Auerbuch, Farnsworth and the other attorneys which we hope to hire shortly would restrict their comments to Service Center cases."[45] After finding out that the AFL-CIO was paying Cohen's salary, Dunbar was clearly upset and replied, "I was especially interested in reading that your salary is paid by the AFL-CIO. I had not, perhaps because of inattention, known that, and there seems nothing in our file regarding it. Could you give us a summary of the financing of the legal work going on?"[46] Cohen's response confirmed that the AFL-CIO paid his salary to work on union cases and that the Field Foundation's current $35,000 and the Mexican American Legal Defense and Education Fund's (MALDEF) $41,000 were spent on legal staff and litigation and office costs. Not satisfied with these answers, Dunbar wrote to Chavez to remind him that:

> To you, it may seem an artificial distinction the Union from the Center (NFWSC). If it is, in fact, an artificial distinction then I believe we may be in trouble. I think you would see why if you asked yourself how many other unions, AFL-CIO or otherwise, get foundation support. Few if any.... I believe your movement (and I believe in it as a strong and good movement) will be much easier for this or any other foundation to assist if the Service Center (NFWSC) salaried staff members are not paid from union funds.... I would therefore suggest that the Service Center administer your medical, welfare, and educational programs and that lawyers attached to the Service Center be only those whose principle [*sic*] work is in connection with these medical, welfare, and educational programs and with the civil liberties and civil rights of farmworkers.... These practices would I think serve to protect your tax-exemption, and would accord with the Service Center's own articles of incorporation, which say that it will not "engage in activities—not in the furtherance of its specific and primary

educational and charitable purposes." ... We want to be able
to assist without at the same time giving our support to any other
economic organization, such as the AFL-CIO or any other national
union.[47]

Despite multiple attempts from both Cohen and Chavez to
explain the distinction between Service Center cases—such as
worker injuries, the right to have a decent toilet and shade in the
fields, and the right not be fired for union activity—and union
cases, Dunbar refused to continue funding the UFW-NFWSC
legal program. Dunbar concluded:

> You understand that we do not believe that we can continue, after
> this year, to contribute to the legal program if its principal staff or
> any of them are paid salaries by the AFL-CIO.... We can and
> would want to talk with you about other things, such as – for exam-
> ple – the Service Center's health programs or possibly, the general
> administration costs of the Service Center.[48]

That was the exact direction taken by the Field Foundation.
Many other foundations followed a similar path, making significant grants to the general administration of the growing NFWSC
but not to union activities, boycotts, strikes, legal services, worker
cooperatives, or any form of worker organizing.[49] The Ford Foundation, which had reservations about funding the project because
of its "political nature" (that is, the focus on protecting migrants'
right to strike and organize) continued to fund the UFW's service center work via the CCC. In 1968, the Ford Foundation
assisted the UFW in applying for 501(c)(3) nonprofit status to be
eligible for additional non-union-related charitable funds for
educational and service programs associated with the movement.
After the 1969 incorporation as a 501(c)(3) organization, several
private foundations, including the Ford Foundation, granted support to the service center for more farmworker service program-

ming (for example, the creation of a community school and a clinic) and general administrative support. All of these programs fell within the acceptable logic of philanthropic self-help. Unlike the early mutual aid and cooperative associations, which were owned and led by farmworkers and poor migrant families, these programs depended on resources from outside stakeholders. They also focused primarily on how farmworkers could help themselves improve their own behaviors and conditions, without challenging individual growers or the structure of the agricultural industry. The revolutionary interpretation of mutual aid to foster self-determination and ownership, and the subsequent union approach, were both replaced by a more traditional charitable model.

Despite these successes in attracting foundation funding, the movement was in crisis throughout the 1970s. Foundation grants for the NFWSC, and the seven additional nonprofit organizations eventually founded by UFW leadership, did not face the mounting strategic problems of the movement; they required increased administration and eventually distracted movement leadership from union organizing when the movement faced its most severe challenges.[50] The external challenges included both changes in the farm industry and increasing competition with the Teamsters. In 1970, major conglomerates of growers closed their nonfarm product businesses, making the UFW's previously successful consumer boycott tool ineffective. Disguising production processes and distribution in large international conglomerations was a particularly successful tactic in avoiding protest and boycott of consumer goods. Also in the summer of 1970, two weeks after the Teamsters made a sweetheart deal with major growers in the Salinas Valley, workers initiated a general strike. This strike was organized by emerging farmworker leaders who were not official union organizers and were not approved by Chavez. Angered by the leaders' refusal to end the strike, Chavez denounced the main organizers. This moment represents one of the many rifts among movement leadership that led to the highly criticized "purges"[51] of the entire volunteer legal and organizing staff and consolidation of leadership among Chavez's close associates and family by 1977.[52]

Leading up to the "purges," Chavez and his family moved away from Delano to La Paz to focus on the NFWSC and other institutional wings of the movement. A two-hundred-acre facility thirty miles southeast of Bakersfield rented for almost no cost from a wealthy friend of the movement, La Paz was to be developed as an educational and training facility for farmworkers and their families. During this time Chavez spoke of the importance of building self-sustaining non-union organizations, even suggesting that self-determination through intentional community living and organic gardening was the future of the movement. However, no record of programs for or engagement of farmworkers exists in the NFWSC meeting minutes recorded during this period.[53] At one meeting in 1971, with Cesar Chavez, Larry Itliong, Dolores Huerta, LeRoy Chatfield, Rev. James Drake, Phillip Vera Cruz, and Rev. Wayne (Chris) Hartmeyer, Chavez suggested that all of the Field Foundation funds and the remaining Ford Foundation funds be spent on building maintenance. The "hustling arm of the union" became the hustle.

Not only did foundations' limited definitions of self-help undermine the political organizing of the movement, but their program operation and paperwork requirements also inundated movement leadership. Throughout the 1970s, overwhelmed by internal crisis and external threat, the leadership could not keep up with the administrative duties that the multiple foundation grants required.[54] Between 1970 and 1976, angry letters from foundations were received claiming that there was no documentation of how funds were being spent, no financial accounting, and unapproved re-appropriation of funds to undisclosed projects.[55] In one case, a NFWSC staff person noted: "The $30,000 [from the Stern Foundation] remains intact for several reasons. Decision was made that La Causa's life was seriously threatened and that many of the projects would have to be postponed."[56] Other responses to foundations asked that original plans for worker coops, credit unions, and legal work in other states be redirected back to general administration at the NFWSC. A 1973 NFWSC memo titled "Problems with Foundations" lists staff reports due, funds not spent, and outstanding decisions to be made about previous requests to redirect funds toward administration.[57] The challenges of bureaucratic inundation persist in the case studies featured in later chapters.

As administrative teams were employed at La Paz with foundation grants, crisis in the fields was rising. The UFW's historic grape contracts expired, violence increased on the picket lines, and hired Teamsters vigilantes and local sheriffs attacked striking workers. In 1974 growers approached governor Ronald Reagan to put an end to the picket lines. Reagan did not accomplish a compromise between the growers and the union, but in 1975, with the collaboration of Chavez, new governor Edmund Gerald "Jerry" Brown Jr. supported and signed a statute to establish the Agricultural Labor Relations Board (ALRB) to create peace in the fields, provide farm labor with basic negotiating rights, and protect the safety of workers through new legislation. The ALRB became the new battleground for the UFW. Brown staffed the ALRB with pro-labor UFW people and passed new worker-friendly regulations.[58] However, with more resources being spent on legislative campaigns and on managing the new union-affiliated nonprofits, the movement accrued debt and fewer dues-paying members, making the union increasingly dependent on donations from outside sources.[59] Another blow to the movement came when George Deukmejian was elected governor in 1982 and transformed the UFW-won ALRB into an advocacy arm of grower associations. With the new ALRB, the union was faced with additional contract losses, failed lettuce strikes, and boycotts and fasts. With time, growers developed new tactics and began to take the UFW to court for civil damages.

Concurrently, as intimately told in Frank Bardacke's book, the distance between the administrative offices at La Paz and the fieldworkers widened, in what fieldworker reps of the UFW believed was an insulting battle of theatrics. Administrative directives to dress as peasants, drive aging cars, and appear to be poor, downtrodden people insulted Mexican-born fieldworkers. Many field reps considered agricultural work an honorable profession. Preferring to present themselves as workers seeking economic justice, they were angered that they had to exaggerate their poverty and suffering to gain support from funders and middle-class allies of the boycotts. As Chavez retreated further, suggesting that the future of the movement might be found in creating a model community at La Paz funded by grants, the sale of candles, and an organic garden,[60] the farmworkers' plight was promoted as a charitable cause but not as a movement based on the collective power of workers.[61]

CONCLUSION: THE LONG DECLINE

By the late 1970s, the group of incorporated nonprofit "movement entities," including grower-supported medical, pension, and education funds, a credit union, and the NFWSC, had at least $10 million in assets, including grants from federal agencies to pay off bad loans made by the credit union, to build a microwave telephone system, and for equipment, supplies, maintenance, and basic educational programs for farmworkers.[62] By the early 2000s, UFW membership had shrunk to under 5,000, yet movement organizations were collectively receiving more than $1 million a year for service and educational programs, from funders including the California Endowment, the Packard Foundation, the Kellogg Foundation, and the Annie E. Casey Foundation. Unfortunately, from the late 1970s to the present day, scandals of fraud, nepotism, and mismanagement have plagued the movement institutions.[63]

The legacy of the farmworkers' struggle is its brilliant approach to taking on a seemingly monolithic industrial system of rule through a unique combination of community organizing, migrant self-help, and cultural organizing tactics. Through a new articulation of "mutual aid," CSO-style organizing, strikes, boycotts, and the cultural messages spread through *Teatro Campesino* and the news outlets of the movement, a group of individuals and institutions presented an alternative politics and culture to a population previously thought "unorganizable." Fitting within the particular conjuncture of the well-resourced American War on Poverty and a raging civil rights movement, the farmworkers' self-help and ethnic pride approach took flight and gained support around the nation and world.

As the farmworker movement made a significant break in the history of the agricultural system, it faced internal limits. The tension between a community union focused on ideas of self-help, volunteerism, social services, and member-based ownership and the founding of an AFL-CIO–affiliated union with a formal bureaucratic leadership structure proved too severe for movement leaders to manage. In the face of internal leadership crisis, growing external challenges, and the faltering leadership of Chavez, the union retreated from both worker organizing and the community union vision to nonprofit institutional management. The American War on Poverty brought new resources to Central Valley farmworker communities, but in the process it introduced competition, turf battles, and the politics of philanthropy. Engaging in the carefully nonantagonistic politics and program frameworks required by the Ford Foundation and Field Foundation, in particular, separated the economic and social goals of the movement, union organizing from community service, and movement leaders from organizing in the agricultural fields.

Given that foundation endowments are created and maintained by profits made in private industry, it is not surprising that they do not fund economic rights, boycotts, or labor organizing, despite the deep connection between economic inequality and the social concerns that many foundations seek to address. In fact, during the social movements of the 1960s, funding lines were often drawn at the economic field. The Black Power movement's battle for economic self-determination, Martin Luther King Jr.'s call for a poor people's movement, and many of the citizen projects launched during the War on Poverty were labeled dangerous and violent causes and were eventually defunded, shut down, or co-opted by government officials and private funders.[64] In many cases, such as the Ford and Field Foundations' involvement in the Voter Education Project, investments in more moderate organizing that garnered popular consensus, such as voter registration, overshadowed the economic equality aspects of the movement.[65]

Thus, on the one hand, this research confirms the expected—that private philanthropy will not fund projects that attempt to make significant changes in the economic sphere or address the structural causes of poverty and inequality. On the other hand, a story of top down co-optation and control, as presented in much of the critical philanthropy scholarship, is insufficient in explaining the relationship between the movement and funders in that it neglects the complicated negotiations between foundations and movement leadership. Chavez's doubt in the union model, interest in establishing nonprofit movement institutions, and embattled retreat from the worker/volunteer soul of the movement also contributed to compromised framings of migrant self-help. Chavez even sharpened his interest in developing non-union entities in the course of the 1980s, and became enthralled by "business" theory and techniques to simultaneously improve wage labor and agricultural farm profit, as evidenced by his conversations with management gurus Peter Drucker and Patrick Below and subsequent business partnerships in the rose industry.[66]

As in urban renewal in the early twentieth century, tentatively negotiated agreements among poor people's movement leaders and powerful philanthropic supporters of self-help poverty action eventually generated consent. The self-help formulation that was acceptable to funders, middle-class consumer boycott supporters, and eventually even to a worn-down Chavez consumed with protecting his own power was that of the poor field hand in need of skills, education, and philanthropic charity—but not a movement in struggle for self-determination, community control, and economic power for the workers who proudly harvest the nation's food.

CHAPTER THREE

Foundation-Driven Collaborative Initiatives

Civic Participation for What?

In a private foundation office with sparkling views of the San Francisco Bay Area, a diverse group of immigrant and farmworker advocates gathered to discuss how to attract resources to their initiative, the Immigrant Participation Collaborative (IPC).[1] The IPC's sponsor, the Stewart Kinney Foundation, a California-based foundation, had convened the meeting. The IPC members had traveled to San Francisco from economically struggling urban hubs scattered across the Central Valley—Stockton, Modesto, Fresno, and Bakersfield. All nonprofit professionals, including a Hmong charity worker, a Chicana farmworker organizer, a young Jewish legal aid lawyer, and a handful of white and Latino male nonprofit directors, the IPC members eagerly assembled in their best "meet the funder" clothes. The group knew well that if they wanted the immigrant civic participation initiative to survive beyond the typical five-to-eight-year philanthropic commitment, they would have to appeal to other foundations.

Following oohs and ahs at the staggering view, and bites of catered sandwiches, the IPC's founding program officer, John

Sibley, called the meeting to order. After much discussion in search of a compelling marketing message for the IPC, one member said, "What really brings this all together is poverty. This is what makes it so hard for immigrants to have a voice—to participate. What foundation would turn away from the poorest region in the state—where the need is greatest?"

Everyone agreed, and they began to articulate the causes of enduring poverty in the region: an agricultural system that relies on continuing waves of seasonal low-wage migrant labor; stalled immigration reform; and the historically racist power structure in the region. As they began to form a shared analysis, Patricia, an organizer with years of experience stretching back to the California farmworker movement, reminded the group: "But I know that funders don't like to hear these things. They want to see families and neighbors making a difference—but not confronting 'Ag.'" Again the meeting participants agreed: foundations do not want to hear about organizing against agriculture or the valley status quo.

Silent until this moment, Sibley, who had initiated and continued to advocate for the IPC, concurred. The most successful framework would avoid direct critiques of the agricultural industry that had created the circumstances of poverty that the partnership ultimately hoped to alleviate. With an uneasy smile, he conveyed his own struggle to garner support for the IPC from his board, which was more comfortable with the idea of immigrant civic participation than with community organizing. At the close of the meeting, he agreed to fund the creation of colorful brochures and a "funder bus tour" of the valley to direct the attention of national philanthropies to the IPC. The main message would juxtapose the dire need and poor living conditions with hardworking immigrants engaging in public life.

Through the story of the IPC, this chapter shows how the foundation-led civic participation "collaborative initiative" maintains the myth that poor people can alter their conditions solely by helping themselves. Within the broader context of the turn away from publicly funded poverty programs throughout the 1980s and 1990s, foundations in the United States and development institutions in the global South promoted "participatory" projects to increase civic responsibility among the poor.[2] By the late 1990s poverty scholars began to document the ways in which privately funded "civil society" initiatives professionalize and co-opt poor people's movements.[3] In some cases the empowerment ideals of the movements of the '60s and '70s were transformed into neutral self-help programs that avoid collective analysis of class, structural inequality, or imperialism. The most radical critiques, as in James Petras's studies in Latin American, claim that benign self-help programs destroy social movements by co-opting grass-roots leadership and facilitating collaboration with capitalist interests.[4]

Civic engagement programs are often managed through privately funded multi-organizational partnerships. An individual foundation or development institution will recruit or in some cases mandate nonprofits to participate in coordinated work to deliver a specific set of outcomes, commonly over the course of five to eight years. While the 1990s saw a number of partnerships focused on civic participation, sometimes funders organize nonprofits around delivering services previously provided by the state.[5] In other cases, foundation initiatives propose to address a set of regionally defined issues. Alternately termed "partnerships,"[6] "comprehensive community initiatives,"[7] or "collaboratives,"[8] many of these programs are admitted disasters that require nonprofit organizations to work toward abstract "theories of change" and fail to produce any measured change in the poverty or regional inequality that the funders claimed to address.[9] In California alone, both the Hewlett Foundation and the James Irvine Foundation have published reports describing how their investments in multiple-partner initiatives drastically failed to achieve their stated goals.[10] These reports most commonly refer to the need for more planning, more technical assistance, and "improved theories of change."

While several professional reports document how collaborative initiatives fail, few studies look at the very nature of the collaborative funding structure. In my research, featured in this chapter and the next, I found that three main professional practices of the "collaborative initiative" compromised farmworker and immigrant organizing across the region. First, the foundation-promoted "civic participation" theory of change turned attention away from workers and the industry and toward the civic responsibilities of poor immigrants. However, unlike much of the critical philanthropy and development scholarship popular today, I found that the terms of civic participation were not always accepted, and "grantees" were not always duped or co-opted. As the opening vignette of this chapter shows, even the foundation program officer understood that "civic participation" is a partial myth used to convince "community organizing shy" boards of trustees to invest in farmworker and immigrant advocacy organizations. The civic participation frame was strategically negotiated and sometimes provided specific opportunities to launch new organizing campaigns. Yet, it was ultimately incapable of addressing the long-standing structural inequalities experienced by valley farmworkers and immigrants.

The second practice that constrained organizing agendas was the simple dynamic of organizing around money. A collaborative grant contract holds advocacy organizations accountable to funders, not communities, members, or constituents. Critical development scholars call this shift the move from downward accountability (to the grass-roots) to upward accountability (to funders and development agencies).[11] To gain entry into foundation collaboratives, smaller organizations are also usually required to participate in "capacity building" training that changes the nature of their daily work. Capacity building often means training staff around accepted professional practice in governance, evaluation, reporting, and financial management. As I learned from the smaller partnering organizations of the IPC, increasing professionalized management takes significant time and resources away from field organizing. Additionally, the constant chase after money (grant renewals) creates distrust and competition between partnering organizations and stifles opportunities for unified action as they arise.

The third professional arrangement is foundation selection of partners. Unlike alliances shaped in social movements or direct organizing campaigns, where shared identity, issue analysis, or enemy often define partnerships, and unlike a union with its clear membership, constituents, and leadership, philanthropic collaborative partners are often selected by foundation staff. Often, program officers have little knowledge of organizing strategy, fit, or previous relationships (or rifts) between selected organizations. As one IPC member described it to me, the program officer is a "matchmaker" who convenes collaborative meetings, which function like blind dates. Partners engage in courting, tentatively agreeing to work together as they wait for commonalities to emerge. The result is often a reluctant marriage that lasts as long as the funding commitment to each individual organization.

Unlike much of the critical scholarship, I show how these forms of professionalization do not necessarily create unitary controlling subjects of neoliberal reform. As you will see in the following pages, the IPC partners were sometimes constrained and frustrated by the foundation's civic participation framework. And sometimes they brilliantly reinterpreted its meaning to serve immigrant rights organizing agendas emerging across the region. In the end, though not co-opted by a unified agenda of control, the collaborative initiative shapes programs around innocuous conceptual frameworks that appease foundation trustees' fear of community organizing. Beyond political limitations, the time and resources involved in collaborative meetings, reporting structures, evaluation metrics, and decision-making among hesitant partnerships rearranges the daily work of members—pulling staff away from their own missions and toward a temporary collaborative structure. One partner aptly calls this dilemma "working for the collaborative beast."

This chapter explores the civic participation "collaborative initiative" through the IPC, which received over $5 million each year from 1996 through 2003. Before introducing the IPC, I provide a brief history of the political, economic, and social factors that converged to set the context for funding immigrant civic participation. I then introduce the IPC and show how the partners accepted, rejected, and negotiated the civic participation framework. The significant limits posed by organizing around money (or upward accountability) are explored through the IPC's small grants and cultural programs.

FROM WORKER RIGHTS TO CIVIC PARTICIPATION: SOCIAL CAPITAL AND THE NEW INVISIBLE WORKER

The particular conjuncture of the downsizing of the welfare state, the expansion of the philanthropic and nonprofit sectors, and an increasing reliance on undocumented low-wage labor in the agricultural industry provided the context for foundations to move away from funding farmworker issues and toward a more broadly defined immigrant civic participation agenda. This section provides a brief description of these converging forces that informed the founding of the IPC in 1996 and the broader context for farmworker and immigrant organizing across the valley.

Between 1970 and the mid-1990s several political and economic shifts paved the way for the expansion and professionalization of the nonprofit and philanthropic sectors in the United States. The "trickle-down economics" and anti-state policies of the Ronald Reagan administration (1981–1989) gave significant "breaks" to the upper tax brackets and began a three-decade trend of a shrinking public sector, wage stagnation, increase in low-wage jobs, deepening poverty, and expanding inequality.[12] With the conservative assault on public taxation and the Great Society programs of the War on Poverty, the idea that wide-scale protection from poverty should not be considered a public good became popular ideology.[13] Following Ronald Reagan's pejorative stories about families dependent on welfare on his 1976 campaign trail, a new wave of political discourse stigmatized poverty (and even criminalized it, when linked to policing the "war on drugs"), especially in communities of color.[14] "Dependency" on the state, "welfare queen," "poverty pimp," and "illegal alien" rhetoric was matched with severe cuts and limited access to public programming. Additional attacks on "entitlements" and the responsibilities of the poor continued through the 1996 Personal Responsibility and Work Opportunity Reconciliation Act (Welfare Reform Act), inspiring unprecedented philanthropic investments in nonprofit organizations contracted to deliver services once provided by the state.

As the economic divide in the United States rapidly expanded, so did wealth in the philanthropic sector.[15] The expansion and professionalization of the philanthropic and nonprofit sectors throughout the 1980s and 1990s and the simultaneous attack on the welfare state marked a significant shift away from the approach of foundations supporting emergent social movement organizations during the 1960s. In the United States, critical scholars began to talk about a "shadow state" composed of privately funded nonprofit and voluntary organizations professionally trained and spatially coordinated to provide previously guaranteed public services.[16] Within the global context of debt restructuring and liberal market reforms, critical development scholars similarly observed a rapid "NGO-ization" as privately funded "civil society" organizations were recruited or established to fill the gaps created by scaled-down state apparatus in the global South.[17] As the public safety net was pulled out from under poor and working-class families, foundations coordinated a large number of service delivery and civic renewal initiatives in poor regions.

Even though California saw an increase in philanthropic activity, most grants were made in Southern California or the San Francisco Bay Area.[18] However, the Rosenberg Foundation, introduced in the previous chapter, paved the way for a series of large-scale farmworker and immigrant initiatives sponsored by major foundations from the late 1980s to the present. As early as

1978, the foundation would draw attention to a new "invisible worker," as articulated here in an annual report:

> There are new migrant farmworkers, the "undocumented" Mexicans who have come across the border and are increasingly the source of labor for California farms. But there is a difference between them and the people of *The Grapes of Wrath* and the Mexican Americans of the 1960s. These new people do not exist officially. Everyone involved—government, the growers, the farm unions, and even the migrants have a stake in pretending they do not exist. And if they do not exist, they have no problems, which are anyone's responsibility but their own.[19]

The Rosenberg report reveals that in 1978 unsanctioned but accepted immigration brought more farm laborers to California than the bracero program ever did. With the increase in undocumented migration, farm labor abuses were on the rise, including fewer units of housing and an increase in mistreatment by growers, including deporting workers before payday and neglecting to provide shade, water, or rest in the fields. From 1978 to 1986, under the leadership of Kirke Wilson, the Rosenberg Foundation increased grants to Central Valley migrant programs. By 1982 other funders, including the Field Foundation and the New World Foundation, joined the Rosenberg Foundation to support the Citizen Committee for Immigration Reform, a coalition of advocacy organizations attempting to build a new immigration reform platform. Throughout the 1980s, the Ford and Rosenberg Foundations shifted their funding priorities away from regional farmworker projects and toward national organizations such as the Farmworker Justice Fund, which worked on immigration reform and monitoring federal farm labor programs.[20]

In 1986 president Ronald Reagan signed the Immigration Reform and Control Act (IRCA). IRCA included several recommendations proposed by both immigrant advocacy coalitions and Reagan's political base of business owners reliant on low-wage, non-unionized seasonal workers, including "amnesty" for people who had entered the country without documentation and a pathway-to-citizenship program. The bill also imposed fines for growers who hired undocumented workers and new resources for policing the US–Mexico border. On passage of IRCA, Kirke Wilson launched a comprehensive citizenship initiative to fund Central Valley nonprofit organizations to provide legal, educational, and immigration services to immigrants eligible for citizenship under IRCA. This project enabled a large number of immigrants to naturalize, and provided resources for nonprofits to deliver services statewide. Rosenberg Foundation funding indirectly contributed to organizing against Proposition 187, a 1994 California ballot initiative, otherwise known as Save Our State, which proposed to increase reporting and screening of—and to limit public service provision to—immigrants without legal documentation. Prop. 187 did pass but was then challenged on constitutional grounds, limiting many of the more severe restrictions.

These investments (alongside the work of community-based immigrant advocacy groups) marked a fundamental shift in funding priorities toward professional immigration and citizenship services and immigrant rights and away from farm labor. While immigration reform did provide legitimate opportunities and mobility for many, it did not improve conditions for farmworkers or decrease poverty across the Central Valley. In fact, the California farm industry's active recruitment of low-wage immigrant labor intensified throughout the 1980s and 1990s, creating new pockets of poverty.[21] Mexican migration to the United States was also driven by new patterns of poverty in rural Mexico, which were created through the neoliberal market reforms of the 1990s. In negotiations with the United States and Canada leading up to the North American Free Trade Agreement (NAFTA), Mexican president Carlos Salinas de Gotari eroded the rights and entitlements of *ejidos,* land grants held by subsistence farmers won through the Mexican Revolution. When NAFTA was implemented in 1994, cheap imports and tax-subsidized farm products from the United States flooded the now privatized Mexican agricultural market. Rural subsistence farmers in Mexico struggled to survive, accelerating migration north.[22]

In a study of the relationships between farm labor, immigration, welfare, and poverty published in 2000, Edward Taylor and Philip Martin reveal that the small gains made through unionization and wage increases in the 1970s

> were reversed in the 1980s and 1990s, as an elastic (highly responsive) supply of low-skilled labor from Mexico and a proliferation of farm labor contractors created surplus labor conditions. Today, California farmworkers face not only declining real earnings but also a lack of housing and other benefits many once enjoyed. For these workers, real take-home earnings, after housing costs, have fallen substantially in the last two decades. Instead of living on the farms where they work, impoverished farmworkers and their families crowd into small rural towns, creating a new concentrated poverty.

In a cyclical fashion, as opportunities on large farms drew new immigrants into Central Valley towns, farmers expanded the production of labor-intensive agricultural products such as fruits, nuts, and vegetables, leading to the creation of additional low-wage seasonal farm jobs and attracting even more migrant workers. The California agricultural labor market has a triangular shape, with many low-wage seasonal jobs at the bottom and fewer agricultural services and management jobs at the top. During the 1980s and 1990s the triangle expanded at the bottom, with less mobility, fewer services, no or substandard housing, rising pesticide poisoning, and poor treatment of the rapidly increasing population of undocumented immigrant field workers. Indigenous people from Oaxaca, Mexico, began to migrate to Central Valley farms during this time, further exacerbating inequalities, as they were commonly mistreated on racial and ethic lines.[23]

The new pockets of immigrant poverty were hidden, as growers and workers alike attempted to work out of sight of the Immigration and Naturalization Service, which increased policing and deportations during the politically anti-immigrant climate of the 1990s. In response to the growing hostility toward immigrants, community-based immigrant advocacy groups began to form new alliances with labor and church organizations. Leaders from the early days of the farmworker movement, including Eliseo Medina and Fred Ross Jr., played an important role in forging these new coalitions.[24] Within this context, foundation staff interested in supporting immigrant-based work began to formulate their own "safe" theories of change. For example, Grantmakers Concerned with Immigrants and Refugees (GCIR) was founded in 1990 to educate foundation staff on how to shape immigrant programs in ways that are approved by often conservative or traditionally anti-immigrant boards of directors. One of the main GCIR messages features hard-working immigrants who "made America the land of opportunity: a nation renowned for self-reliance, freedom, and democracy."[25] GCIR presents a framework for showing how investing in immigrant communities is vital to local economies and the social and cultural fabric of American society. Rather than listing the various conditions, concerns, or rights of immigrants, GCIR proposes that foundations could contribute to building cohesive communities in the face of increased immigration through "pathways to integration," including a central focus on "civic participation."

After the terrorist attacks on the World Trade Center and the Pentagon on September 11, 2001, disguising immigrant rights organizing in assimilationist frameworks became increasingly important. Generalized fear of border-crossing terrorists fueled localized discrimination against immigrants in places like the Central Valley and enabled the US Congress to increase security measures through the quick passage of the Patriot Act in late 2001. Provisions of the Patriot Act included increased border security, expanded rights of police officers to search individuals and business establishments without consent, increased access of federal law enforcement to financial and business records, and indefinite detention of immigrants.

Many provisions of the Patriot Act were supposed to sunset in 2005, but the Republican Party–backed Sensenbrenner Bill, HR 4437, threatened to restore the more anti-immigrant elements of the policy and further restrict service provision to undocumented immigrants. Under HR 4437 undocumented immigrants and anyone who helped them were to be classified as felons. The passage of HR 4437 by the House of Representatives ignited a mass mobilization in 2006 where growing alliances among immigrant advocacy, labor, church, and many other civil society organizations activated millions of people in marches across the country. While HR 4437 did not pass in the Senate, the bill catalyzed an immigrant rights movement that is still active and building today, including DREAM Act campaigns led by undocumented college-student "Dreamers" seeking permanent residency, college tuition benefits, and additional rights and privileges. The early days of the immigrant rights movement intersected with the work of the IPC, and the main program officer was an advocate for funding immigrant rights in progressive philanthropy circles.

Beyond the timeframe of the IPC, the Ford Foundation, Open Society Foundations, Atlantic Philanthropies, and Carnegie Corporation of New York collectively invested over $300 million in organizations fighting for immigrant rights and legislative reform to include a pathway to citizenship for undocumented immigrants. The groups funded include major national organizations, including the National Council of La Raza, Mexican American Legal Defense and Education Fund, National Immigration Law Center, and Center for Community Change. Although funds are still being directed toward helping immigrants sign up for services won in recent deportation reprieves granted by President Obama, most of these foundations scaled down their immigrant organizing funding when political agreement on a more comprehensive immigration reform bill was not reached.[26]

Within the context of the emergent immigrant rights movement, foundation program officers played a central role in translating the new immigrant integration language into fundable efforts to address farmworker and immigrant poverty across California. Alongside critical development scholar Michael Goldman,[27] the foundation staff I interviewed that were associated with the IPC and other immigration initiatives across California agreed that the "myths and fictions" embraced by funders are often very different from what advocates working on the ground experience. In this case "engaging immigrants in civic life" is privileged over addressing the abuses of the farm labor system, unequal opportunity structures, increased policing of immigrant communities, weakened labor power under neoliberal market reforms, and immigrant rights.

The ideas program officers most commonly referenced when shaping the immigrant civic participation "theory of change" were drawn from globally renowned "social capital" research. Sociologists employed by the World Bank[28] theorize the economy as "embedded in networks of social relations that collectively make up the social structure."[29] Focusing on the weak or untrusting relationships between individuals in poor communities, rather than the restructuring of societies and institutions through capitalist development, social capital projects appeal to funders adverse to holding powerful institutions accountable.[30] By naming social capital and "trust" as the glue for economic development and social progress, the role of global capitalist competition in damaging existing social ties and creating poverty is disguised. Productive social organization is also limited to integration or mobility approaches where resistance against structures of powers is seen as counter-productive.[31]

In the context of the United States, Robert Putnam is particularly influential in foundation circles. Based on his studies of local government in Italy, Putnam claims that levels of social trust, reciprocal relationships, and membership in civic associations are critical to effective governments and economies.[32] In his best-selling book *Bowling Alone*,[33] Putnam laments the decline in membership in bowling clubs and homeowner associations, arguing that 1960s activism elevated individual rights over community ties. Calling for mutual support, cooperation, and trust over conflict and grievances, Putnam and his social capital research team at Harvard University's Saguaro Seminar inspired a wide array of "civic renewal" and "civic participation" philan-thropic projects.

One program officer I interviewed, Diane Clancey, suggested that "the integration and relationship-building model became the road map for successfully funding immigrant and refugee work." She explained that when shaping a new immigrant fund-ing area she had at first found it difficult to find language outside the worker rights framework she was familiar with from her past life as an advocate. Eventually she called on Urban Institute reports by authors such as Jeffrey Passel and Michael Fix to help her frame a program "in terms of the American Way."[34] She told me, "The immigrants that come to this country are ... the most industrious, hard working, risk takers and dreamers. These are the people who made it here.... They are not lazy, future wel-fare recipients. So I frame things in terms of the values people on the board hold most dear: family, hard work, individuals helping each other and helping themselves. So our programming is around that kind of American civic support and empowerment."

Following up on Clancey's framing, which conjoins self-help and democratic civic virtues, I asked what she would then *not* be able to talk about with her board of trustees. In keeping with the other program officers interviewed, she replied, "I would never attempt to bring a grant proposal to my board that speaks of challenging economic inequity through direct action organiz-ing, labor or welfare rights, or holding businesses or major indus-tries such as agriculture accountable. Such proposals have been known to cost many a program officer their jobs." While not always with the same intentions, the program officers' new fram-ings obscure questions of structural inequality and revive the persistent self-help "bootstrap capitalism" approach to alleviat-ing poverty articulated by Andrew Carnegie in 1889. To give away the end of the story that follows, John Sibley did eventually lose his job, but not until after an eight-year run with the IPC.

FROM SHITKICKERS TO RELATIONSHIP BUILDERS: FOUNDING THE IMMIGRANT PARTICIPATION COLLABORATIVE

Through investments in the unprecedented real estate, dot-com, and finance boom, the assets of California foundation endowments nearly doubled between 1990 and 2000.[35] Also during this period, the Central Valley was one of the few regions where poverty rates increased. In addition to the trends in the agricultural industry, rapid development from the San Francisco Bay Area and Los Angeles encroached on valley communities. Commuters and displaced low-wage workers left the wealthier regions experiencing skyrocketing rental prices for the poorer towns strung along the interior valley highways. Today the Central Valley contains some of the poorest rural districts in the country, with more families living below the federal poverty line than anywhere else in the United States.[36]

One of the most popular strategies to meet the required "spend out" of the enormous windfalls in foundation endowments was through the form of the "collaborative initiative." Historically the most poorly funded region in California, the Central Valley received an unprecedented amount of foundation grants in the form of large-scale initiatives.[37] According to Marsha Collins, another Kinney Foundation program officer, the new approach emerged during a strategic planning process in the early 1990s. Through this process the foundation decided to end funding to individual direct-action organizing institutions and instead invest in broad-based civic collaborations that might provide integrated support systems to communities struggling with declining public resources. The foundation also proposed that collaboratives would have more impact, in that organizations would be required to work together. This collaborative approach was partially inspired by the social capital literature of the day[38] and was initially tested through civic engagement projects to ease tensions in the wake of the 1992 Los Angeles "riots."[39]

In this context, John Sibley was able to sell the Central Valley immigrant collaborative to his board by turning attention to an impoverished region the foundation had not significantly funded before, and to the many organizations already working collaboratively to deliver citizenship services after the passage of the 1986 IRCA legislation. Yet the process of getting the initiative framed and approved was far from easy. According to Sibley, and validated by interviews with over twelve additional staff at other foundations, program officers like Sibley are inevitably challenged when they attempt to collaborate with potential grantees mostly interested in impressing them. One program officer put it this way: "When I went into foundation work my IQ immediately increased. People all of a sudden seemed to always agree with me. This felt good and I thought I was really coming up with some good ideas. Then I realized what was going on and became frustrated, because I need a reality check when I am way off. I needed it to come from them. But people don't want to tell you that." While several organizations were excited about working with Sibley, it was mainly his idea, immediately validated by interested grantees, which framed the initiative.

With unchecked decision-making power in relationship to the grantee communities (despite his desire for partners to take ownership of the initiative), Sibley experienced quite a different power position within the foundation. Built up and constantly pitched to by people seeking funding, he was simultaneously deflated in relation to the executive staff and board. Several steps removed from the decision-making conducted by trustees, program officers must find ways to convince those who make the decisions: the board. Within the board there are usually one or two "decision-making" members who play the role of chief financial officer or board president. These decision-making members, according to Sibley and my additional program officer interviews, usually and in the case of the Kinney Foundation, have the most connections in the business community and with industry—from a banking and finance background, major media networks, and through longtime connections in the broader philanthropic community.

One step below the board of trustees is the foundation president or CEO. The job of the president is to take the pulse of the board and make sure that all proposals brought to their attention are in keeping with what they will accept. The president is the gatekeeper, assuming the responsibility of never letting a board member "alight" on a particularly radical or questionable idea proposed by program staff. Between the president and the program staff is the vice president. The vice president keeps the president up to date on the ideas and plans of program staff as far in advance as possible so that the president can swiftly communicate between the board and the vice president. Below the vice president is the program officer, who may not meet the board of trustees more than once, depending on the foundation. The soaring ego of the program officer in relationship to grantees is brought back to earth as they work in relative isolation from the decision-making process within the foundation.

As they attempt to frame funding initiatives to address issues of socioeconomic inequity that will resonate with their conservative boards yet meet the expectations and needs of community groups, many program officers experience a great deal of anxiety. According to one California program officer I interviewed,

> My personal belief is so different from the board that I always need to be reading everyone at all levels to figure out how to reframe things.... It's like walking on a tightrope, always mis-stepping and falling into landmines.... No other time in my life have I had to dichotomize myself in two—me and the foundation's beliefs. I need to understand both, know where I stand, and find ways to work between the two.... I am really not very good at understanding and reading what is going on in here [the foundation]. It's just such a different perspective and environment that I find my own values being pushed and challenged. It started to really wear me down, to get to me, and I didn't even realize what was going on. It was in my subconscious.

Pitched to by multiple immigrant and farmworker advocacy organizations seeking funding, and working with his vice president to shape the project in ways acceptable to the board, Sibley proposed that the foundation support an experimental immigrant civic participation initiative in the Central Valley. After much framing and negotiation up and down the leadership ladder I have just described, funding was approved. It was the right timing, with increased endowment output requirements and the new social capital ideas in the air. The board approved what would be named (by the president of the foundation) the Immigrant Participation Collaborative.

According to Sibley, after the new Kinney Foundation strategic plan put a few regional collaboratives in place, never again did they fund individual "shitkicker institutions like the Center for Third World Organizing." According to Sibley, his pitch to the IPC was successful because it was more about civic learning and social integration, not "shitkicking" or direct-action organizing. In the context of the anti-community-organizing legacy of the Reagan era, welfare reform's revived self-help ideology, and in the aftermath of the organizing against the anti-immigrant Proposition 187,[40] it was important that Sibley speak in terms of engaging immigrants in civil society, as opposed to organizing immigrant and farmworker populations. Sibley explained that the new problem statement that the foundation leadership and board approved read something like this:

> In a place of such diversity, the way to go is to build a pluralistic democracy—the board buys stuff like this—you build the democracy as you build the community. This is the way I talk, but I also believe in it. You can choose to talk about direct-action organizing or you can instead talk about problem solving. The key is to never frame things in a way that you bring up a red flag for the board. He [the CEO] always said to never let the board alight on any particular issues. Once the board disagrees with a program officer they are gone.

Sibley was in tune with what his board of directors would or would not approve, but he also believed in the new approach based on what he had seen when visiting a farm labor camp in the Central Valley town of Woodville. At Sibley's suggestion, several leaders from the grant-seeking organizations designed a trip for him to learn about their work in the valley. In Woodville he found a hub of activity—farmworker children and families joining together in recreational programs, men and women dusty from a day in the fields studying for citizenship classes, committees working to plan for infrastructure repairs in crumbling migrant housing, and leaders speaking of taking on regional officials to address pesticide poisoning cases in the camp. (Interestingly, both Kirke Wilson and a program officer from the Western Foundation who is featured in the next chapter took their boards to this same migrant camp, eight years apart.) The image of the migrant center in Woodville remained in Sibley's mind and heart as he shaped his vision for the IPC.

Echoing the farmworker movement's "mutual aid" philosophy, Sibley proposed that "only immigrants could improve conditions in immigrant communities—that relationship building, education, and shared action are the keys to lasting change." The IPC's approach to solving the long-standing problems faced by farmworkers and other immigrants to the valley was further described as "building a broad, strong, and diverse network of relationships to promote civic problem-solving and immigrant engagement in public life." IPC partners (including organizations built during the early days of the farmworker movement, social service organizations, and legal aid agencies born out of the War on Poverty) were originally recruited by foundation staff and asked to outline ways in which increased "immigrant civic participation" might improve poor conditions in valley communities, and how they might learn from and assist one another. They were not required to provide an analysis of problems or of the political, social, and economic relationships at play in the valley, or corresponding strategies to effect change. Civic engagement, learning from one another, and building relationships were understood as the goals. The IPC partners were also encouraged to govern themselves and create new projects and campaigns for the foundation to support.

In 1996, after the partnership vision was discussed with a couple of the invited organizations and its "theory of change" approved at the foundation, the IPC was officially launched. In addition to his own theory of change, Sibley explained the approach of the IPC as building on the work initiated by Kirke Wilson of the Rosenberg Foundation. Sibley convinced the Kinney Foundation to invest over $3 million a year in the project. The IPC grew from four partners in 1996 to twenty-one in 2002, including community organizing, legal assistance, popular education, social service, religious charity, and applied research nonprofit agencies—some who had worked together in the farmworker movement and some who had never worked together nor perhaps ever anticipated doing so. Together, partners designed new programs (such as leadership training, re-granting programs, youth organizing, and a cultural arts festival) and launched organizing campaigns around issues, including an effort to count "under-counted" populations in the US Census, and Senate Bill 245i, which proposed legal family reunification for undocumented residents. From 1996 to 2002 the IPC received in excess of $5 million a year in individual organizational grants, private consulting, and program support. The remainder of this chapter discusses how IPC partnering organizations were limited yet also sometimes took advantage of the model of the philanthropic collaborative initiative.

IDEAS THAT DON'T STICK: NEGOTIATING THE CIVIC PARTICIPATION FRAMEWORK

Instead of a grass-roots nonprofit sector co-opted by neoliberal agendas, as is commonly reported in the critical philanthropy and development literature today, I found that the partners of the IPC did not naturally adopt the framework promoted by the foundation. Instead, I found that civic participation was presented, received, and rearticulated within multiple and often contradictory frameworks. Sometimes civic participation served to obscure issues of farmworker and immigrant poverty; sometimes it divided rather than united partners; and sometimes it provided new opportunities to organize in the region.

The limits presented by the "immigrant civic participation" framework were partially due to the political constraints placed on Sibley, who was obligated to represent the IPC differently in different contexts. To all audiences, he proposed that the way to solve the long-standing problems faced by farm laborers and other immigrants to the valley is to build a diverse network of relationships among leaders, organizations, communities, and allies to promote immigrant and farmworker driven problem-solving and engagement in public life. When speaking with IPC partners and allies in the valley, he extended the "participation" goals to confronting the structural problems of the farm labor system and the intensifying persecution of undocumented immigrants. When conversing with Kinney Foundation leadership or philanthropic networks, he spoke only of the inherent ability of "participation" and "trusting relationships" to strengthen social and economic life. For example, the IPC's cultural exchange festival was highlighted in the foundation's annual report, but a fledgling immigrant rights coalition founded by partnering organizations was *not* to be represented in the public IPC. The opening vignette to this chapter, where most partners recognized that *no* foundation would publically support the *real* organizing work, is telling of the broad-scale dilemma of the coded "civic participation" language still widely popular in funding circles.

Thus, internally, the IPC aimed to build social capital against the inequities wrought by capitalism (in keeping with Pierre

Bourdieu's original theorization of social capital).[41] Yet publicly the partnership claimed to foster mainstream integration and social mobility within the current system—a message that partners did not wholly reject but deemed evasive and incomplete. Many IPC partners respected the program officer's spoken commitment to issues of inequity but felt that the "participation" approach touted publicly and in all official foundation documents masked the real issues at stake and ultimately served the interest of remaining "politically neutral." In keeping with the Gramscian understanding of philanthropy,[42] the foundation maintains the status quo by recognizing and then incorporating a radical stance within common-sense mainstream ideology. While the program officer's spoken intention was to protect organizers whose work might be deemed too confrontational by the board of trustees of the foundation, the result is akin to what Gramscian political scientist Joan Roelofs calls "the mask of pluralism." By translating organizing agendas into unthreatening civic participation language the program officer convinces outside audiences that they are taking on the hard issues while at the same time muting the voices of direct action organizers. Despite Sibley's own analysis, desires, and heartfelt personal commitments to taking on the injustices he observed through his work with IPC partners, he was unable to confront, let alone name, the real issues at stake through the foundation.

Though organizing themselves under the "immigrant civic participation" banner in order to receive funds, partners also did not buy into the conjoining of the two terms. For Sibley, the coupling of "civic participation" and "immigrants" includes the notion that by building human capital (individual skills, voice, attitudes, and behaviors), social capital (networks of relationships), and institutional capital (membership-based organizations), immigrants can "become full, contributing members of democratic life and ... improve conditions in matters affecting their lives." While many partners agreed on the importance of building the voice, networks, and institutions of valley immigrants, they showed their frustration with the terminology by constantly asking, "civic participation for what?"[43] Some suggested that the language avoided the material conditions and concerns of their constituents and suggested that the partnership take a stand on participation for immigrant rights in the face of the Immigration and Naturalization Service (later Immigration and Customs Enforcement) raids that increased after 9/11, for amnesty leading up to the immigrant mobilizations of 2006, or for strengthening "the Union" for those who came up out of the UFW movement.

By breaking down the "immigrant civic participation" phraseology, partners also revealed contradictory meanings. Several partners believed that the "citizenship" frame separated out undocumented migrants from those granted formal citizenship, working against the IPC's spoken commitment to democratic participation. Some felt that the term "immigrant" universalizes a group of diverse identities, including migrant farmworkers, Southeast Asian refugees, and American citizens from different home countries and with different needs, interests, and identities. This became a particularly contentious problem as Sibley recruited and funded Southeast Asian and indigenous immigrant partners to work alongside the traditional Mexican-farmworker-serving organizations that grew out of the movement. One partner's experience with the reluctance of long-time farmworker movement leaders to embrace refugee and indigenous populations reflects the difficulty in framing the partnership around a unified concept of immigrants:

I was a speaker at a conference of [two partnering organizations] and said that [they] need to involve Mixteco groups because the indigenous population is growing so rapidly and are the most abused farmworkers today, and they both said no. I even brought some Mixteco leaders to the meeting to talk about the demands of their communities. [One staff person] who had been there since the movement days stood up and says, referring to the new indigenous worker population, "These people will work for anything. They are driving down wages and standards." I think these movement people and governors of [the established organizations] have professional-ized jobs and they don't see what is going on in front of them any-more, how racist they have become. Racist and professionalized.

In this instance, the well-established movement institution rejected the concept of "immigrant" as an organizing framework as they were more concerned with time of migration and labor status. In their minds, it would be against their best interest to join in a partnership to engage a broader spectrum of immi-grants; yet at IPC meetings they still spoke the language of uni-fied immigrant civic participation. Similar comments were made by other partners about the Southeast Asian refugee orga-nizations being privileged by their historical relationship with the public welfare system and that therefore they should not be given priority by the foundation. Others questioned a faith-based partner organization's white evangelical leadership and their interest in joining the partnership. The history of competi-tion and turf battles between partnering organizations was extremely difficult to overcome—especially in the absence of a unified analysis or agenda. For many, the new language only served to mask or repress the broader struggles for farmworkers that some partners have been involved in for years.

The conjoining of "immigrant" and "civic participation" also created significant organizing opportunities. For example, several

IPC partners came together to pass a state bill to allow undocumented immigrants to get state driver's licenses. Joining other advocates across the state, partners turned the campaign into a public safety issue. Using the language of "immigrant civic participation," IPC partners argued that due to lack of public transportation many immigrants drive without licenses to get to work, to pick up their children at school, or to go to church, which presents a hazard for pedestrians and for other drivers. Their public organizing messages claimed that to protect public safety immigrants must be provided with official licenses so they can behave like responsible citizens. The immigrant "they" must drive safely, as a licensed driver, like "us," and responsibly carry the proper identification that provides both the rights and responsibilities of citizens. With intense organizing across the IPC network, and in the context of a heated state governor election, the bill was passed.

However, as political articulations are never fixed and are open to constant re-appropriation, newly elected governor Arnold Schwarzenegger's team turned the conception of public safety on its head, arguing that is not the unsafe driving environment but the immigrants themselves that we must fear. At the time of my research, the evolving "War on Terror," increasing Immigration and Customs Enforcement raids, and the image of terrorists hiding behind the undocumented immigrants applying for driver's licenses helped this re-articulation to temporarily stick, and the bill was repealed. The next turn in the driver's license legislation was a proposal from conservative legislators to pass the bill with a new clause stipulating that the cards of non-documented residents carry a special mark or color labeling the cardholder as different and easily identifiable to law enforcement.

In the last couple of years of funding for the IPC, partners began to coalesce around the emerging immigration reform mobilizations that eventually took hold in major cities in 2006. Long before achieving national recognition, many of the partnering organizations were deeply involved in leadership development training and speaking to policymakers for the fledgling DREAM Act organizers, or "Dreamers"—undocumented college students fighting for immigration reform and access to higher education and jobs. A small group of IPC partners formed an environmental justice coalition that is still engaged in action research around air quality and pesticide use across the region. Yet as the partners attempted to find ways to organize through the immigrant civic participation framework, Sibley continued to struggle to "hide" the community organizing work from his board.

One of the ways that Sibley convinced trustees to continue to invest in grass-roots organizing groups, beyond reframing the language of partners' work, was to build their professional management capacity. According to Anna Rosa Sanchez, a program officer at a regional foundation Sibley collaborated closely with, "the ultimate goal is to develop more organizations that the bigger foundations can fund for their valley initiatives. There are virtually none professionally capable in some parts of the valley—but lots of small groups of people doing good things. So now we need to help them become fundable organizations—from Bakersfield all the way up to Shasta." Sanchez describes the bulk of her work this way:

> Teaching people what kind of language to use in grant applications, how to put together a work plan, goals, objectives, activities … how to do more large-scale financial management, accounting, etc., so that they can handle larger grants.… For example, [a major foundation] told us that if we spend the time building the capacity

of [an indigenous Mexican organizing group] then they will be able to fund them. So I helped them learn larger-scale management techniques, got them a few small grants, even nominated [a local organizer] for a Ford Foundation award, which he got, and now they are fundable.

The nature of the capacity-building technique used by program officers reveals a contradictory duality. While "capacity building" does in fact provide greater access to resources and power for small organizing groups like the indigenous Mexican group mentioned above, it also changes the nature of the organization's work. A staff person with this organization expressed dismay with being "stuck doing desk work and not organizing anymore." She is grateful that her organization now has more funds and legitimacy but is fearful that it is no longer serving the direct and changing needs of the indigenous farmworker communities they claim to serve. A long-time farmworker organizer and director of an IPC member organization expressed similar sentiments about the changes he has seen:

> After I left the UFW, I got a job working with the Office of Economic Opportunity. They paid farmworker organizers big salaries, so most stayed on. But they kept us away from the strikes, so I left, after too much time sneaking out to do the real organizing.... Later foundations came in and were equally rigid but in different ways. It became all literacy and services and no organizing. Now people are trapped on computers.... planning programs and writing reports. We need to be accountable to communities, to people and their schedules and not to our meetings and foundation deadlines. We can only see the damage this kind of thing does when something dramatic happens. Like that year when there was a bad winter freeze and all of a sudden there was no farm work. We need to be flexible enough to say, "To hell with the English or civics classes. These people need to eat!"

Another organizer put it this way:

> What is frustrating about our work right now is that nobody is really organizing. All this civic participation planning, and trainings, and no organizing. If new money comes to us through the new [Western Foundation] farmworker project I want it to go to organizing. And you can't train an organizer overnight or at a training like some people think you can. You have to walk in the muck, get contaminated with pesticides like everyone else.

MONEY AS AN ORGANIZING TOOL

Beyond the realm of professionalized program frameworks and discourse, collaborative initiatives also bring individuals and organizations together in new ways. The IPC was generally organized through quarterly meetings in one of the partners' hometowns, usually Sacramento, Modesto, or Fresno. For the first few years, partnership meetings focused primarily on learning about one another and building relationships. Quarterly partnership meetings were a space for individual organizations to receive training on using the media, grass-roots fundraising, demographic issues concerning immigrants in the valley, and other topics of concern to individual organizations or clusters of partnering organizations. The first unified effort was a campaign to renew an expired 1994 legal provision that allowed non-citizen family members of US citizens to reapply for their resident status without having to return to their home country for an often lengthy time before being allowed to return to the United States. Referred to as 245(i), this bill helped immigrant families with both legal and undocumented members stay together. The 245(i) campaign prompted action among members of the IPC and other immigrant advocacy groups across the state and nation. It was the first (and the last, according to some) successful joint organizing effort of the IPC.

At the suggestion of and with additional grants from Sibley, partners also designed and managed collaborative projects, including a re-granting program, a leadership fellowship program, and a cultural exchange festival. While these collaborative projects were valuable in many ways, they were also the most problematic. Many believed that although these efforts were important, they reorganized program staff and took time away from developing a common agenda across the partnership. While each of these projects brought new resources to valley immigrant communities, they also heightened competition and even ignited new turf battles between partners. The following section shows how involvement in the IPC collaborative projects (the Public Engagement Network and the Cultural Festival) took time and resources away from organizing alliances across the region.

THE PUBLIC ENGAGEMENT NETWORK AND THE CULTURAL FESTIVAL

At the initial suggestion of Sibley, the IPC developed and implemented a small grants program for emerging immigrant groups across the valley. A committee of staff representatives from each partnering organization developed the grant awards criteria, communicated calls for proposals, and with additional Kinney Foundation funding made 228 grants to 149 small civic and community-based groups. This program was first called the IPC Grants Program and later renamed the Public Engagement Network (PEN).[44] The funded projects were all local and immigrant-led and included areas such as cultural heritage education, community organizing for political representation on local boards, environmental justice, pesticide awareness, and youth leadership. Aside from getting resources to small, emerging organizations, the goal of the granting program was to expand the IPC's organizing capacity and network down to the grass roots. Sibley explained, "The IPC partners are actually what I call the 'grass tips.' They have been around a while and have fairly established institutions. Through PEN we can now reach the grass roots."

Making small grants was rewarding for the IPC partners in that they were able to see how much a small amount of support can do for very grass-roots groups. However, the act of organizing a network around grants proved to have unanticipated consequences. One partner explained how a hierarchical dynamic between IPC partners and PEN grantees was established through the granting program:

> We used to do this thing where we'd bring the [PEN] grantees to our partnership meetings to hear about what they had achieved at the end of the grant cycle. Sometimes it was a total disaster. One of the [IPC] partners, or I'm not sure who, but there was one big circle of chairs around the perimeter of the room for [IPC] partners and another circle of chairs inside of it. They had to sit there with us watching from the outside, talking amongst ourselves. It was like to them we were this judging authority looking in at them, like they were on display, "Oh, look at this cute little group from Kern or Madera." And then some [IPC] partners would talk amongst themselves and not listen when they were presenting. It was awful.

Through PEN, IPC partners got a taste for becoming philanthropists. Because they invited new immigrant leaders, youth, and budding civic organizations to the partnership as recipients of IPC funding with set reporting and evaluation requirements, a hierarchy based on a monetary relationship was immediately established. The IPC network of 21 organizations had indeed expanded to almost 150 new grass-roots immigrant organizations, with incredible potential to organize if the right moment or shared cause emerged. However, even when attacks against immigrants deepened as the Patriot Act was passed after 9/11 and the Immigration and Customs Enforcement raids chased already isolated immigrant communities into hiding, the IPC/PEN network was unable to mobilize. Instead of building alliances, the PEN grantees became competitive with one another for IPC funding. IPC partners became mini-philanthropists, and partners continued to compete with one another and now with PEN groups for the attention of the foundation.

Another aspect of PEN that unintentionally reinforced monetary over strategic organizing alliances was the technical assistance component of the program. As a part of receiving grants, the PEN recipients were required to attend technical assistance and networking gatherings hosted by one of the IPC organizations. The Valley Immigrant Center (VIC) received funding and consultants from the Kinney Foundation to organize and facilitate the required PEN retreats. The center's director, Maria Suarez, initially saw this as a great opportunity to simultaneously reach out to new groups across the valley and strengthen the IPC network and her own organization. However, she discovered early on that the very nature of "training grantees" was set up to fail. Reflecting on the divisive nature of philanthropic relationships, Suarez described one of the main consequences of organizing around money:

> We were responsible for bringing all of these grantees together and that made a forty-plus-person workshop, when we know that twenty is about the most that makes for a good popular education

learning environment.... These gatherings were mandatory in the foundation contracts, which meant that people had to come for the money, not because they wanted to. For most it was thought of as just another "required meeting." It was hard to get many of the grantees away from this attitude of just coming for the money.... The main problem was that people now think of us [VIC] as [the Kinney Foundation], always asking us for money and resources, and have a certain kind of expectation from us that makes it difficult for us to do the kind of work we want to do. People want to know what we can do for them, not what we could do together.

In this scenario, both the organization hired to facilitate the re-granting process and the grantees themselves move from an organizing or educational relationship to a grantor/grantee relationship. Organizations also risk becoming competitive and protective of their work as they seek approval and future grants from the foundation, as monitored through VIC. The IPC partner representatives who sat on the PEN committee were well aware of these challenges and constantly asked themselves, "How can we stop calling PEN members 'grantees'? Even if we don't say it to them in person, we are still thinking of them as grantees. We need to find a new way of thinking about this." With money as the primary organizing tool, it would take a lot of work for partners to get outside of the philanthropic framework.

One attempt to bring immigrant groups together across the IPC-PEN network and beyond was the IPC's Cultural Festival. In the wake of 9/11, anti-immigrant sentiments increased in many parts of the country. California's Central Valley was no exception. At one PEN gathering in late 2001, conversation converged around the idea that in the current political climate, with increased violent attacks and home raids, immigrants were "hiding out" and afraid to express their concerns or enact cultural practices in public. From this meeting the idea emerged to found an annual festival where immigrants would perform their native dances, songs, and stories, and engage the general public in workshops around the issues of concern to immigrant communities. The VIC, a cluster of IPC and PEN partners, and a host of Kinney Foundation consultants worked to make this idea a reality. First they convened youth, women, and organizational leaders from the Hmong, Mixteco, Mexican, Cambodian, and Pakistani communities across the valley. Next they formed a committee and interviewed people in each community, came up with a series of themes of interest to each, and designed a three-day event to bring the issues, concerns, and cultures of Central Valley immigrants to the public stage. The event drew over 3,000 Central Valley residents.

While the Cultural Festival was an inspirational and for some a transformative experience, it could not escape the fallout of using money as a central organizing tool. The Kinney Foundation staff and consultants chose VIC as the main convener for the festival and made an initial grant of $350,000 to produce the festival. Two other IPC partners with a long history of cultural arts through the Chicano and farmworker movements resented VIC for receiving the grant and refused to organize their constituents in the North Valley. Other partners asked why they should be involved if VIC received all the funds to organize the event. And yet others directly asked VIC for money, imagining that they had a huge surplus of resources from the foundation for organizing both the PEN gatherings and the festival.

Individual cultural presentation groups, including Mixteco and Hmong dancers, a Mexican *banda*, a farmworker-movement-style *teatro*, and a Cambodian opera, all expressed the importance of having a public stage beyond their immediate communities. The feelings of pride and acceptance, of making friends across cultural lines, of taking over a public space in

Fresno for three days, countered the isolation and marginalization many immigrant communities experience. But as VIC offered stipends to presenting groups, the word got out that they had a large grant from the foundation and they were accused of hand-picking cultural groups to perform. For the first time, VIC was receiving numerous calls from community groups and individuals asking for stipends or complaining that another community group was getting more attention or money than they were. Local professionals vied for consulting contracts to do the lighting, the electrical work, and the staging of festival productions, and VIC found itself playing the role of a large production agency. IPC partners slowly withdrew their participation as they realized that they would not receive additional funds for being involved. After three years of convening the festival, the director of VIC found herself overwhelmed by festival organizing duties, a changed relationship with local groups vying for stipends to participate, and an organizational program increasingly distant from their mission to convene immigrant leaders in popular education and movement building across the region.

Ironically, despite the unanticipated divisive fall-out of the project, the Cultural Festival, surrounded by positive publicity in foundation networks, was one of VIC's most productive hooks for attracting new funds. The "multicultural" artistic expression framework gained more mainstream attention than the original immigrant rights concerns the project was founded on. A reader of critical philanthropy scholarship might easily conclude, as Joan Roelofs proposes in her frequently cited book *Foundations and Public Policy: The Mask of Pluralism,* that the cultural program represents a typical neoliberal move to fragment organizing alliances through identity politics. In Roelofs' critique, private foundations increasingly promoted multicultural programming as a way to fragment groups and divert attention away from dissent against capitalism in the 1990s. Fitting neatly within a neoliberal ethic of individualism and blind faith in markets, blaming society for not respecting individual cultures and identities was embraced where critiquing markets was not.

However, like the simplistic critique of self-help that fails to recognize its radical self-determination variants (as in the Black Panthers and the early years of the farmworker movement), this analysis neglects the long histories and radical potential of cultural organizing. Creative expression, the arts, and identity-based organizing have also been used to forge cross-ethnic solidarity and movement building, for example in the Black feminist tradition of collective consciousness and solidarity[45] or the mural movement that forged alliances between Black and Chicano groups in the 1960s. Using art and culture as a means for building movement alliances has matured to the point where the term "cultural organizing" is shared among its diverse practitioners, including members of labor unions, grass-roots community development initiatives, and international human rights campaigns.[46] Many of the participants of the VIC describe their cultural work as an expression of liberation necessary for movement building, and continue to host cultural exchanges that aim to strengthen immigrant voice and leadership in the Central Valley. Whether they can ignite the more radical change they seek through a foundation-funded, time-intensive program is yet to be seen.

CONCLUSION: THE BUBBLE BURSTS AND PARTNERS DISPERSE

In 2001 the California dot-com bubble burst. The Kinney Foundation's endowment shrank, and 9/11 made it increasingly unpopular to fund immigrant organizing. Just as in 1995, when the foundation had embarked on a strategic planning process to redirect funds toward collaborative initiatives, it went through an overhaul in 2002–2003. Never completely sold on the immigrant organizing focus, the foundation's leadership made the IPC a primary target in a severe downsizing and reorganization. Just before the foundation decided to end funding to the IPC and to eventually retire (that is, to fire) its main program officer, Sibley predicted: "I feel like I am on the train tracks with a train coming at me at full speed, and there is nothing I can do but watch it hit me. They've been after me for some time now. And now, with the change of fortunes at the foundation, and it being even less popular to fund immigrant groups, they have their window."

The tool that the Kinney Foundation used to end funding to the IPC and to lay off staff was the still-popular "outcomes-based evaluation" model. Perhaps ironically, in 2002 the foundation board required Sibley to show quantitative measurable outcomes for the relational vision of civic participation championed by the foundation in the 1990s. Consultants were hired, and partners were interviewed. Sibley came up with a PowerPoint presentation showing three primary measures of success: new immigrant volunteers, participation in public events and forums, and immigrants served in citizenship and education courses. These "participatory" outcomes were not "concrete" enough for either the Kinney board of directors or the outside funders the IPC was attempting to attract. Just as the partners had asked themselves in the early days, the board and the potential funders asked Sibley and the IPC, "Civic participation for what?"

The IPC shared the same fate as many collaborative initiatives of the 1990s. It had based its success on social relationships, not quantitative "measurable outcomes," as became the standard when the business-oriented approach to evaluating philanthropic investments took hold during the economic downturn of the early 2000s.[47] Unfortunately, because IPC partners were organized by money and not by a shared analysis of immigrant concerns and collective organizing strategies, they had difficulty attracting new funding and slowly disbanded. The lack of a unified vision or strategy was observed by a potential funder and communicated in a long email:

> I have to say that from my perspective there is a sense that the leadership is at the edges, i.e., within various organizational members, each pulling and pushing the [IPC] in several directions at once (which makes it seem almost like a field of tornadoes where funnels are constantly emerging and disappearing, but with no apparent center and capable of heading off in an unforeseen direction at any given moment), rather than having a clear center, like a hurricane, where there is a clear direction and concentrated energy with a clear forward momentum, which even if it turns, turns as one. I don't want to go too far with this analogy since I clearly see the [IPC] energy as creative and not destructive, but I hope you get my meaning about having a clearly visible and compelling or driving center. The second point is really the whole issue of making some tough decisions about priorities and the most important work of the [IPC].... I think that without demonstrating some real progress on both issues, the discussion about funding might be a tough one.

The author of the email went on to suggest that after five years of Kinney funding, the partners "get free" of the single-foundation paradigm, and that individual member organizations should not be provided support through the IPC without having built a "collaborative center." The Kinney Foundation ended funding to the IPC in 2003, and the partners found themselves "Kinney-dependent," exhausted from years of reorganizing themselves around temporary monetary alliances. This dynamic was further complicated when other foundations, such as the Western Foundation, suggested that the IPC map out a new set of goals around its own collaborative initiatives, as explored in the next chapter. In a recent interview, Juanita Gonzales, the director of an IPC partner organization, suggested that it appears as if "all the partners want to do now is get funding from the Western Foundation. I have a feeling that now we are going to be all about farmworker health and completely drop immigrant organizing altogether."

Returning to the first of the three dilemmas presented at the start of this chapter, can the "theories of change" acceptable to philanthropic institutions ever match up with the struggles of social movement leaders and institutions? Could the Kinney Foundation's "immigrant civic participation" truly empower farmworkers and immigrants, without confronting the agricultural system and immigrant policing that contribute to entrenched systems of inequality? Looking back to the previous chapter, could the myth of a "community union" embraced by the Field Foundation meet the demands made by Cesar Chavez for a unionized and respected workforce across the agricultural sector? In this case, the myth broke down when strikes, boycotts, and union drives scared off private funders, and redirected Chavez, and the notion of a community union fell apart. The study of the IPC has shown that without including an analysis of the structural inequalities that breed inaction, improving conditions for poor farmworkers and immigrations through civic participation remains an idealized self-help myth.

Ultimately, the funders of the IPC were interested in ameliorating but not solving regional poverty. While Sibley might have been interested in organizing farmworkers, the president and the board never were. Sibley was able to create an opening for immigrant and farmworker organizing because of his skill at shaping an idealized vision of a pluralist democratic sphere. However, in Michael Goldman's words, "As long as we perpetuate the claims that there is no connection between increased poverty in the South and increased accumulation in the North … we are merely retelling imperial-modernization myths."[48] The same claim can be made about retelling the American myth of "participation" without making the connection between poverty and plenty, between low-wage undocumented immigrant labor and a globalized agricultural industry.

Returning to the second proposition made at the start of this chapter, can strategic coalitions be built from monetarily-driven partnerships? This study has shown that in the end, money proved to be an ineffective and at times disruptive organizing tool. In the case of the IPC, I observed the ways that organizing through a funder prevented the formation of collective strategies to address enduring immigrant and farmworker poverty in the valley. Long-time farmworker organizers made desperate calls to action, accusing other partners of wasting time, money, and political alliances that would have been harnessed and organized into a collective political strategy back in the "movement days."[49] Questions like "What are we waiting for?" and "Are you in for the long haul or just the [Kinney] paycheck?" and statements like "We just need a shared vision" were not uncommon. Despite the dramatic calls for unified action, very little time was spent analyzing issues of common concern, understanding each other's approaches to community organizing,[50] or strategizing beyond the specific funded programs and reports they were required to produce.

If strategic action had been taken on issues identified by partners, the foundation would likely have pulled out for fear that the organizers were too "radical." Most partners knew that Sibley was closely watched within his own foundation by a board suspicious of his efforts to "sneak in" community organizing. Under great stress during the last years of the initiative, one of Sibley's strategies as he straddled the gap between the board and the partners was to simply "throw money where the energy was," hoping that the additional resources would give new life to "authentic" partner-driven efforts. Instead of spurring new organizing, money became the end, rather than the means. Partners focused so heavily on keeping the resources coming that all of their energy was spent on staying in the game. When the funding dried up and partners struggled to keep programs going, and in some cases to keep their organizations from shutting down, they realized that the cost of collaboration was too high. During his very difficult last days at the foundation, Sibley noted that "perhaps money is a very blunt organizing tool."

And finally, what can we conclude about foundation staff selecting and "match-making" collaborative partners? What do foundation professionals actually see and expect when they recruit diverse organizations to participate in a collaborative? What is an authentic grass-roots (or "grass tips") organization? Who do immigrant and farmworker organizations actually represent? What capacity does an organization have to mobilize constituents? Despite all of the problems introduced through foundation funding structures and the institutional arrangements required, a question very few of the partners I interviewed wanted to address was what the foundation-recruited partner organizations were actually doing, with or without foundation funding. IPC partner Daniel Ortega revealed:

I think the program officer confused immigrant organizations with immigrants. He was dealing with organizations that don't always listen to their constituents and are often competitive with one another over who they are representing and who is getting the most funding and recognition. Oftentimes they don't represent anyone, and funders think they do. [One organization] that is built up as *the* group that organizes indigenous Mexicans only represents a small slice of Oaxacans, for example. And some organizations are made up of two to three people.

The nonprofit organizational framework itself poses limits where partners are ultimately accountable to their own boards and funders. The funder in turn is accountable to no one, except for their investors and the market. In this configuration there are ultimately no constituents or people to collectively represent. In the absence of shared articulation of their identity, common enemy, and purpose—a central component in most social movements[51]—it is difficult to imagine the partnership finding its "collaborative center" or set of organizing principles. Urban theorist Manuel Castells[52] has argued that institutionalized community-based organizations are incapable of generating real social movement or change. Similarly, Piven and Cloward, in their historic study *Poor People's Movements,*[53] show how social movement organizations inevitably solidify into rigid bureaucracies unable to move with the concerns of the people they originally set out to represent. Others have further argued that most development or social service organizations contribute to the larger capitalist state project that foundations maintain.[54]

Similar to various social movements that emerged in the 1960s,[55] the growth, professionalization, bureaucratization, and distancing from constituents (often in relationship with public and private funding requirements) of movement organization have severely changed the organizing terrain across the Central Valley. With historic institutions attracting the majority of grants, few emerging groups are able to compete. In the absence of a regional or national movement and in the context of established institutional boundaries, funders feel more entitled to propose the ways in which initiatives are designed. In a resource-poor region of great need like the Central Valley, established organizational leaders are less apt to turn down foundation grants from philanthropic initiatives or chart new territory.

The model of the "collaborative initiative" in particular provides insight into the limits and possibilities of social change within the predominant philanthropy framework. It helps explain the ways in which mainstream foundations, reluctant to directly address the market forces and economic relationships on which they rely, reshape organizing through program frameworks that ultimately ask poor people to help themselves, through monetary alliances and foundation-selected nonprofit leadership. By uncovering the places where grantees did not always "buy into" but were able to capitalize on philanthropic relationships and theories, we also see how collaboratives can open up and strategically navigate spaces of possibility.

The next chapter is a case study of an initiative designed by an ambitious program officer who planned to learn from the mistakes of the IPC. Felipe Cordero recognized the capacity of the IPC's civic and relational approach to engage a greater diversity of stakeholders. While Sibley believed in civic participation as a broad-based grass-roots (or grass-tips) organizing tool, Cordero saw the framework as an opportunity to make an explicit shift away from protest politics and toward mutually beneficial or "win-win" partnerships between farmworker-serving organizations and the agricultural industry. At a time when the UFW and industry stakeholders were forming an unprecedented alliance around agriculture-friendly immigration reform, Cordero translated the IPC model to correspond with the central tenet of "philanthrocapitalism": by helping industry we can help the poor. As has been the case in earlier philanthropic self-help efforts, the participation of the poor can be about political action or incorporation through broad-based partnerships with mainstream stakeholders. Cordero's project took up many of the recommendations of the IPC partners, including more governance, training, planning, and asset building. However, by virtue of his determination to produce results agreeable to both industry and workers, this project unfortunately found even less success than the IPC, which at least launched two successful campaigns and several productive projects during its short lifetime.[56]

CHAPTER FOUR

Selling Mutual Prosperity

Worker–Grower Partnerships and
the "Win-Win" Paradigm

Water glasses, forks, and knives clinked amidst the chatter in the ballroom of a Hilton hotel in Sacramento, California. In a room slightly darkened for a luncheon plenary session, farmworker advocates, agricultural industry representatives, state politicians, and foundation staff gathered to learn about a new initiative launched by the Western Foundation.[1] The Farm Worker Community Building Initiative (FWCBI) aimed to improve poor living conditions in California's agricultural communities through an unprecedented partnership between farmworker advocates, farmers, and public service providers. A politician opened the panel, thanking the foundation for bringing attention to the unequal health outcomes for the people who harvest the nation's fresh fruits and vegetables. A member of the Farm Bureau spoke of his own efforts to provide healthcare and housing for the workers on his almond farm. A recognizable leader from the farmworker movement joined in the praise of the foundation, rousing the audience with the movement's "unity clap" and "¡Sí, se puede!" chant. The president of the Western Foundation closed, admonishing the audience to "use the opportunities and resources at hand to tackle the agricultural poverty that has plagued Americans for the last century."

Breaking the ebullient mood, a young Latino immigrant rights organizer suddenly shouted from the back of the dimly lit room. Addressing the panel, he demanded, "How can you work with growers when children are sick with pesticides? Campesinos [farmworkers] are sleeping in cars. People are hiding out [from federal immigration raids]. This is going to be just like all of the other projects that come in but never change anything." As I listened to the fiery attack I anticipated heated rebuttals from the panel. Instead, a former farmworker now contracted with the new initiative moved the center of gravity. In front of a tense audience, he shouted to the room: "I'm not worried about us migrants—us campesinos. We are strong people. We will survive. I'm worried about you growers who will be devastated if we [undocumented immigrant field workers] are all forced to leave. How will you keep your farms in California when you could do better in Mexico? How can we help you win this fight?"

This agenda-shifting moment came in 2007, just over a decade after the US-led North American Free Trade Agreement aggressively advanced deregulation of global agricultural trade, devastating poor farming villages in Mexico.[2] Unable to compete with the flood of US-grown, tax-subsidized, and genetically modified corn, subsistence farming in Mexico collapsed, especially in the indigenous regions of Oaxaca. In the face of deepening poverty and insecurity, many families from these agricultural regions struggle to survive, forcing an unprecedented number of villagers north in search of work. Following a decade of trade liberalization, Central Valley farms experiencing competition in globalized markets and displaced migrants from decimated subsistence farms in Mexico need each other more than ever. Militarization of the border through Homeland Security and intensified policing of migrant communities ensure that both farms needing low-wage labor and migrants fearful of dangerous border crossings stay in California longer.

In my research on the most recent moment of philanthropic investments in addressing poverty across California's Central Valley, I found that despite worsening conditions for farmworkers and new racialized abuse of indigenous Oaxacans, even advocates believe that building partnerships with growers is the only viable strategy for improving the lives of farmworkers. For the first time, farmworker-organizing strategy includes saving California agriculture from the threat of global competition and the need to ensure a sustainable workforce through new guest-worker programs. In keeping with the now hegemonic "win-win" or "double-bottom-line development" trend in poverty alleviation, which proposes that what is good for capital is good for the poor, the FWCBI sought to alleviate poverty while also benefiting the farm industry.

Filipe Cordero, the founding program officer of the FWCBI, was partially inspired by the "win-win" approach of the United Farm Workers–grower alliance in the AgJOBS legislation drafted to address the current immigration crisis.[3] Beyond AgJOBS, new worker–industry partnerships organized by United Farm Workers' nonprofit organizations aim to improve production strategies and industrial efficiency, increasing the profit and competitiveness of farmers while improving the output (and theoretically the wages) of workers. As implied by the former farmworker who shifted the agenda at the FWCBI conference, the new theory goes something like this. In the context of the rapid globalization of agriculture, in which the cost of doing business (e.g. for land, water, equipment, labor, and regulation costs) is higher in California than in the global South, the human worker is the only malleable input to increase competitiveness. Growers need to stay competitive, so they cannot risk the cost of change. Workers on the other hand can simultaneously improve their own lives and boost production by learning new skills and showing leadership in the workplace and in agricultural communities. Theoretically, this approach offers a win-win, improving farm profit, and workers' wages and living conditions, at the same time. Yet, in this turn of events, self-help takes a strange twist, with the poor responsible not only for themselves but for saving the industry.

The double-bottom-line approach is particularly popular in the field of philanthropy. Domestically, this trend, commonly termed "philanthrocapitalism," is represented in foundations' embrace of business-oriented practices such as outcomes-based or impact investing over traditional charity.[4] At the global scale, a wide array of philanthrocapitalists such as Bill Gates propose that "creative capitalism," defined by entrepreneurial projects accountable to "doing well while doing good," is the solution to growing inequality and global poverty.[5] Some double-bottom-line capitalists seek profit in "the bottom billion" or the poorest of the poor, including pyramid schemes that "empower" slum residents in the global South to sell affordable single-use-size shampoo bottles[6] or engage in micro-credit programs that create new financial markets (and debt structures).[7]

In this chapter I interrogate the explicitly "win-win" approach of the FWCBI. Through extensive interviews and observation between 2007 and 2009, I found that the $10 million project created institutional governing structures and professional program frameworks that prohibited organizations from addressing the long-standing practices that have kept farmworkers living in unhealthful and unjust conditions. A stringent focus on community "assets" over organizing and an excessive concern with multi-stakeholder consensus building frustrated grass-roots organizations already challenged by a pessimistic political-economic climate. Some projects within this framework do propose incentives for industry to become more environmentally friendly. Some present ways to increase worker productivity and thus wages. None hold the industry accountable for its continued abuses and failure to implement the health and safety legislation passed under the leadership of the California farmworker movement. Obviously, none address worker ownership, cooperatives, a corrupt labor contractor system, below-minimum wages, international market liberalization, and the related patterns of immigration that make agricultural wealth possible.[8] Though inconceivable today for most of the people I interviewed, these alternative approaches were imaginable by the farmworker movement only a few decades ago.

While farmers never found reason to fully participate in the FWCBI, the foundation's concern with appeasing them (and other mainstream stakeholders) consumed and eventually destroyed the initiative. This chapter interrogates the "win-win" framework and the ways in which the FWCBI attempted to engage diverse stakeholders in improving the valley's poor agricultural communities. I first show how a foundation-appointed multi-stakeholder "task force" translated empirical research on farmworker conditions into policy recommendations that required workers to take responsibility for their own well-being and excluded questions that held growers account-able. Before describing the implementation of the project, I trace the lineage of its "win-win" approach not to neoliberal reforms in agriculture but to worker–industry partnerships inspired by business management consultants, including Peter Drucker and Patrick Below, recruited to the inner circle of the United Farm Workers by Cesar Chavez.

After describing the historical dimensions of the model, I introduce Campesino Rising, a local site of the FWCBI. I show how the "asset-based community development" model engaged partnering organizations in professional processes to document their own strengths and resources, but disallowed the identifica-tion of collective problems. Beyond the limits of the asset model, each "organizing" partner of the initiative was required to bring "authentic" farmworker leaders to the table, exacerbating exist-ing competition among regional nonprofit organizations.

Through the story of the FWCBI, this chapter shows that the neoliberal framework is not always presented through conspira-torial agendas but is solidified by reworking movement strate-gies into programs acceptable to both workers and industry.[9] The "win-win" paradigm brought new ways of speaking about poverty in agricultural communities, simultaneously silencing older notions of "antagonistic" organizing and producing new frameworks that lack a radical social imagination. The new state of mind is not always fully embraced, yet is maintained through fears of financial insecurity and deportation among undocu-mented workers and growers alike. Echoing the funding rela-tionships during the early farmworker movement, philanthropic power is shown to operate through what it asks the poor to do for themselves, as much as through what it excludes.

FROM *LABORING IN THE SHADOWS TO
THE BOUNTY OF FOOD*: DILUTING RESEARCH
THROUGH THE STAKEHOLDER TASK FORCE

The Western Foundation (WF) is a relatively new foundation that makes grants to service-providing nonprofit organizations and research institutes, often with a specific focus on the social, economic, and environmental health of regions. When made aware of the WF's interest in the Central Valley, several long-time farmworker advocates with connections in philanthropic networks (some, members of the Immigrant Participation Collaborative featured in the previous chapter) lobbied and eventually convinced WF program officers to make an explicit commitment to address farmworker concerns in California. In this section, I show how the WF's original commitment to addressing farmworker poverty was watered down and depoliticized by the foundation-led task force.

In 1998, a team of agricultural researchers associated with the California Research Center approached the WF to see whether it would fund a California-based agricultural worker ethnographic research project. The WF agreed and funded the center to conduct extensive research and publish *Laboring in the Shadows: Enduring Farm Worker Poverty*,[10] which documented the extremely poor health and living conditions of California farmworkers. The report attracted wide support and provided a rationale for the WF to shape farmworker programs. WF program officer Felipe Cordero explained, "I have everyone we are going to fund, all of the partners and consultants, read this report in order to understand the real lineage of this work." Included in this report was a rousing call to action from the foundation's president:

> We pay tribute to those who have struggled to bring dignity and rights to the lives of California's farm workers as we present this

report, *Laboring in the Shadows.* ... In this report we ask all Californians to look deeply at the often hidden lives of the more than 1 million migrant agricultural workers of California.... As a result of their low-wage work and undocumented status, farm workers face more barriers than any other group of workers in America.... They continue to labor in our fields—often silent in the shadows, but ever present. The contradiction is unavoidable: that their labor provides our nation and the world with a bounty of food, yet still they suffer in ways most Americans would never tolerate.

The main findings of the report included the following:

- One in five male subjects had at least two of three risk factors for chronic disease.
- A large majority of research subjects showed significantly higher iron deficiency anemia than most US adults—mostly due to serious food insecurity and hunger.
- Nearly 70 percent of all subjects lacked health insurance.
- 18.5 percent reported having a workplace injury.
- 41 percent reported pain lasting at least a week in one or more body parts.
- The six most commonly reported health concerns included dental problems, back pain, itchy eyes, knee pain, foot pain, and hand pain.
- The three most common mental health concerns were agitation or irritability, frustration or anger, and depression. Many reported financial, physical, and psychological abuse in the fields.
- When asked about workplace health, 23 percent of subjects complained of itchy eyes and 15 percent of headaches. In one research location, 60 percent of the subjects said that they were required to "test the

produce" by eating unwashed grapes to determine whether they were sweet enough to harvest.

· Only 7 percent were enrolled in any government program serving low-income people, and only one in six said that their employer offered any form of health insurance.

Using these serious, and to some startling, findings, Cordero embarked on a campaign to educate his board of directors and secure funds to design a large-scale farmworker initiative. Like John Sibley of the Immigrant Participation Collaborative (chapter 3), he arranged "trustee tours" to farmworker communities to convince his board of both the need and the potential in farmworker organizations:

> We took interested board members to the valley, many whom had never been beyond Los Angeles or the Bay Area in California, to become familiar first-hand with how real the need was. They were taken to Tall Trees to see the environmental damage, the absentee-landlord system, and the horrible living conditions. Then afterwards they were brought to Cutler-Orosi to see a model housing development. Then the CRC [California Research Center] presented the research findings from *Laboring in the Shadows*. This was enough to get the board to direct $50 million to address the health of farmworkers.

By 2001, Cordero was responsible for "cutting up the fifty million" into a statewide farmworker program. Instead of immediately investing in regional organizations to address the serious health, living, and work conditions revealed in *Laboring in the Shadows*, the foundation convened a multi-stakeholder task force. With the assistance of a professional facilitator associated with a large communications agency, a planning team, and a host of technical advisors, the task force's twenty-two members discussed the findings of *Laboring in the Shadows* with the goal of building multi-sector consensus on program and policy recommendations for the foundation. The members included academics, health care professionals, growers, elected officials, and farmworker advocates. In the final report from the task force, *Farm Workers and the Bounty of Food,* the chair, a retired congressman, opens with an open letter to the president of the WF. The letter states, "The most surprising finding was that we could actually reach consensus in such a short time frame and on such difficult issues." So, what did the growers, worker advocates, health care providers, and public officials all agree on? According to the report, "Everyone agreed fully on two issues. First, the Task Force agreed that there is a general shortage of culturally competent health care professionals in agricultural areas. Second, it was agreed that the general health infrastructure is weak in rural agricultural areas, particularly with respect to comprehensive medical facilities."

The specific agreed-on program and policy recommendations for the WF to fund and promote included: increasing the number of farmworker-serving, culturally competent health care providers; improving access to medical care where farmworkers live; funding of health education and prevention; analysis of existing insurance coverage plans, with the goal of increasing the participation of farmworker families; identifying governmental funding to increase farmworker access to public programs; developing a process for reserving Social Security contributions of workers for health insurance programs; and creating binational relationships with the United States and Mexico to address health education. The report also proposed establishing a state-level Farm Worker Health Commission to create policies and programs to improve and monitor health and safety laws in agriculture, and policy to target "bad actor" employers who regularly violate occupational health and safety laws.

At first glance, it appears as if the task force addressed the pressing issues revealed in *Laboring in the Shadows*. Growers even agreed to form new policies to target "bad actors" that do not enforce existing labor protection laws. However, when compared to the original findings of *Laboring in the Shadows*, the issues that required changing the way the agricultural system operates were avoided, watered down, or disguised. Nowhere did the task force recommendations call for addressing the "insufficient diet" and the extreme food-insecurity risk in farmworker communities. Though they were mentioned in the introduction of *Laboring in the Shadows*, there was no mention in the task force's report of the uncompensated overtime hours farmworkers need to work in order to feed their families, or the growing number of undocumented workers who are often paid well below minimum wage and who for many months out of the year cannot afford to meet their families' basic needs.

The task force included many policy recommendations to increase access to health care and insurance coverage but never mentioned the continuing use of pesticide spraying and ground pumping where farmworkers work and live. There was also no mention of the "fruit testing" practices growers demand, putting workers at risk. The structure of the workday, breaks, and the causes of chronic back, knee, foot, and hand pain were also not mentioned. The dramatic mental health problems that often emerge as a result of abuse and manipulation of workers in the fields, though described in *Laboring in the Shadows*, did not show up in the pages of the task force's report. While it is known that fieldwork is by its nature very difficult and stressful work, the frequent references in *Laboring in the Shadows* to agitation, anger, and depression in connection with continuing abuse in the fields were ignored.

All of the policy recommendations of the task force, excluding the final recommendation to "develop policies and programs" to improve (not to directly enforce or control) worker safety regulations,[11] required action and change by health care providers (more services), by the state (providing more housing, insurance, and programs), by local municipalities (changing codes to improve infrastructure in farmworker communities), and mainly by farmworkers themselves (health education and participation in programs). None of the recommendations required change for growers. While all of the recommendations are important and if implemented would improve conditions for many workers and families, none address the structure of the farm labor system, which continues to use poisonous pesticide techniques and illegal wages and working hours, or the financial, sexual, physical, and mental harassment that many workers reported in WF-funded research. In removing every element that might fuel antagonism between the various stakeholders, the process disguised the issues that if addressed would be more likely to improve conditions in agricultural communities in the long run.

A reader knowledgeable in the history of California agriculture and efforts to improve conditions for workers might argue that changing the structure of the system is currently unthinkable. This is the precise point of the "win-win" moment—that the convergence of the current political economic climate, entrenched institutional relationships, and the popular embrace of the double-bottom-line approach have altered common-sense thinking around what kind of change is possible. Turning stark research findings into policy recommendations (agreed on by growers, politicians, advocates, and health care professionals) transformed analysis of a system that breeds poverty in agricultural communities into a set of discrete "solvable problems." Individual actors, most frequently health care providers and workers themselves, are asked to improve conditions through their own efforts. There is no confrontation of the key structural arrangements that produce and maintain poverty: global trade liberalization, the labor contractor system, and abuse of undocumented immigrants, to name a few.

The lack of efficacy in foundation-funded research is not lost on the many people I interviewed in the valley who have witnessed years of outside research that has yet to show local returns. One mental health service provider explained:

> We have seen lots of people come in and ask us questions, but we never see the funding or even the results. [WF] survey people asked us questions and then don't provide anything. He [WF researcher] was crying, overwhelmed. I think he was surprised, when he learned about all our problems and needs, but he had no power. He was just the interviewer. The mental issues we keep talking about have to do with hard work, isolation, mistreatment in the fields, not to mention the sexual abuse of women in the fields—the hard life of an immigrant farm worker.... I didn't even get a copy of the report. Thankfully, I kept the researcher's card and called him to ask for it. He told me that there was all this red tape and that he'd send it soon. Well, three years later we finally saw the report, but it didn't live up to the issues we are really facing, that we talked about. Ultimately, people come and do studies, but then there's no money—that we see over here, anyway. They are doing that [Campesino Rising] project and giving out lots for meetings and things but I'd rather see funds go directly to address what is going on in the fields.

Anita Jimenez, a farmworker advocate at a farm labor center in southern San Joaquin Valley County, shared these sentiments:

I really wonder if they are just doing another study on us. They should already know what is going on down here, coming in with some new project. Didn't they talk to people? Didn't they read *Laboring in the Shadows* a couple years ago? After all that research and not taking on the real issues but holding meaningless meetings instead—people are basically being bribed, with grants from the WF, to get involved.

Much like the World Bank–funded research that critics complain never finds its way back to the people whose voices and participation are enlisted,[12] Cordero did not incorporate the realities conveyed locally into his plan to engage diverse stakeholders. Maria Chacon, a farmworker advocate with a graduate degree in agricultural economics, explained to me why long-time farmworker organizers have the patience to engage in grower-friendly studies and programs mandated through foundation grants. She suggested that if we want to keep farms and farm jobs in California, it's going to be hard to change the industry any time soon. Agriculture is a competitive export-based economy, and, as she described to me (before the worst years of the drought), California has the best weather and the best landscape with the capacity to grow what others cannot. Chacon concluded that it is very difficult to solve local problems around labor enforcement in a highly competitive global export-based market.

Everything is born out of this system—our benefits and all our problems.... It took forever to get growers to join AgJobs. And we agree with all the compromises except maybe the potential abuses of a new guest-worker program. But there has been nothing more unifying for farmers and farmworkers than immigration reform. So this is all we've got right now.

The particular conjuncture of globalized agriculture and worker fears of deportation inspired an unprecedented consensus.

Unable, or unwilling, to take on immigration reform policy or the structure of California-style industrial agriculture,[13] Felipe Cordero of the WF struggled to find paths to address farmworker poverty in ways acceptable to his board, and to growers, politicians, health care providers, and long-time farmworker organizers and advocates. After four years of planning and discussion with multiple stakeholders, a statewide program was launched. Before analyzing the FWCBI through one of its local sites, Campesino Rising, I trace the origins of the model—not to the agricultural industry but back to the farmworker movement itself.

THE NEW WIN-WIN PARADIGM:
THE UFW'S FIELD

One might assume that the current "win-win" approach emerged as a direct ploy of industry to control labor in the neoliberal era of trade liberalization and intensified policing of immigrant communities. Yet one of Felipe Cordero's inspirations, as he met with and listened to farmworker organizers and service providers across the state, was the "new win-win paradigm" of the UFW's Farmworker Institute for Education and Leadership Development (FIELD). FIELD's win-win model was inspired by the late Cesar Chavez, who himself toyed with the idea of worker–industry partnerships. In the early 1990s, the UFW was struggling to retain contracts due to increased competition with the Teamsters, the legacy of the leadership purges that occurred in 1979 through the 1980s, and a general failure to organize members. During this time Chavez became enamored of the "management theory" that proposed ways to improve conditions for workers and profit for owners simultaneously. This new-found interest, inspired by his friendships with famous management guru Peter Drucker and another management advisor and author, Patrick Below, was not always well received. To many union leaders, "management" was a dirty word. Some writers even claim that his obsession with business management led to the movement's demise.[14]

Though Chavez began to experiment with management theory, it was not fully tested until after his death, in an experiment with a rose farm, Bear Creek Roses. Before Chavez's death in 1994 he recruited an inner circle of family members of UFW founders. These new "family" leaders were groomed by Chavez to manage the multiple "movement institutions." The training they received was based on what Chavez learned from Drucker and Below. In 1994, one year after Chavez's death, the UFW gained a contract with Bear Creek Roses in the Central Valley town of Wasco. In the beginning the union brought up a large number of grievances, creating conflict between the union and the grower. David Villarino, one of the management-trained UFW organizers and the subsequent director of FIELD, believes that losing the contract would have been an immense, if not final, blow for the union.[15] In an attempt to save the relationship, Patrick Below was called in to help the union address worker–management issues at Bear Creek Roses. Similar to classic management theory popular today, Below proposed that an organization must be understood as a whole and not just the sum of its parts. Successful strategic change would be not about the concerns or grievances of workers or owners separately but about a cooperative attempt to improve the business and industry as a whole. According to Villarino, "The most important thing that Below did at Bear Creek was facilitate a process where UFW workers and owners together created a mission of mutual prosperity and respect, and innovative thinking for improving the company."[16] Villarino recalls:

This was genius thinking because we don't usually work with growers in this kind of context of mutual prosperity. It was also genius because we created a $1.5 million profit after implementing a 30-percent production increase for the two types of roses they produce. The workers were better educated and more trained, and in the end the worker crews were making decisions and did not even need a foreman anymore. This helped raise wages and earnings for the piecemeal work and doubled vacation time. The normal lost days in December that year decreased by 1,000 percent. This was a huge paradigm shift because the company was using the farmworkers' knowledge, utilizing it to the benefit of the enterprise. And the company committed to sharing the gains and maintaining employment for workers. For us this was a revolutionary lesson for the Union.[17]

The Bear Creek project eventually broke down when it became clear that the project followed the grower's vision, with workers helping them reach it. Villarino believes that when management publicly took credit for the project, they lost the trust of the workers and hindered future collaboration at Bear Creek.[18] Despite the failure to give workers equal voice or recognition, the idea of "win-win" planning became central to the new approach of the UFW. In 2000, nearly a decade after the Bear Creek experience, the UFW engaged all of its various institutions (the union and eight nonprofit "movement office" organizations) and leaders in a strategic planning process. At this meeting it was agreed that "everyone has failed farmworkers. The growers have not changed, educational institutions are failing farmworker children, training and workforce development efforts have done nothing for farmworkers ... and the union failed with 98% of the industry with no contracts."[19] At this meeting it was decided that the UFW would focus less on contracts and direct organizing and instead look at poverty, the whole life of the farmworker, and how to make farmwork a livable career. One of the ways proposed for implementing this new direction was to use the Bear Creek model through the union-associated nonprofit, FIELD. David Villarino was asked to lead this effort.

> It was proposed that I use the existing UFW nonprofit FIELD to implement the Bear Creek Roses model across the industry. Cesar founded the original FIELD in 1979, with support of the Carter and Brown administrations. At first he was doing a lot of workforce development stuff like auto-mechanic training, word processing, culinary careers. In the 1970s Cesar was very serious about the need to make agriculture a career, a job that has dignity, so this was his "workforce development" wing of the movement. The revived FIELD originally got DOL [Department of Labor] money from the Clinton administration to fill the skill gap between workforce development and industry needs. We used the theory behind Bear Creek—that if we cross train workers in roses and in grapes then we can increase production and the average workweek.[20]

FIELD convened a research consortium to conduct the first-ever in-depth study on the agricultural workforce, charting the various skill sets and demographics of workers. Through this research it became clear that agricultural skill sets had never been identified by any state, federal, or other workforce agency. During the Manpower workforce-development project of the 1950s, the industry was practically ignored. Instead of investing in the agricultural workforce, policymakers assumed that everything would be rapidly mechanized and that farm jobs would shrink to insignificance. However, in time low-wage, labor-intensive crops showed economic growth. While the California seed, pesticide, and land-use technologies had once given the United States a competitive advantage globally, others countries now caught up on these fronts—Mexico, Spain, and China. Agricultural industrialists quickly realized that the one area they had never fully developed, and that could be used to their competitive advantage, was the labor force.[21]

From these findings, FIELD developed programs to simultaneously improve worker productivity, worker–manager relations, and industry profit. The Bear Creek concept was solidified through FIELD-facilitated "industrial partnerships" with major farms in California. As FIELD staff set out to build collaborations with large growers and farm bureaus, they initially faced the problem that they were identified with the UFW. To counter this identification, FIELD staff surrounded themselves with industry people to show that they were not about grievances or confrontation. Even though the president of the UFW and other UFW leaders sit on FIELD's board of directors, and even though FIELD is described as a Movement Office of the United Farm Workers, staff described its relationship to the union as inconsequential.

The lead "industrial partners" coordinator at the time when this research was being conducted, Joaquin Garza, a former field worker, Foster Farms manager, and business school graduate, is particularly adept at building relationships with growers and explaining the FIELD model in non-confrontational business terms. As communicated in FIELD trainings and brochures, the main goal is to find the common ground between workers and growers to keep farms in California and improve the agricultural industry through labor–management alliances. According to Garza, FIELD's leadership training is less about organizing and more about business development and conflict resolution, with the ultimate goal of creating better workers and better worker–employer relations. Garza revealed that while collaboration generally means identifying projects and improvements that workers and employers agree on, growers are less interested in addressing worker concerns and primarily concerned with their bottom-line needs as a business. In the interest of keeping growers at the table, Garza prioritizes projects that he can convincingly describe as improving the growers' bottom line. His "win-win" leadership programs train workers in a culture of compromise, focusing on ways they can improve their own skills, productivity, lives, and communities through leadership development programs.

While Felipe Cordero of the FWCBI cited FIELD's "new win-win paradigm" as one of his main inspirations, he also mentioned wanting to re-inspire the radical movement for farmworker rights that had been ignited almost half a century before. However, as will be described through the local project site, Campesino Rising, the relentless focus on consensus and community assets frustrated the funded community organizing partners and ultimately crippled the FWCBI.

THE WESTERN FOUNDATION'S
CAMPESINO RISING

Campesino Rising is a huge investment in the valley right now. The program officer is a risk-taker in that he wants to support farmworker organizing but the effort is currently being designed to demonstrate success for the foundation and does not want to look too close into the faces of the people. They are nervous about how farmworkers will feel about the program because there will be no rapid results.... Part of this is because he is trying to please everyone—his dance between the foundation board and staff, the community-based organizations, the growers, the hired consultants, the health service agencies. I'm afraid that we are complicit in creating this myth that the foundation is really addressing the

> issues. I'm afraid that in the negotiation between all
> these groups we are like the sound and the fury
> signifying nothing.
>
>> Interview, John Jeffries, evaluation consultant to
>> the WF, FWCBI

I began observing the FWCBI's Campesino Rising (CR) project in the agriculturally productive San Joaquin region of the Central Valley in the spring of 2007, after a brutal winter freeze caused loss of crops and thus weeks of lost pay for field workers. Many families struggled to keep their housing and pay for food. It was also one year after the mobilizations across the United States in protest against the anti-immigrant Sensenbrenner Bill (HR 4437), which proposed to raise penalties and increase felony classifications for immigrants who entered the United States illegally. Shortly after these mobilizations, Immigration and Customs Enforcement (the former Immigration and Naturalization Service, reorganized under the post-9/11 Patriot Act) increased raids on undocumented immigrants' homes, intensifying a sense of fear in farmworker settlements. Central Valley farmworker advocate Sophia Guerrero described the situation in the San Joaquin Valley, home to the largest migrant farmworker population in the state of California:

> Things are really bad right now. People have created a secret underground hiding place that I've seen but was sworn to keep to myself. It's like a bomb shelter and there are appointed spotters and siren systems for people fearful of raids.... The freeze has made things even harder because people have not worked much and can't feed their children. And the freeze crisis is turning into a drought crisis. They are afraid to go get help, or go to clinics. Everybody is hiding out.

Before the mass mobilizations, Immigration and Customs Enforcement raids, and the freeze and subsequent drought, a smaller geographical site in the greater San Joaquin Valley was picked as a location for the CR project due to its large farmworker population and entrenched poverty. It is estimated that at least 57,000 farmworkers live in the selected project area. The number could be greater, as the agricultural base is spread out across the county and many workers are undocumented.[22] Farmworker families live in the many unincorporated towns scattered between farms, often lacking infrastructure such as clean water, housing, and social services. With one of the largest agricultural production values of any single county in the United States, the CR project site is also one of the worst places to live and work in terms of pesticide ground pumping, spraying, and drift. The farms in this region grow predominantly high-pesticide-use crops such as citrus fruit and grapes. In addition to pesticide poisoning, farmworkers report concerns in the fields including poor sanitation and safety, mistreatment by farm contractors and field managers, financial exploitation, physical abuse, psychological manipulation, and illegal charges and bribes around transportation, housing, food and drink, and farm equipment. Unfair dismissal, intimidation, and age, ethnicity, and gender discrimination are also commonly reported.[23]

Despite the number of critical issues that CR could have addressed, the project quickly became bogged down in professional training and planning processes. According to several granted partners I interviewed, there was no CR involvement in the immigrant rights organizing of 2006 or 2007 or in "challenging anything that would improve conditions for farmworkers." So what were the CR project and its partnering organizations doing from late 2005, when the local project was launched, until 2009? According to the paid staff, most of their time was spent "with a lot of pressure to implement the asset model."

From its inception, the $50 million FWCBI was troubled with the contradictions presented by funding issue-oriented organizers to participate in a complex multi-layered asset-based process. After the task force translated the *Laboring in the Shadows* findings into recommendations and the WF board approved the statewide project, Cordero began to design the initiative. As he learned from historic movement organizers, interested growers, and service providers, he envisioned multiple, and in some instances conflicting, approaches to addressing farmworker poverty. In an interview, he initially told me, "Since the UFW days we have not seen any change in conditions or any comparable organizing. So we really want to ramp up what people organizing farm workers are doing—to revitalize a social movement." However, instead of laying out social movement or community organizing strategies such as problem analysis, issue-oriented campaigns, activism, strategic alliance building toward specific targets, legislative change, and tactics like strikes and boycotts, Cordero proposed ways to build consensus among advocates, growers, and service providers. His idea was to "tap into the recognition among agricultural business leaders that workers are their most precious resource and it would therefore be in their best interest to take better care of them." This approach was alternately described as an "asset-based" or "win-win" model that strives to help both growers and workers change the way they view farmworker communities—the worker gaining dignity and pride in the work; and the grower investing in health, safety, and opportunities for farmworkers and their families. To do this, Cordero proposed that "we need to mobilize resources to make a unified statement about the importance of and dignity in farm work, like AgJOBS but at the local level."

While CR rhetoric included mention of revitalizing a social movement, funded organizations were asked to focus only on "assets" and were prohibited from acting on any individual or collective concern or issue that emerged. Many of the partners of the CR project were issue-based and action-oriented institutions and found this approach confusing, diffuse, and frustrating. The remainder of this section explains the vision and design of the CR project. The following section discusses how issue-based organizers and the asset-based model clashed, revealing the internal contradictions of the "win-win" approach.

The first grants made to the broader FWCBI went to organizations that the program officer identified as the "champions," including nonprofit organizations associated with the farmworker movement, legal aid agencies, and a Spanish-language radio station. These grants were open-ended; they were intended to get the historic farmworker institutions on board and enable them to increase their work on improving conditions for farmworkers. Cordero recalls, "We made three-year grants of $600,000 each to several of these agencies during the start-up period." Some believed that, as one evaluation consultant put it, "Felipe [Cordero] wanted to make grants for political reasons, to get in with the UFW, and allowed them to submit skeletal applications that said nothing at all. And if you look at the actual investments, most of it is going to their work on immigration issues. This is really bad, but Felipe just lets them do whatever they want and had his assistant write up the content and contract with goals and objectives." In essence, Cordero agreed that these grants were generally made to show the foundations' support for the historic farmworker movement and to allow them to "ramp up what they are already doing" to build worker–industry partnerships.

One year after this funding of the "champions," two demo sites were announced. Cordero recalls that after the San Joaquin Valley CR demo site was selected, "the service-provider people swarmed like flies to honey—all the nonprofits would swarm. But there were no *campesinos* there. It was a mistake for us to start talking so early. The cat was out of the bag. We had to start making a statement loud and clear that this project was not going to be about services but about long-term community building. It was important that we used the right language because we found out who fundamentally wanted to do this work." Instead of posting an open call for proposals, Cordero spent a year networking and deciding which organizations to invite. I interviewed staff from all nineteen of the partnering organizations, and three-fourths of them said that Cordero individually courted their organization. Long-standing farmworker advocacy organizations that were not invited to participate suggested that "the WF's new partners are selected on the basis of who has the best verbiage. It's about language, proposals, how you argue and present it, and also connections you have, who you know." Interviews with partners revealed that some were selected based on their social movement history and connections, some for their skill at communicating "community building" theory, and some based on recent success in organizing farmworker populations.

Inspired by the "lessons learned" by the Immigrant Participation Collaborative (see chapter 3) and articulated in several philanthropic reports on regional partnerships,[24] Cordero articulated three fundamental "community-building" beliefs to guide the detailed structure of a multiple-stakeholder regional partnership. First, he proposed that the voice of the people (farmworkers) must be at the center. Second, the effort should be sustainable after the foundation funding was gone. And finally, the project would use an "asset-based" model, drawing on the work of Cornelia Butler Flora and Robert Putnam.[25] As introduced in the previous chapter, the social capital theory of Flora and Putnam proposes that the most socially and economically vibrant communities are those that recognize and mobilize internal strengths and trusting relationships within the community. Drawing on Flora's work, the five assets (or forms of community capital) to be mobilized toward improving farmworker health and living conditions were public, environmental, community, social, and economic capital. The project was guided by the belief that by identifying and strengthening community assets, as opposed to identifying problems, diverse stakeholders can develop trust and common interests toward mutually beneficial lasting change. The plan for achieving these partnerships was imagined in three phases: relationship building, asset mapping, and finally action planning. Multiple stakeholders, including the agricultural industry, were to be included.

The project was to operate through a complex institutional structure. In an umbrella-styled configuration, the WF and supporting consultants and staff would envision, guide, and support the overall project. Underneath this layer of leadership, the "champions," also called strategic partners, were to provide technical assistance and support to other partnering organizations. Working under the foundation and the strategic partners, a local branch of a major national charity was funded as the convening partner. This partner was to staff, convene, and manage the entire initiative through one hired director and a number of project coordinators. Other grantees, including local and regional community organizing institutions and service providers, were to recruit farmworker participation and engage in the relationship building, asset mapping, and action planning.

Committees were to be organized by the community organizing partner institutions. These committees would be neighborhood-resident groups that organized local farmworker leadership. A farmworker assembly would provide training to build farmworker capacity to participate at the council level. The assembly level was conceived as an afterthought when planners decided that farmworkers needed more training before moving to the council level. The council would operate at the town level (three towns in the project region were selected to participate) and have farmworker representation plus members from other sectors including the schools, social services, businesspeople, agribusiness, and health care providers. This group was tasked with mapping local assets and aligning them with strategies to address local and regional issues. Ultimately, it was proposed that a regional coalition would form, with representatives from each local council. This group would plan at a broader level and ideally maintain the interests and voice of farmworkers.

Imagine the regional coalition as an umbrella, with the three councils directly underneath, one farmworker assembly underneath the councils, and several neighborhood committees under the assembly. All together, the various project groupings were to work toward regional decision-making around population health (e.g. reduced occupational injury, improved mental health), community health (e.g. improvements in housing and social support), and "systems change" (e.g. improving worker–employer relationships, preserving employment, creating responsive public policy).

The committees were organized and staffed by community-organizing grantee institutions. Paid staff of the convening partner facilitated the assembly and councils. Over $10 million was dedicated to the local CR project, and grants were made to nineteen partnering organizations, including the "champions" and additional community-based and health care organizations. According to Alice Richards, the staff director of the project, housed with the convening partner organization, "The idea ultimately is that a regional body, with farmworkers, growers, service providers, policy makers, would come up with a broad and unified picture about improving farmworker health and then develop and implement action plans, or get the resources needed to make a difference."

The first stumbling block in the multi-stakeholder model was revealed immediately. One year into the implementation of the CR project, it was determined by convening partner staff that the farmworker representatives were "not ready" to voice their concerns as equals alongside the more powerful collaborative members. In response to this realization, initiative resources were allocated to leadership training for local farmworker representatives in farmworker assemblies. Hence, the assembly level of the process, as described above, was created as an afterthought. By this time, multi-stakeholder councils had already formed, but they lacked farmworker representation because the farmworkers were being held back for training at the assembly level. Already, the decision-making bodies lacked the voice of the farmworker. The convening partner realized that without addressing the power imbalance between workers and growers, and even between workers and local officials and service providers, there would be no way to build true multi-stakeholder consensus, as farmworker participants tended to remain silent in collaborative meetings. The following section shows how the asset-mapping and consensus-building model continued to marginalize the voices of farmworkers and frustrate community-organizer grantees.

LIKE OIL AND WATER: PROFESSIONAL
"GIRLS," ASSETS NOT ISSUES, AND
MEMBERSHIP COMPETITION

The broad goal of CR was ambitious: to both revive a social movement and build regional policymaking partnerships between workers, growers, and service providers to improve conditions in agricultural communities. Problems arose quickly for issue-based and member-based organizers, who had little patience with the overwhelming focus on asset models and consensus-building processes. In addition to their frustration with the slow pace of the project, the organizer institutions battled with one another for members. The assembly struggled to retain staff and participants. The councils remained mired in asset mapping, and growers did not find reason to join the effort. A regional coalition never formed before the funds dried up and partners moved on to other things.

Ultimately, without a shared purpose or identity, specific issues, or defined targets to rally around, the project became all process, and partners disengaged. The foundation attempted to infuse energy into the project by supporting local pesticide organizing, but it was too late in the game. When the funding was discontinued due to lack of "measurable outcomes" at the foundation level, partners pulled out as their individual grant contracts ended. In my research, I observed (and describe below) how the goals of the project were eroded through three specific approaches promoted in the CR project. The first was the overwhelming preference given to young professionals over seasoned organizers. The second was the focus on community assets over issues, which ultimately drove the program officer to re-evaluate the project in the face of criticism from both grantees and the foundation. The third problematic approach was the

project's focus on institutional membership, which conflicted
with existing member organizations' strategies.

PROFESSIONAL "GIRLS,"
NOT SEASONED ORGANIZERS

I was surprised to see them hire all these young girls
that have no experience in the community like us
"old ladies" do. They have no idea how to work with
farmworkers. They go to meetings with all the fancy
clothing and language but really don't know
anything.

> Interview, Gracie Hermosa, director of a
> historic farmworker organization, 2007

Early on in the implementation of Campesino Rising, the foundation required the convening partner to hire "professional
girls" as project coordinators. The idea was that seasoned organizers would not be able to facilitate a process based on assets and
broad stakeholder agreement as opposed to confrontational
issues. The staff was expected to be "neutral and professional,"
with the educational training to understand the multi-layered
project design and the skills to facilitate meetings with diverse
groups of people. The four coordinators hired were all recent
college graduates from either Fresno State University or University of the Pacific, in Stockton. They had bachelor's degrees
in sociology, social welfare, and/or public health. Two were
daughters of farmworkers. All had grown up in the Central Valley. Each had worked in a social service office in an administrative capacity. None had community organizing, development, or
public or political affairs experience.

From the start, the staff of granted partnering organizations
did not trust or respect these young women coordinators.
The coordinators in turn became frustrated with their lack of

experience working with the seasoned and sometimes fiery leadership of the partnering organizations. I interviewed four of the "second-round" coordinators multiple times in 2007–2008; the first four had already quit due to lack of direction, problems working with partnering organizations, and/or "personal reasons." The coordinators I interviewed did not have a significantly better experience than those who came before them. By the end of my research, only one remained with the project.

The main problem the coordinators faced was how to communicate what they perceived as a complex consensus-building model to granted organizations interested in action, and how to embody the role of the neutral facilitator. The WF required each coordinator to attend facilitation training at a consulting agency in San Francisco, a meeting with staff at the foundation to review the model, and a meeting at a large public health agency to understand a broad and integrated concept of health. They were also required to read reports from partnering organizations and WF, including *Laboring in the Shadows*. After the training phase, coordinators were expected to bring the partnership to life through the various institutional structures and processes described in the previous section. Though armed with the theoretical program design and professional training, the coordinators immediately discovered that they were not prepared for working with the partnering organizations, many of which had long-standing turf battles and competition between one another.[26] One coordinator, Lupe Vega, described her experience this way:

> I was sent away for a week to get trained. I had to review the model and I had a lot of questions, but now I get it. It's asset-based, not action-based. We were told not to say "I" or "my." So my role is just to explain this and facilitate. Since we are focusing on the asset-based approach, I don't know what organizing partners are working

on—I don't have opinions either way.... My main challenge is that people did not trust me and were like, "What are you really going to do for the community?"

Sandra Frank, a slightly savvier coordinator, described her experiences this way:

> It's hard to work with organizations that don't want to work with you. And the reason they have trouble with us is because of this whole model thing. And from the beginning the program officer keeps changing things. It's been three years now, and the organizations that are a part of it are still asking, "So what is it?" What are we supposed to be doing now? It's scary to go to the [foundation] meetings because they are changing things all the time. When [Cordero] gets an idea he's like, "Let's change this!" Then we have training, a new part to the model that we have to communicate. For example, we didn't have the [assembly] part at the beginning. Then they realized that the farmworkers involved needed capacity building before they could get involved with other people at the table. It's like we are communicating to people who work with farmworkers that we think campesinos are not "prepared" to participate. And that in front of all these people, that have been involved for years, that *we* are the ones that need to *train* them.

The second coordinator quoted clearly understood what she was up against: a complex theoretical model that kept changing, an approach that prevented community organizers from organizing, professionalized processes that dismissed long-embedded leadership, and a facilitation style that prevented the coordinators from acting on the concerns of project participants. While all of the coordinators were born and raised in the Central Valley—three in the local project area—and two were the children of farmworkers, the professionalized role they were required to play bred distrust and disrespect from almost all of the partners. They were often described in terms such as these:

Gracie Hermosa, CR grantee and director of a farmworker
organization: "These girls with jewelry and pantyhose who go
into poor people's houses like they don't want to get dirty. So in
the end because they are not like organizers who get dirty in
the fields with workers, we end up with the same old thing as
usual: outside people getting input from immigrants but not
doing a damn thing about it."

Daniella Tores, CR grantee and community organizer: "They are
gatekeepers and are preventing anything from happening. The
drumbeat is 'the people aren't ready,' so they spend hours and
hours at the partner meetings trying to get the asset language
down."

Susan Katz, CR grantee and health educator: "They are trying to
build community connections. The thing is we *are* very well
connected already; we work with all these agencies. Why go
through a whole new door?"

In hiring recent college graduates with no experience working
with farmworker organizers, CR threw the coordinators into the
lions' den. Each of the partnering organizations embraced a different community-organizing methodology, from action research,
to Industrial Areas Foundation–style organizing (defined by
issue identification and institution building through one-on-one
and house meetings), to popular education and service-center
approaches. They also had their own (often competing, as will be
described in the next section) constituency and local leadership.
To require these groups to work together collaboratively was the
first challenge. To require them to operate according to a vague
and changing model that prevents action was an even bigger challenge. Ironically, the professional "neutral" facilitators experienced more conflict and antagonism than "old-school organizers"
might have, as a result of the partners' distaste for the professionalized processes and theories presented.

Despite the inherent challenge of funding community organizers to not organize, grantee Gracie Hermosa suggested that if an "organic immigrant leader" was hired instead of a "pretty young thing," then the project might have half a chance. Hermosa recommended Maria Lopez, an indigenous Mixteco woman whom I met through a friend in Fresno and hired to watch my then eight-month-old daughter while I conducted interviews and attended meetings.

> I'd hire Maria. She is a perfect example of someone who came here as a migrant, looking to improve the lives of her family and her people. Look how she organized against the raids and for Mixteco culture in Madera. If we can't pay the Maria Lopezes of the world beyond cooks, cleaners, and taking care of our children, then we are stuck. This is the kind of woman that needs to take over. But many of these women, like Maria, are also stuck in our macho culture where she can't do a lot until she's talked to Alfredo [a Mixteco leader] or her husband.

Throughout my research into the CR project, an assumed gendered politics was visible where young, college-educated women were deemed neutral and professionalizable, while organizers referred to as "old-school ladies" were viewed as too confrontational and embedded in local politics and turf battles. Emerging women leaders from the indigenous Oaxacan (Mixteco, Trique, and Zapotec) communities were often sidelined by the gender roles prescribed by their traditional cultures. I also found that the hired coordinators were only successful in recruiting women into the process. Coordinator Anna Martinez explained: "I noticed one day that when a couple of the women were leaving, their husbands were in the car waiting for them. I said, 'Now why didn't you just come in!' But it's part of the Mexican culture. They just don't do the community stuff." Because the project was communicated as a "community improvement" effort and not as an attempt to address the grievances of workers (this was avoided for fears of alienating growers), Mexican men assumed that it was a "women's thing," designed for traditional community caregivers.

Ultimately, in an attempt to create a neutral "win-win" politics, the professionalized and gendered hiring decisions limited the project's ability to successfully engage historic community organizing institutions and male farmworkers. As has been observed in the context of international development poverty programs, strategically gendered professionalism can depoliticize and "domesticate" activist approaches and networks in local regions.[27] In this case it also represents the mixed or dual efforts of philanthropic self-help: women who grew up in poor Central Valley communities were empowered to lead through their own professionalization but were required to direct time and resources toward bureaucratic operations and not causes of concern within farmworker communities.

TAKE YOUR TIME BUT HURRY UP: ASSET-BASED COMMUNITY DEVELOPMENT WITH DIRECT-ACTION ORGANIZERS

Theoretically, all of the granted partners were implementing the CR model by attracting farmworker leaders to neighborhood committees, assigning farmworker representatives to receive training at the assembly, and participating in city councils. In reality, partners did not understand the model, and resisted it.

> Gracie Hermosa, CR partner and program director at a Mixteco service provider and organizing institution: "It was not clear what to expect or what kinds of outcomes they wanted to see. It

got off to a slow start. Especially for the organizing partners, because we were not supposed to focus on any issues until the [committees and assemblies and councils] were formed. We had all this money and not much to do."

Jefferey Cohen, CR partner and legal aid staff person: "I think that what [CR] is really trying to do is just create a model and eventually to create non-confrontational issues, things to do like creating work plans. I think what they want us to do is help them move to a place where this model can play out."

Francine Donez, CR partner and community organizer: "When it was first proposed it was really out there in the clouds. I could not grasp what they wanted. It's like climate change and social change, very pie in the sky. There are so many components I can't figure out what I'm supposed to be doing."

From the start, partners rejected the professional staff and project design. The organizers were frustrated that they were funded as "organizing partners" but were prohibited from allowing their members to identify issues, such as pesticides, water rights, and abuse of workers in the fields. Service providers were wary of a project that required many meetings but did not include planning or resources around service delivery. City officials did not want to spend their time on processes that had no immediate implications for their constituents. The coordinators described what occurred at the assembly and council levels and inspired such widespread critique:

Alicia Perez, assembly coordinator: "We need to start with the basics. Some people here don't even know what an agenda is, so we are starting with explaining what an agenda is and how to use Robert's Rules of Order. We have an 18-month funding timeline so we need to get people up to speed. We are also working on building a structure for our meetings, ground rules and things. Then we will get to talking about what they like about their community—what assets they would want to preserve and use to improve things."

Anya Walker, council coordinator: "I would describe our meetings as getting everybody trained enough to do this work for themselves. So we spend time getting the same language of assets down, how to create a mission statement, how to create guidelines to work by. I have to review the model again—that it's assets, not action-based. The meeting tonight, we are going to talk about the model of the council and how it should work; then we'll discuss our mission and vision, do an asset training, and then plan our first celebration."

Over a six-month period I attended several council meetings and the mandated monthly partner meetings. At each of these meetings, one of the paid staff would conduct an ad hoc "quiz" on the five community health assets, while participants and partnering organizational staff mumbled to themselves and slowly volunteered answers like stubborn schoolchildren: public—environmental—community—social—economic. When I pushed project coordinators to discuss what kinds of things council or assembly participants would like to work on, some specific issues did emerge. But it was immediately determined that "it's not time to act yet" because the consensus-building process needed to be played out first. Here is one example.

Erica: Have any critical issues ever emerged from a meeting that people want to work on?

Assembly coordinator: At one meeting a *mayordomo* [field supervisor] came and after listening to everybody he was like, "Wow, I had no idea these things were happening on the job." The rest of the workers were talking about how the water is dirty, there are no toilets in the fields, women are being taken advantage of and abused. This is still going on and in many cases for women it is the only way to get ahead.

Erica: Are these issues, like sexual and other abuses in the fields, things that the council will bring up as priorities to work on?

Assembly coordinator: Well, these are not the kinds of issues that we'd take to the council. There we will work on asset maps and health plans. The challenge is that we need to wait for the assembly reps to get done training the worker reps, and then they can join the council. They can't do anything without the reps there ... and now the councils don't have the ag voice at all, workers or growers, and this is supposed to be community-based, so we can't do anything without them at the table.

Here is another example, from an interview with a council coordinator.

Erica: So, when you ask people what they'd like to see improved, what has come up thus far?

Council coordinator: One woman talked about the high grass in her backyard and how there were drug dealers and prostitutes that used it every day. And this is an unincorporated area, so they don't really have police or any help. So then I turn it around and say, "How can we see this place as an asset?" She answered my question by envisioning a clean yard with a place for kids to play. So we can then turn these problems into assets.

Erica: Is this something that they are now going to work on together?

Council coordinator: No, we are not about doing things right now. Maybe in the future this is the kind of thing they might want to do. But lots of people are just affected by looking at things differently. The goal is to build the capacity for them to be ready to do things for themselves first—hold meetings, understand plans, see assets instead of just problems, and provide a structure before they work on issues.

This planning process had been going on for a year before I began conducting research in the spring of 2007, and it was still underway when I completed most of my fieldwork in 2009. Over and over, farmworkers and service providers were told to learn new skills, speak new languages, and professionalize their behaviors. In this new iteration of self-help, people are asked to improve their own conditions by identifying the meager resources they already have but never by speaking or acting against the industry or mainstream institutions. Whereas the self-help philanthropy during the social movement of the 1960s imposed limits only once the participation of the poor went beyond what was acceptable to foundations and mainstream institutions, the new self-help forecloses problem identification and protest by proscribing all engagement around assets and relationships with industry.

BREEDING COMPETITION AMONGST MEMBERSHIP-BASED INSTITUTIONS

Because the granted organizing partners rejected this slow and, to them, patronizing process, they quickly became hesitant to bring their "best leaders" to the assembly or to the councils, for fear of losing them to CR. In the words of Juanita Olmos, lead organizer of a community organizing CR-granted partner:

> In our [committee] we train for organizing and action. But at the [council] level we can't even talk. At the [council] we have to sit around learning about "assets." Leaders that I send there say to me, "We are tired of being breast-fed, we are growing and need more substance. They are talking about the same thing each time, no action." The leaders say to me, "Don't send me there." So I have to be careful about losing leaders for our own organizational membership if they get anxious about so many meetings with no action.

Despite the organizing partners' frustration with the assembly and council process, they were required by their grant contracts to send farmworker representatives to these meetings and ended up competing with one another for "authentic" local leaders. This dynamic bred intense competition and even slander among the organizing grantees. In the words of organizers from three different partners:

> Diana Herrero, PICO-trained granted partner: "I'm not really sure that the other organizing partners really have [committees] like we do. You saw how no one really wants to talk about what they are doing at [CR] meetings.... We have a process and have been building leadership for real."

> Gracie Hermosa, granted partner organizer from a historic migrant organization: "Juanita [another organizer] has no relations in the community. And people know they don't really do much organizing and just give workers a bad name. So now they go in the back door through these other guises to get their own membership quota."

> Abel Fernandez, organizer from a partner organization from a historic farmworker movement institution: "We get to the meeting and they are like, "So how many people are you bringing? Which are your leaders?" And we claim them all, because the others are not bringing anybody. The ones they want to bring, well, I know them from way back from my years in the community, and those people are not the ones that are going to do anything—just the same old regulars that join everything. But these guys [other organizers] don't know, because they are just going in and starting all over again what has been done before. Anyways, they had only one person, and I had four."

In addition to the competition and distrust among organizers, they were also conflicted by commitments to other funders. Many received large grants from the state of California under the First Five early childhood education program, which required funded organizations to produce educational materials and deliver trainings. While some of the membership-based organizations preferred to keep members for themselves rather than lose them to CR, others were accused of only convening people to provide the services prescribed by other funders, like First Five and other private foundations, and not organizing CR committees.

Community organizers were not the only ones having difficulty bringing representatives to the table. For all of the win–win worker–grower talk, none of the councils could attract membership from agribusiness. Grower representatives found no reason to collaborate with worker advocates and had no tolerance for meetings and planning processes during busy planting and harvest seasons.

WHEN CAPITAL SMACKS UP AGAINST THE WALL: A LAST-DITCH PESTICIDE ORGANIZING ATTEMPT

With project coordinators advised to "stick to mapping assets" until workers and growers were at the table, the project stalled. In the midst of this standstill, and with an ultimatum from the foundation board to show measurable outcomes if funding was to be continued, Cordero called together a small group of advisors. They decided to break from the model and required partners to take on anti-pesticide organizing. However, this last-ditch attempt to rally partners did not work, due to the partners' sense of betrayal that Cordero was leading with an issue while claiming to be participatory. Partners also criticized the foundation's lack of knowledge about anti-pesticide strategy and its unwavering fear of confrontation with growers. According to Cordero:

I mentioned, as an example of something that they could start to work on together, potential action on a particular bill on pesticide drift. Last year, a bill was signed by the governor, with very few people following it. It was an emergency alert bill on pesticide drift—but it was flawed. Usually the public health official is the point person for any drift emergency. But in this bill it was said to be the agricultural commissioner! So I told everyone that they could educate people about this bill at the [CR] sites, train people how to recognize drift, file reports, hold the alert system accountable. And then when there is no response to an emergency, they mobilize to complain and go to legislation to fix the bill.... But the organizational leaders were upset because me, from the foundation, was bringing in issues while I've always talked about it coming from the people.... It's hard, because at the foundation I am constantly pushed to show success. The board can say that they believe in a long-term community-building approach, but at the same time they press for measured outcomes. I am not even secure that the money for the future of this project is guaranteed. I need to figure out how to show that conditions are improved. I'd like to do something similar to environmental justice approach.... And because my project is about farmworkers and not just service providers, it's more controversial, and I'm under more scrutiny to show results.

My interviews with partners confirmed that while some supported organizing around the pesticide-drift alert system, they resented being told by the foundation what to focus on after Cordero's insistence on a participatory, community-driven model. As brilliantly described by international development scholar Uma Kothari, participatory "moderators" and "facilitators" employed by funding bodies, like Cordero and the young professional coordinators, often find themselves in a bind where they are "unable to share ideas with 'locals' to promote a more participative exchange because in order for them to express and maintain their professionalism, they need to retain an authoritative distance.

This may create a tense ambivalence because of the twin demands to be participative and authoritative."[28] In this instance, Cordero was widely criticized for stepping out of his role as the silent, "participative" authority.

However, a more fatal assessment of the foundation's last-minute attempt to take on the pesticide-drift alert system came from partners with experience working on the issue. Amy Jennings, a staff person with a pesticide action group hired as a technical assistance partner to CR, found the foundation-driven pesticide organizing even more frustrating:

> I am at the Policy Committee meeting that [Felipe Cordero] just formed to deal with finally getting something done through the initiative. I was so frustrated.... We are all asked to talk about what it would look like if we really brought assets to an issue. They [Cordero and a hired consultant] wanted to take SB 391 as the hypothetical to work on. What was so frustrating is that we [a pesticide organization] already have a strategy for this, and SB 391 lends itself terribly to collective action with [CR] partners. I would have picked the buffer-zones issue because people could identify necessary buffer zones in their communities to work on. But SB 391 all happens at area guidelines that are already developed, and for this what is needed is to develop talking points and turn people out at hearings. But it is not a broad and creative issue. We are the pesticide partner, why not talk to us about which pesticide issues would lend itself to collective action? ... So then I asked if this is a hypothetical exercise or are we really working on this? In response, [Cordero], in a fit of excitement, says, "Let's work on this! Let's get to work!" And then I'm like, "Oh my god, these people have no idea." But they acted excited. And then the next day the entire partnership was mandated to work on this.... Later there was the push-back from the [convening partner]. They kind of were frustrated with us because we were trying to make it happen and it goes against the model. Plus every partner has a separate grant

agreement and are now all of a sudden supposed to work together. So they are all asking, so what is it that we are now supposed to do? Who gets the credit for it? I also had to tell the evaluator consultant that the model is getting in the way. That the [convening partner] is stopping things from happening. This is the first time that we talked to an evaluator consultant about problems related to doing direct service versus organizing and that what we are doing is not ever going to be about social capital! I also told her that SB 391 is not good, and that buffer zones is. She kind of went, "Whooops!"

The three partnering organizations with a history in anti-pesticide organizing agreed on the larger underlying dilemma: It is impossible to address pesticide poisoning through the "win-win" framework. In the words of organizer David Sweet:

The problem is that this model is silent on where capital won't budge—the things that we can't win through dialogue. I really wonder if [Cordero] understands this? ... People in the valley are acting all nice about the project in public, from the people who want money from the initiative. But pesticide activists in San Francisco are asking, "What happens when capital smacks up against a wall?"

Similarly, organizer David Vega proposed:

For anything to really happen we are going to need to make some demands, protest, but of course that doesn't fit with the model. "We are not there yet," is what they'd say. The local County Board of Supervisors is made up of all Republican, conservative growers. So collectively taking on pesticides through collaboration is laughable when we can't even get growers or supervisors to participate. We are just so far apart from those in power. We need to shake things up, but the foundation won't let us push on anything.

The failure of Cordero's pesticide organizing attempt reveals that the win-win approach was flawed and worked against the grain of community organizing. At a larger level it reveals that, in the context of industrialized agriculture and its deeply embedded political support system, consensus among diverse and unequal groups is nearly impossible and sometimes undesirable. Truly addressing the living, working, and health problems experienced by workers would raise too many issues and immediately scare off growers. "Win-win" development is duplicitous in contexts where the prosperity of the stakeholders who refuse to come to the table is dependent on the suffering of weaker stakeholders that the process aims to ameliorate. This initiative's failure to address pesticide organizing joins an embattled lineage of historical cases, from the Black Power movement's involvement in the Gray Areas Program to participatory development projects in the global South, where efforts to address structural inequalities are disrupted by the ideological and political limits presented by foundations.

CONCLUSION

Complicating the basic structural limitations of the FWCBI model is the unfortunate reality that many community-organizing institutions are also not addressing the issues of most concern to farmworkers. In the context of unannounced raids on immigrant households, a predominantly un-unionized workforce, growing job insecurity, financial crisis, and now harvest-threatening drought, organizers have managed to take on only safe issues, such as putting up stop signs and streetlights in farmworker neighborhoods. Every partner I interviewed criticized all the others as only organizing themselves to gain institutional membership and foundation grants. The competitive and project-oriented funding culture makes building a farmworker power base even more difficult.

In an unimaginative environment where everyone is fearful of confronting growers, it has become common sense to ask farm-workers to build relationships with industry as the best way to help themselves.

Even champions of the consensus-based model—such as Michael Dimock, who runs a statewide sustainable-agriculture project called Roots of Change, designed to bring diverse stake-holders to the table around sustainable agriculture systems in California—suggest that the model is not always workable.

> The Central Valley is a lot tougher. We tried to start an AFA [collaborative committee] in Merced, but that folded.... We had some farmworker advocates and growers, but they were so very polarized. In the Merced case there were simply too many extremes. You see, in Ventura and on the many small and organic farms we've worked with we were able to take the power away from the poles. We need to take the power away from the edges and bring it to the center. Our philosophy and organizing approach is inspired by the work of Dee Hock[29]—that the poles of debate stop everything. Poles control the process and you always end with a stalemate. And politicians won't take leadership because it is too risky. But in the Central Valley we had no "center," no real way to move away from the poles in a way that was authentic.[30]

While the "win-win" or "new center" agenda proposes to simultaneously save jobs, industry, and for Dimock also the environment (a triple bottom line), what is not conceivable to produce through consensus or collaboration? What does it exclude, hide, or make unthinkable? Given the current desperation of both workers and growers, very few of my interview subjects questioned the very goal of making it easier for industrial farms in California to generate profit. With the intertwined relationship between poor Mexican pueblos and the farm fields of California, advocates have become increasingly interested in making business easier for growers in order to secure jobs, maintain the viability of binational networks established around the industry, and protect migrants whose families on both sides of the border rely on farm labor. Without Central Valley farm jobs, migrant families will become more nomadic, travelling across states and borders at each harvest. In the face of financial crisis and drought, this is already happening.

On the other hand, if the large industrial farms of California were forced to change or leave, the enduring poverty, marginalization, and abuses in farmworker communities might be alleviated. Yet, in the whole two-year course of my fieldwork, only one of my informants asked the question, "Why should we spend our time saving these big farms?" Rebecca Rosado, a long-time farmworker and recently trained community organizer from Tulare County, proposed:

> Saying that to help us all out we should help keep big farms here is like saying that you have this baseball team that you go to see, and then you end up fighting for the team to hire some star player who makes the owner tons of money that none of us ever see. Then on top of that now with the new popularity we have to pay $150 for a ticket, and with all the building and parking they are polluting our town. What do we really get in the end? I say it should be about helping the workers or nothing at all. We should be clear about that. We need to ask if we really want to partner with farms here. The reason that people like him [FIELD staff person] say that we are no longer in time to fight is only because they grew up, got good jobs, drive good cars, or formed these big organizations like FIELD or the UFW. They've been there and then got comfortable.

Only this one farmworker organizer proposed that pressuring industrialized farms to change or leave is a viable solution. A few are—not so publicly—critiquing the AgJOBS partnership and are fighting for guest worker–free immigration reform. Both industry insiders and farmworker advocates are unsure whether farmworkers will benefit significantly from the recent immigration-reform proposals presented by president Barack Obama.[31] In the current post–financial crisis moment where the security of the "big guys" has been temporarily shaken, the call to "save industry to save jobs" is similarly playing out in other sectors. Terms such as "social entrepreneurship," "bottom-line development," and "philanthrocapitalism" make common sense. While unique and unprecedented cross-sector partnerships are emerging, such as the worker-ownership arrangements of the United Auto Workers and recent agreements between farmworker organizers in Florida (Coalition of Immokalee Workers) and food chains like Burger King and Chipotle, much is kept off the table. The complex relationships between particular political-economic moments in time, entrenched immigration and labor patterns, the maturation of social movement organizations, and the specific management ideas of planners, facilitators, and funders across a region as divided as California's Central Valley shape the very possibilities for social change.

Dolores Huerta, cofounder of the UFW, is going back to the basics, organizing farmworker communities and building grassroots farmworker and immigrant leadership through her Dolores Huerta Foundation. Reflecting the original "mutual aid" motivations of the farmworker movement, Huerta still believes that "when immigrant, farmworker, and low-income people empower themselves they can add so much to the community. We have seen people in Weed Patch, for example, pass a local bond issue for the school district, build a gymnasium, a swimming pool—it gets so hot here—and build sidewalks and gutters for a whole community." Yet Huerta, a seasoned organizer, also finds the current moment challenging. In her words, "When we find growers who really want to partner with us, it does make things easier—would add a lot of strength to organizing in the community. Unfortunately, that is not always the case but rather the exception."

Is it possible to simultaneously address farmworker poverty and increase agricultural prosperity in the Central Valley, one of the largest food-production regions in the world, whose success relies on low-wage seasonal back-breaking labor? And should the most marginalized workers in the United States be responsible for both improving their own lives and saving an industry? As a pesticide partner of CR suggests, "The problem is that this model is silent on where capital won't budge—the things that we can't win through dialogue.... What happens when capital smacks up against a wall?" Relationships between private foundations, professionalized advocacy organizations, and other regional stakeholders have solidified a limited understanding of what is possible in addressing enduring poverty and inequality. Yet, new ideas and movements are taking shape beyond the Central Valley, as will be touched on in the concluding chapter.

CHAPTER FIVE

Conclusion

REGIONAL ABANDONMENT AND THE NEW SELF-HELP

Real poverty is the belief that the purpose of life is acquiring wealth and owning things. Real wealth is not the possession of property but the recognition that our deepest need, as human beings, is to keep developing our natural and acquired powers to relate to other human beings.

Grace Lee Boggs[1]

History will judge societies and governments—and their institutions—not by how big they are or how well they serve the rich and powerful, but by how effectively they respond to the needs of the poor and the helpless.

Cesar Chavez[2]

Every summer and winter I return to California's Central Valley with my daughter, Emilia, and husband, Jose. Jose's mother, Soledad, was a farmworker who courageously raised seven children while migrating between Mexico and California. Leaving rural Mexico in search of a better life she found farm and eventually cannery work up and down the state of California. Known to work significantly harder than her then husband, Soledad harvested fruits, vegetables, and nuts—sometimes with her elder children at her side. Following a season picking peaches and plums in the fruit orchards of San Mateo County, Soledad found work in a cannery in San Jose. After a serious injury at the cannery and separation from her husband, she moved to the Central Valley town of Lodi to be near a church community and a gracious family, also from Mexico, who provided the extra support she needed. Soledad's home was always open to her seven children, their growing families, and the many people in need she met through her church and her seamstress work. Eventually, the hard physical work took its toll on Soledad's health. After her passing, the family committed to joining together once a year to celebrate her life.

For the annual reunion, we stay with family in Stockton, which is near Lodi, in northern San Joaquin County. While the city of Stockton has long been troubled by the persistent poverty that plagues most towns built around the agricultural industry, it recently declared bankruptcy, and a growing sense of insecurity and desperation is palpable. My nephews, usually eager to see the latest blockbuster movie at the Regal Cinemas complex, recently warned us not to venture to downtown Stockton at night. When stopping at a gas station, they say, remember to lock the car. I am told of frequent robberies, car thefts, and murders in Central Valley towns. In an environment of few job opportunities, often-unstable housing, and poorly funded schools and social services, increasing numbers of young people are turning to gangs and the streets.

While the daily challenges that many people face living in the valley are not visible to someone passing through, a quick drive around Stockton, Modesto, Merced or Fresno reveals numerous foreclosed homes and empty storefronts. Tract homes, built during the housing boom on farmland recently abandoned in the face of global agricultural competition and drought, remain vacant.[3] In the top five on the *Forbes* list of "America's most miserable cities" for three years in a row, Stockton has among the worst unemployment, home foreclosure, and violent crime rates in the United States. Of course these patterns are not unique to California's Central Valley. From Oakland to Cleveland to the South Bronx to Detroit, the effects of the current economic downturn are felt most deeply in places suffering from globalization of regional industry and subsequent abandonment. With unemployment rates lingering around 14 percent (not to mention an increasing reliance on part-time and below-living-wage jobs and the undercount of undocumented and recent immigrants), budget cuts to public schools and social services, and aging, uninhabitable or inaccessible housing stock, residents in places like Stockton and the South Bronx live in a state of insecurity.[4] They are also working multiple jobs, taking care of elders and children, maintaining social networks and support systems, and building community.

Even as the financial crisis and subsequent economic recession (or depression) has had grave effects on poor regions, it has also opened new doors. With the housing and stock market crash in 2008 came the recognition that markets fail—that the invisible hand of free market capitalism is not always so steady or so free. For the first time since its hegemonic rise in the 1980s, neoliberal ideology based on the blind promotion of market deregulation, privatization, downsizing of the state, and the role of the private sector in correcting all that ails society was popularly challenged. The cracks in the system opened up spaces for a new cadre of public intellectuals who question the role of unchecked corporate capitalism and a political system that protects the elite at the expense of the rest.[5] Books, blogs, essays, and films on this topic have found new and growing audiences. Bernie Sanders, a self-described "democratic socialist," is a viable candidate for the Democratic Party's nomination for President in the 2016 elections.

When poverty is revealed as the result of structural abandonment, the contradictions of a hegemonic system are exposed. In our current moment, the forces both to preserve and to challenge the dominant "self-help" framework for alleviating poverty are negotiated along what Antonio Gramsci calls the "terrain of the conjunctural."[6] New "entrepreneurial" programs that ask the poor to work harder to compete in fully privatized school districts, for example (in Wisconsin, Philadelphia, and Washington, DC), represent the forces to preserve the legitimacy of the free market. Alternative forms of self-help have also taken root. Occupy Wall Street called attention to the relationship between the "1%" and the "99%," attracting long-time activists and disaffected youth to collectively camp, cook, clean, dialogue, and protest toward a new society. Many have moved on from Zuccotti Park to start or join anti–police brutality, tenants' rights, and creative arts campaigns across the country. The #fightfor15 minimum-wage campaign and the #BlackLivesMatter movement against police brutality and mass incarceration have recently gained momentum, inspiring growing numbers of people to challenge structural inequities within our social, political, and economic systems.

With sentiments similar to the Occupy movement, Grace Lee Boggs, the 100-year-old renowned social movement leader and scholar, proposes that Detroit is setting the stage for "the next American Revolution." She believes that in the face of unfathomable urban abandonment and abuses at the hands of major social institutions like the prison–industrial complex, there is a limit to oppositional protest and demands-based or reformist politics. She instead calls for cultural renewal. Boggs and a growing network of do-it-yourself "solutionaries" spend less time fighting against systems that have proven to fail poor people and more attempting to redesign the very notions of work, jobs, education, and safety in ways that are individually satisfying and collectively beneficial. They are doing this through person-to-person helping relationships, neighborhood-run gardens, community policing, and cooperative schools. Interestingly, this approach is not all that different from the earliest motivations of Cesar Chavez. Like Boggs, Chavez's initial vision was to bring education, pride, meaning, systems of mutual support, and just rewards to a people whose potential was limited by their back-breaking work and a culture that does not recognize them as full human beings. In the beginning and toward his embattled end, Chavez remained more interested in creating alternative cooperative institutions run by and for farmworkers, and in making agricultural work a dignified, respected, and sustainable profession, than in union organizing. Others, such as the Arizona-based Puente Human Rights Movement, believe that both a closed-fist approach (protest and demands) and an open-fist approach (creating new alternatives) are necessary to protect the human rights of and build positive futures for immigrants today. In places like Detroit and Arizona, grass-roots social movements are reclaiming the human dignity, mutual aid, and self-determination aspects of the self-help approach to empower poor and marginalized communities that philanthropic efforts have often denied.

NEGOTIATING THE POLITICS OF PHILANTHROPY AND THE SELF-HELP MYTH

Findings from my research on philanthropic investments in addressing migrant poverty in California's Central Valley reveal how privately funded self-help partnerships evade addressing the very problems they claim to solve. I found that the partnerships between foundations, social movements, and advocacy organizations featured in the three case studies are ultimately untenable. Instead of building long-term strategies to address regional poverty, they busied local leaders, staff, and constituents with programs prohibited from taking on the production of wealth that both regional poverty and private foundations are created upon. My research uncovered how leaders and professional staff seeking private funding during the social movements of the 1960s, the civic-participation initiatives of the 1990s, and the entrepreneurial "double bottom line" development projects of today have had to promote programs that ask the poor to help themselves while evading the root causes of poverty and inequality. I discovered that over time, while foundation investments have not alone altered the terrain of farmworker organizing, they have promoted theoretical frameworks, institutional arrangements, and professionalized practices that constrain the work of organizers around notions of developing and integrating migrant leadership—but not to strike, organize, or challenge any aspect of agricultural production, and not to create alternatives to the predominant system.

I also found that these projects are not always the result of top-down, imperialist, neoliberal agendas. They are more commonly the failed negotiations of sympathetic foundation and nonprofit staff whose hands are tied (and busied) by the institutions in which they work. The three cases documented the various ways in which foundation initiatives and philanthropic professionals are required to disguise, hide or shift priorities away from the root causes of poverty. The often heated correspondence between Field Foundation program officer Leslie Dunbar and Cesar Chavez, featured in chapter 2, showed that foundation staff see themselves as important actors in social movements. That so many funders could express deep appreciation for a farmworker movement based on workers' rights and dignity, yet withhold all funding to organizing, boycotts, strikes, and union legal cases, evinces a deeper dilemma of organizing through private wealth.

My archival research on the farmworker movement taught me a profound lesson about the tightropes and land mines that both foundation staff and movement leaders must negotiate as they battle to obtain desperately needed resources while not letting the interests and perceptions of people and institutions of wealth alter the nature of the struggle. Ultimately, creating new non-profit organizations to separate economic from social justice (the union from the movement) was a successful and even innovative strategy in the eyes of both the donors and Chavez. Yet, this strategy ultimately failed the movement. These divides are alive and real today. Funders who attempt to reform the public schools, improve juvenile justice systems, or address food insecurity, joblessness, and poor health outcomes of the American and global poor often evade structural analysis of industrial abandonment, widening inequality, and historically unequal opportunity structures along the lines of race, class and immigration status.

Program officer John Sibley of the Kinney Foundation had an even harder translating job than the staff of the Field Foundation during the farmworker movement years. In an era of philanthropic retrenchment away from funding organizing and immigrants, not to mention workers, Sibley tried to sell a benign civic participation "theory of change" to secure funding for the Immigrant Participation Collaborative (IPC). The constant brokering between the organizations he believed in and the board that he needed to appease took a heavy emotional toll. Before he was let go from the foundation, Sibley won a high-profile national foundation award for his work with the IPC. He felt as if the recognition represented a token of the outward recognition foundations often seek for engaging marginalized communities, while sealing the deal of his firing from his own foundation. Sibley's analysis mirrors foundations' role in maintaining cultural hegemony by appearing to address pressing issues while disabling those prepared to take them on.

Felipe Cordero of the Western Foundation defined his work as an improvement on Sibley's IPC. Like Sibley, he authentically believed in reigniting the farmworker movement. However, his vision for a complicated, multi-layered project proved even more problematic. Initially defining his success by the complexity of the model, Cordero made the mistake of neglecting the existing relationships, talents, strategies, and wisdom of the funded partners. Without collaboration or buy-in there was no progress; for all the process, there was no action. Cordero also believed that he could produce a viable win-win between the poorest people in the United States and some of the wealthiest farmers in the world. Overwhelmed by the challenges, Cordero realized that the consensus-building approach he so enthusiastically promoted was not easily achieved or, according to some, even desirable. Like the Kinney Foundation with the IPC, the Western Foundation decided to drop the project. Cordero was also let go from the foundation. His is another case of the casualties involved in the politics of funding long-term poverty alleviation work through private institutions that demand apolitical, non-confrontational, short-term, measurable outcomes.

In the three cases featured in this book, working within the lines of what is acceptable to their foundations, the program officer was revealed as a consummate mythmaker. During the social movement times, they theorized how developing farmworker leadership and concretizing the self-help infrastructure development approach would improve conditions in agricultural communities. But they would not recognize strikes, boycotts, or union organizing. In the post-9/11 anti-immigrant moment, foundation professionals interested in funding immigrant and farmworker organizing highlighted the responsible, hard-working and civically engaged immigrant. But that civic engagement could not include organizing in the emerging immigrant rights mobilizations or efforts to address enduring abuses of farm labor. Through the process of developing fundable self-help theories of change, the program officers simultaneously guaranteed foundation grants to advocacy and organizing groups and limited what they could achieve while funded.

Professional "capacity building" made grass-roots immigrant organizations fundable while simultaneously limiting their ability to organize. As phrased by Antonio Gramsci, training and development can either serve to position "working class people [to] become intellectually autonomous so that they could lead their own movements without having to delegate decision making to career intellectuals," or they can resemble "technical schools that become incubators of little monsters aridly trained for a job, with no general ideas, no general culture, no intellectual stimulation."[7] The foundation program officer's dilemma of determining how to introduce acceptable program frameworks and professional management requirements while retaining the interests, strategies, and wisdom of local organizers and residents reveals the internal ethics of the nonprofit professional. For the most part, time-consuming and short-term grant reporting, evaluation, and partnership program requirements distracted organizers from building collective understandings of regional issues and forming creative strategies that truly engage, empower, and benefit farmworkers and immigrants.

Some program officers I interviewed could see themselves in this brokering role. They embraced a refashioned American self-help ideology and helped staff learn new professional skills as a way to sneak in social and economic justice organizing. Others lost themselves in the process and quit, or were fired for sticking to a principle. Through my current research on self-described "radical" or "social justice"–oriented program officers, previously or currently working at major New York City–based foundations, I am learning how they negotiate these lines in their grantmaking work. Thus far, the mainstream "self-help" myth seems to remain a staple—that, and "innovation." One program officer told me that even for the most radical community organizing projects, if he calls it "innovation" he has a better chance of getting the grant approved.

Through this research I have also become acutely aware of the professional, personal, and even emotional challenges experienced by foundation professionals who constantly "code-switch" between the struggles and agendas of grass-roots organizers and confrontation-shy boards of trustees. Preliminary interviews in my new research suggest that the toll is greatest for people of color, who become worn down by constantly having to present themselves in non-threatening, apolitical, and rationalistic terms as they try to make their way in predominantly white and wealthy boardrooms.[8] According to one veteran Latina program officer, "If you are perceived as a person of color with a political agenda, you are out. You have to find a way to be neutral in all ways—the way you talk, what you wear, the way you present your ideas.... Ultimately these wealthy board members are fearful of mass insurrection—that you will enable people to come after their money and their children—so they watch you."

Some program officers see their role simply as doing what you have to do to get money to people who need it. Others are more conflicted and ask themselves what global poverty scholar Ananya Roy asks of development practitioners and planners: "Is it possible to disassociate the innocent professional from the political regimes within which they work?"[9] Through the framework of Erving Goffman's *The Presentation of Self in Everyday Life*[10] I am exploring this question by investigating the professional roles, identities, and relationships of power that foundation staff negotiate within their own institutions. Caught in a web of contradictions, these program officers struggle to present the institutional front of benevolent philanthropist, while producing what Goffman describes as a politically compromised "working consensus" between the grass-roots organizations they seek to fund and the wealthy trustees they attempt to win over.

As someone who currently teaches nonprofit management and who helps attract foundation grants to allies I still work with in the Central Valley, I am personally complicit in these contradictions and conundrums. When we convince foundations that the struggles of farmworkers and immigrants can be addressed through their participation in a new program, we are implicitly claiming that the funds could not be better spent on directly supporting people already working hard to build a future for themselves and their families amid great adversity. In asking for leadership development resources we imply that indigenous leadership does not exist, or if it does, it is not acceptable, or effective. When we agree to participate in foundation-led collaboratives, we work over and around existing networks and alliances. While these claims are not intentional or always accurate, they risk replicating the troubling patterns of philanthropic intervention featured in this book.

As a result of at least four decades of working through the privately funded nonprofit model, many farmworker and immigrant organizers and advocates I spoke with ultimately expressed feeling "stuck" and hopeless that any funded project can address the poverty and marginalization maintained through industrial agriculture. They would like to think that the next "big initiative" will bring new opportunities to help the people they see suffering on a daily basis, but they do not expect it. They are frustrated with having to work within "the game" of speaking to foundation program guidelines and with mounting administrative management requirements. Very few spoke of doing this work without foundation funding. With institutional structures to maintain, constituents to serve, and salaries to pay, this is simply the way that organizing is done, however ineffectively. In the context of the financial crisis, and now drought, they also see no way to change the largely unmonitored agricultural system that both growers and migrants have come to rely on.

Even as I found my research deeply sobering, I still have hope. My hope comes from my enduring belief in the radical variations of self-help that inspired my own work as a popular educator and organizer, described in the preface of this book, and new movements taking shape today. Tempered by a cautious concern that uplifting individual efforts might conceal or mystify the need for a more aggressive collective politics, I am also inspired by the radical self-determination of local people I have worked alongside and that I met through my research in the Central Valley. Most of them do not work for nonprofit organizations or foundations. They are mothers, soccer coaches, long-time farmworkers, direct service providers, and caregivers. Like Grace Lee Boggs's revival in Detroit, they are youth, parents, neighbors, and local leaders dedicating their lives to changing conditions and building support systems for those struggling with financial insecurity.

I found hope, and yet also concern, for people in the rural agricultural communities across the Central Valley who are helping one another, taking care of children, and organizing people on a daily basis, with few resources and often threatened legal status. I am inspired by a woman I met in the town of Woodlake who told me that she keeps serving migrants at a local clinic because every time an old man or woman comes through the door, she thinks of her *campesino* father, who, despite the chronic health problems of a fruit picker, worked the fields to a ripe age in order to pay her way through college. I am inspired by Rosa, who, while taking care of my newborn daughter while I conducted interviews and attended meetings, was also organizing youth gatherings, cultural events, and protests against the raids in her indigenous Mixteco community in Madera. I am inspired by Pablo Espinoza, who told me his story of coming to the valley as a teenage migrant worker and being recruited to organize the protest against the tin-roof housing that ignited the movement in 1964. His pleas for farmworker organizations to move away from their desks and paperwork, back to the fields and Laundromats, to build a new organizing base, feel alive and possible every time I hear him speak.

Without listening to the people who still have passion, dreams, and hope, and who are not consumed with grant-reporting obligations and the next funding trend, we will not know what is possible. Although they often work outside formal advocacy roles, these people are not without leadership skills, networks, organizations, and community-development practices. On the contrary, they have inherited and continue to build on deep traditions of "self-help" and "mutual aid." Of course, sometimes grass-roots leaders and volunteers are successfully recruited by formal institutions and find the transition to becoming a professional advocate difficult. Others work multiple low-wage jobs. And yet others find their way into the private sector, supporting their volunteer work through insurance, money transfers, cellular phones, and credit schemes directed at migrants.

Yet the individual community volunteer is no panacea. While the rigidity or dependency of the nonprofit institutional model often stifles or redirects new organizing, without strong organizations individuals can only get so far. Industrial agribusiness has its own lobbying institutions, deep connections to state and federal policymakers, and in some instances generous publicly subsidized programs. It is naive to propose that a much weaker party, migrant farmworkers, or other poor communities might be better off without similarly powerful institutions. Instead, I propose that it is time for long-standing social movement organizations to re-evaluate whom they are truly representing, what kinds of ideas might ignite popular support, and what kind of work they need to be doing to better connect with and serve their constituents. I also believe that it is time for new organizing and grass-roots community development institutions to be built (and there are a few, as described below), and for federal and international development agencies who care about eradicating poverty to take a look at unlikely places like the Central Valley—the interior of a state often thought of as the land of opportunity yet where so many suffer without recognition.

FARMWORKER ORGANIZING AND THE
NEW FOOD JUSTICE MOVEMENTS

One example of an organization that is creatively taking on farmworker poverty and the abuses of the agricultural industry is the Coalition of Immokalee Workers (CIW) in Florida.[11] In contrast to the UFW approach, the CIW considers its work "anti-slavery" and "fair food" organizing. Without the history of an ethnically driven La Causa, industrial unionization, or collaboration with growers, the CIW is a grass-roots community-based organization composed of mainly Latino, Mayan, and Haitian field workers. It also includes low-wage workers from other sectors across the state of Florida. Like the farmworker movement, the CIW has a goal of fighting for fair wages, stronger labor protections, and better housing and community infrastructure. However, the CIW strategically articulates much of its work in the global context of indentured servitude. Their approach to addressing the common withholding of pay, sexual abuse, harassment, poor conditions, and literal slavery that still exist in agriculture is also framed in the now-popular consumer context of "fair food" and "food justice."

Farmworker organizers in the Central Valley, through the desperation of the agricultural economy and partnerships with growers around immigration reform, have painted a picture of corporate agriculture reliant on low-wage immigrant labor as an inevitable reality. In contrast, the organizing campaigns of the Coalition of Immokalee Workers disrupt the totalizing and commonly accepted picture of industrial agriculture through images of enslavement and abuse. Like Teatro Campesino at the height of the farmworker movement, the CIW engages new images and theatrical representations through multimedia campaigns and public demonstration. By using social media, targeting specific audiences, and exposing old problems in new and relevant ways, the CIW has successfully won legal cases against food outlets such as McDonald's and Chipotle that buy tomatoes from growers that abuse workers. The CIW has also re-articulated its organizing with the growing Slow Food and Food Justice movements, taking environmentally conscious advocates to task to "dine with dignity" and include the rights and well-being of workers in their messaging.

In stark contrast to the farmworker organizers I interviewed in California, the CIW claims that in "Immokalee today ... nothing is impossible." Under the motto of "Consciousness + Commitment = Change," the CIW's Campaign for Fair Food and anti-slavery organizing has transformed one of the poorest, most politically powerless communities in the country into "a new and important public presence with forceful, committed leadership directly from the base of our community—young, immigrant workers forging a future of livable wages and modern labor relations in Florida's fields." In recognition of their work, "three CIW members were presented the prestigious 2003 Robert F. Kennedy Human Rights Award, the first time the award had gone to a U.S.-based organization in its 20 years of existence."[12] Strategically articulating their work in the context of global social movements, the CIW has changed the agenda for farmworker organizing, using images and ideas that disrupt the picture of "nothing is possible" and give hope to new generations of migrant activists. Their vigils, protests, and localized community-building represent a new politics—disrupting a hegemonic fast food industry that separates the consumption of food from the people and earth from which it is produced. Places like Immokalee give hope that a new movement will disrupt the story told in this book.

Aligning farmworker rights, health, and safety with the increasingly popular food movements is a particularly hopeful strategy. From Michael Pollan's widely popular *Omnivore's Dilemma* and *In Defense of Food*[13] to Alice Waters's edible school-yard, to farmers' markets and restaurants that serve locally grown organic foods, to urban gardens and produce distribution programs that aim to address unequal access and food insecurity, new food movements have captured the public imagination. Yet linking industrial agricultural worker rights and conditions with the food movement has not been and will not be easy. In the 1970s, when Cesar Chavez launched "organic produce" campaigns focusing on anti-pesticide organizing, the UFW was swamped with a record number of calls from the general public. However, according to a long-time farmworker organizer,[14] a large majority of the callers were interested in where they could buy organic produce and not how they could participate in anti-pesticide organizing. Food advocates are often more concerned with the culture of eating, building personal responsibility, and attacking common American-diet-related diseases such as diabetes through the American dinner table, small-scale farming, urban gardening, and selling and buying local.[15] These are all critically important causes, but they are less interested in the conditions of workers in the large-scale, export-based farms—by far the most common form of agriculture in California, and where the overwhelming majority of farmworkers labor.

Even when philanthropic attention has been paid to large-scale farms, focus on worker conditions has been insignificant. For example, the director of Roots of Change, a foundation-initiated partnership to create a sustainable food system in California, told me that they were close to reaching their sustainability goals (which at least on paper concern addressing worker health, safety, and rights) with growers in the Napa County grape industry.[16] This was the same year that journalist David Bacon was promoting his new photo series picturing Oaxacan workers sleeping in the drainage ditches that surround those very Napa Valley vineyards.[17] Again, and as Julie Guthman has shown in her study of "agro-food philanthropy," outward philanthropic claims to address the issues can convince the public that broad-scale change has occurred while masking what is going on in the fields.[18] Like during the farmworker movement of the 1960s, aligning labor rights with a broader mainstream food movement will not come easily. It will have to be fought for.

When I attended the Council on Foundations meeting in 2013, I was pleasantly surprised to hear the Kellogg Foundation support a more radical food justice movement. President Sterling Speirn even described food justice as "working to dismantle racism and deep inequalities in the food system." For Kellogg, he explained, "fair food treats food production workers right, is healthy, is available to all and is affordable." I was impressed to learn that under Speirn's leadership Kellogg made significant grants to the Coalition of Immokalee Workers. I also discovered that the projects funded by Kellogg, including those presented at the conference and grants reported in online annual reports, mainly focus on poor and marginalized communities helping one another plant gardens, educate youth, and improve access to healthy produce. Again, these are all very important issues. But in keeping with the tradition of mainstream self-help, they do not hold the food industry accountable for poor treatment of workers or for unhealthful food production practices. After I had returned from the conference and shared with colleagues how impressed with Speirn I had become, I was informed that he was stepping down as president of the Kellogg Foundation. I have no doubt that he chose to retire.

But I do wonder whether he was emboldened to speak of taking on the food industry in anticipation of his departure.

Many others are taking food justice seriously in the United States.[19] Risa Lavizzo-Mourney, president of the Robert Wood Johnson Foundation, pronounced that "food is the civil rights issue of the 21st Century."[20] Groups like the Coalition of Immokalee Workers, Familias Unidos por la Justicia (in Washington State), and even mayors' offices across the country are embracing a more structural analysis of inequality within regional food systems. I left the 2013 Council on Foundations conference inspired by Paula Daniels of the Los Angeles Food Policy Council. Daniels urged the funders in the room to recognize that "we have an industrialized food system that does not work for all of us." She reminded the group that small farmers struggle, the environment and our health suffer, food insecurity abounds, and "in places like the Central Valley, you have the most productive agricultural regions and the most food deserts." The new food justice movement may represent a rupture from the efforts of the past fifty years that failed to make changes that are meaningful for those who plant, harvest, package, and sell our food.

Alternatively, if the concerns of middle-class consumers and well-funded programs that ask poor people to improve their own lives by buying, planting, and cooking healthy food overshadow the financial, physical, and environmental abuses and corresponding loss of human dignity experienced in agricultural labor that Cesar Chavez proposed to transform through radical farmworker self-help, we have a long way to go. For Chavez, and also for other poor people's movements, human dignity and self-determination are ultimately at stake. For someone often not accorded respect, in treatment, in pay, in rights and opportunities, it becomes very difficult to respect oneself. Without self-respect, Chavez proposed, it is hard to demand it. And herein lies the distinction between the philanthropic and the radical approach to addressing poverty and inequality through self-help. The one tells people how to help themselves in order to change their purportedly bad behaviors, neutralize conflict, and maintain systems of power. The other calls for people to analyze their own relationship to power in order to transform it. Most often we are caught somewhere in between.

NOTES

CHAPTER I

1. The Council on Foundations (www.cof.org) is a connecting hub for philanthropy professionals in the United States. Their annual conference provides an opportunity for foundations to showcase their work, and for professionals working in philanthropy to learn from one another.

2. For foundational "culture of poverty" studies, see Michael Harrington, *The Other America: Poverty in the United States* (New York: McMillan, 1964); Oscar Lewis, *Five Families: Mexican Case Studies in the Culture of Poverty* (New York: Basic Books, 1959, 1975).

3. For a study of self-help poverty programming in the United States, see Barbara Cruickshank, *The Will to Empower: Democratic Citizens and Other Subjects* (Ithaca, NY: Cornell University Press, 1999). For an international perspective, see Lamia Karim, "Demystifying Micro-Credit: The Grameen Bank, NGOs, and Neoliberalism in Bangladesh," *Cultural Dynamics* 20, no. 1 (2008); Tanya Murray Li, *The Will to Improve: Governmentality, Development, and the Practice of Politics* (Durham, NC: Duke University Press, 2007.)

4. Robert Reich, *Supercapitalism: The Transformation of Business, Democracy, and Everyday Life* (New York: Vintage Books/Random

House, 2007); Robert Reich, "Why the Rich are Getting Richer, and the Poor, Poorer," in *The Way Class Works: Readings on School, Family, and the Economy,* ed. Lois Weis (New York: Routledge, 2007).

5. For a comprehensive historical study of the transformations towards individualistic and behavioral approaches to addressing poverty policy and research in United States, see Alice O'Connor, *Poverty Knowledge: Social Science, Social Policy, and the Poor in Twentieth-Century U.S. History* (Princeton, NJ: Princeton University Press, 2002).

6. For studies on patterns of professionalization in the nonprofit sector, see (1) *Antipode* 37, no. 3 (2005) and the many useful articles in this issue with the theme Working the Spaces of Neoliberalism: Activism, Professionalization and Incorporation; (2) Aziz Choudry and Dip Kapoor, eds., *NGO-ization: Complicity, Contradictions and Prospects* (London: Zed Books, 2013); (3) INCITE! Women of Color Against Violence, ed., *The Revolution Will Not Be Funded: Beyond the Non-Profit Industrial Complex* (Cambridge, MA: South End Press, 2007), particularly the chapters by Gilmore and Rodriguez; and (4) Nidhi Srinivas, "The Possibilities of the Past: Two Routes to a Past and What They Tell Us," *Management and Organizational History* 7, no. 3, 237–249 (2012).

7. For a recent analysis of how unregulated capitalist economies create vast inequality, see the widely read book by Thomas Piketty, *Capital in the Twenty-First Century* (New York: Harvard University Press, 2014).

8. For a summary of statistics on the growth of the nonprofit sector in the first decade of the twenty-first century, see Peter Kim and Jeffrey Bradach, "Why More Nonprofits Are Getting Bigger," *Stanford Social Innovation Review* (Spring 2012), www.ssireview.org/articles /entry/why_more_nonprofits_are_getting_bigger; Lester M. Salamon, ed., *The State of Nonprofit America,* 2nd ed. (Washington, DC: Brookings Institution Press, 2012). Whereas a majority of philanthropic wealth is invested in large health care and educational institutions, many grass-roots organizations concerned with poverty and inequality increasingly rely on foundation grants. Many local and regional programs aimed at addressing poverty have come to rely on resources from private foundations even though the foundations do not have a particularly strong focus on funding poverty initiatives. For data on

foundation giving and poverty, see the 2007 Foundation Center report, *Focus on Poverty* (http://foundationcenter.org/focus/gpf/poverty/).

9. Alan Berube, *The Enduring Challenge of Concentrated Poverty across America: Case Studies from across the U.S.* (Washington, DC: Brookings Institution, 2008).

10. For news reports based on the 2012 US Census, see www .huffingtonpost.com/2012/09/20/california-poverty_n_1901642.html and www.mercurynews.com/ci_21596949/central-valley-areas-among-poorest.

11. For current research on conditions for farmworkers and immigrants in California's Central Valley, see the reports produced by the California Institute for Rural Studies (www.cirsinc.org). For a study on poverty and sexual abuse of migrant farmworkers, see the 2013 Frontline documentary, *Rape in the Fields* (www.pbs.org/wgbh/pages /frontline/rape-in-the-fields/).

12. For information about indigenous fieldworkers, see Seth Holmes, *Fresh Fruit, Broken Bodies: Migrant Farmworkers in the United States* (Berkeley: University of California Press, 2013).

13. For discussion on strategic articulation and cultural hegemony, see Stuart Hall, "Race, Articulation and Societies Structured in Dominance," in *Sociological Theories: Race and Colonialism* (Paris: UNESCO, 1980; reproduction, Oxford: Blackwell, 2001), 305–45. For a more recent usage of Hall's theory of articulation, see Tania Li, "Articulating Indigenous Identity in Indonesia: Resource Politics and the Tribal Slot," *Comparative Studies in Society and History*, 42 (2000): 149–79. Also see chapter 6 of Raymond Williams' seminal work on cultural hegemony, *Marxism and Literature* (Oxford: Oxford University Press, 1977).

14. Matt Garcia, *From the Jaws of Victory: The Triumph and Tragedy of Cesar Chavez and the Farm Worker Movement* (Berkeley: University of California Press, 2012); Malcolm X and Alex Haley, *The Autobiography of Malcolm X* (New York: Ballantine Books, 1992).

15. For a discussion of the historical tensions between the "racial uplift" and "Black power" traditions of African American self-help, see Kevin K. Gaines, *Uplifting the Race: Black Leadership, Politics, and Culture in the Twentieth Century* (Chapel Hill: University of North Carolina Press, 1996). For a detailed historical account of radical variants of

Black freedom struggles of the South, see Akinyele Omowale Umoja, *We Will Shoot Back: Armed Resistance in the Mississippi Freedom Movement* (New York: New York University Press, 2013).

16. Louise Knight, *Citizen: Jane Addams and the Struggle for Democracy* (Chicago, IL: Chicago University Press, 2005); O'Connor, *Poverty Knowledge.*

17. Barbara Cruikshank, *The Will to Empower: Democratic Citizens and Other Subjects* (Ithaca, NY: Cornell University Press, 1999); Alyosha Goldstein, *Poverty in Common* (Durham, NC: Duke University Press, 2012); Michael Katz, *The Undeserving Poor: From the War on Poverty to the War on Welfare* (New York: Pantheon, 1990).

18. C.K. Prahaland, *The Fortune at the Bottom of the Pyramid* (Upper Saddle River, NJ: Wharton School Publishing, 2005).

19. Kathryn Moeller, "Proving 'The Girl Effect': Corporate Knowledge Production and Educational Intervention," *International Journal of International Development* 33, no. 6, 539–622 (2013).

20. Frances Fox Piven and Richard Cloward, *Poor People's Movements: Why They Succeed, How They Fail* (New York: Vintage Books, 1978).

21. Carmel Borg, Joseph Buttigieg, and Peter Mayo, eds., *Gramsci and Education* (Oxford: Rowman & Littlefield, 2002), 147–78.

22. For examples of social movements incubating through popular education and collective organizing processes, see Aldon Morris, *The Origins of the Civil Rights Movement* (New York: Free Press, 1986), 40–174; Myles Horton, Judith Kohl, and Herbert Kohl, *The Long Haul* (New York: Teachers College Press, 1997).

23. Robert Arnove, ed., *Philanthropy and Cultural Imperialism* (Boston: G.K. Hall, 1980); Edward H. Berman, *The Ideology of Philanthropy: The influence of the Carnegie, Ford, and Rockefeller Foundations on American Foreign Policy* (Albany: State University of New York Press, 1983); Inderjeet Parmar, *Foundations and the American Century: The Ford, Carnegie, and Rockefeller Foundations in the Rise of American Power* (New York: Columbia University Press, 2012); Joan Roelofs, *Foundations and Public Policy: The Mask of Pluralism* (Albany: State University of New York Press, 2003).

24. See Arnove, *Philanthropy and Cultural Imperialism*; Berman, *The Ideology of Philanthropy*; Parmar, *Foundations and the American Century*;

Roelofs, *Foundations and Public Policy*; Behrooz Morvaridi, "Capitalist Philanthropy and Hegemonic Partnerships," *Third World Quarterly* 33 (2012): 1191–1210.

25. For a full discussion on the use of Antonio Gramsci's term "cultural hegemony" as it relates to private philanthropy, see Roelofs, *Foundations and Public Policy*; Arnove, *Philanthropy and Cultural Imperialism*.

26. Morvaridi, "Capitalist Philanthropy."

27. La Via Campesina, "La Via Campesina Denounces Gates Foundation Purchase of Monsanto Company Shares," September 13, 2010, http://viacampesina.org/en/index.php/actions-and-events-mainmenu-26/stop-transnational-corporations-mainmenu-76/917-la-via-campesina-denounces-gates-foundation-purchase-of-monsanto-company-shares.

28. Joanna Barkan, "Got Dough?" *Dissent* 58, no. 1 (2011): 49–57; Joanne Barkan, "Hired Guns on Astroturf: How to Buy and Sell School Reform," *Dissent* 59, no. 2 (2012): 49–57; Stanley N. Katz, "Assessment and General Education," *Liberal Education* 94, no. 3 (2008): 30–37; Stanley N. Katz, "Reshaping US Public Education Policy," *Stanford Social Innovation Review* (Spring 2013), www.ssireview.org/articles/entry/reshaping_u.s._public_education_policy; Sarah Reckhow, *Follow the Money: How Foundation Dollars Change Public School Politics* (New York: Oxford University Press, 2012); K. Saltman, *The Gift of Education: Public Education and Venture Philanthropy* (New York: Palgrave Macmillan, 2010); Janelle Scott, "The Politics of Venture Philanthropy in Charter School Policy and Advocacy," *Educational Policy* 23, no. 1, 106–36 (2009).

29. Vincanne Adams, *Markets of Sorrow, Labors of Faith: New Orleans in the Wake of Katrina* (Durham, NC: Duke University Press, 2013); John Arena, *Driven from New Orleans: How Nonprofits Betray Public Housing and Promote Privatization* (Minneapolis: University of Minnesota Press, 2012); Naomi Klein, *The Shock Doctrine: The Rise of Disaster Capitalism* (London: Picador, 2008).

30. Peter Buffet, "The Charitable-Industrial Complex," *New York Times*, July 26, 2013. More moderate analysis comes from scholars and practitioners who note the diversity within the philanthropic sector and point toward the work of "progressive" or "radical" philanthropies, usually with significantly smaller endowments, and the trend in organizing foundations around "social justice" strategies. To research

some of this work, see the National Committee on Responsive Philanthropy (www.ncrp.org), and Daniel R. Faber and Deborah McCarthy, eds., *Foundations for Social Change: Critical Perspectives on Philanthropy and Popular Movements* (Lanham, MD: Rowman & Littlefield, 2005).

31. Individual and organizational names for the case studies featured in chapters 3 and 4 are disguised in keeping with the Human Subjects Protocol of the University of California, Berkeley, Institutional Review Board.

32. Frank Bardacke, *Trampling Out the Vintage: Cesar Chavez and the Two Souls of the United Farm Workers* (New York: Verso, 2011); Garcia, *Jaws of Victory*; Miriam Pawel, *The Union of Their Dreams: Power, Hope, and Struggle in Cesar Chavez's Farm Worker Movement* (New York: Bloomsbury, 2009).

33. Marshall Ganz, *Five Smooth Stones: Strategic Capacity in the Unionization of California Agriculture*, PhD dissertation, Harvard University, 2008; Pawel, *Union of Their Dreams*.

34. David Villarino, interview with the author, October 2007.

35. Ernesto Laclau, *Politics and Ideology in Marxist Theory: Capitalism, Fascism, Populism* (London: NLB, 1977), 161.

36. Susan Brin Hyatt, "From Citizen to Volunteer: Neoliberal Governance and the Erasure of Poverty," in *The New Poverty Studies: The Ethnography of Power, Politics and Impoverished People in the United States*, ed. Judith G. Goode and Jeff Maskovsky (New York: NYU Press, 2001), 201–35; Cruikshank, *The Will to Empower*.

37. Cruikshank, *The Will to Empower*; Goldstein, *Poverty in Common*; Katz, *Undeserving Poor*; O'Connor, *Poverty Knowledge*.

38. Drawing on Michel Foucault's theory of "governmentality," Barbara Cruickshank (*The Will to Empower*) describes this turn in self-help poverty action as introducing new "technologies of citizenship" that represent relations of power as expressed through a converging set of ideas, institutional structures, and routinized programs that ensure that people govern themselves through local improvement schemes and civic projects as opposed to challenging, claiming, or relying on state structures of governance. Others, such as Susan Brin Hyatt ("From Citizen to Volunteer"), document how neoliberal governance governs the poor through their own volunteerism.

39. In 1913, the Sixteenth Amendment to the US Constitution initiated income tax. In the amendment, the US Department of the Treasury created a tax code that exempted philanthropies, which led to the development of philanthropy and the proliferation of foundations in particular. Since 1913, changes and clarifications have been made to the tax code, such as the Tax Reform Act of 1969, which established rules for private foundations including a minimum payout requirement and a 4 percent excise tax on net investment income. For further details on the development of tax codes relating to foundations, see Oliver Zunz, *Philanthropy in America: A History* (Princeton, NJ: Princeton University Press, 2012).

40. Andrew Carnegie, *The Gospel of Wealth* (New York: Century Press, 1900), 5.

41. Carnegie, *The Gospel of Wealth*, 22–23.

42. Knight, *Citizen*.

43. For scholarship on philanthropy in the early twentieth century, see the collection of articles in Ellen Condliffe Lagemann, *Philanthropic Foundations: New Scholarship, New Possibilities* (Bloomington: Indiana University Press, 1999).

44. Mary Jo Deegan, *Jane Addams and the Men of the Chicago School, 1892–1918* (Chicago, IL: Transaction Press, 1988).

45. Jane Addams, *Philanthropy and Social Progress* (Freeport, NY: Books for Libraries Press, 1893).

46. O'Connor, *Poverty Knowledge*, 48; Jamin Creed Rowan, "Sidewalk Narratives, Tenement Narratives: Seeing Urban Renewal through the Settlement Movement," *Journal of Urban History* 39 (2013): 392–410.

47. A recent study shows how the narratives, marches, parades, and protests of settlement workers and residents were adopted and translated by philanthropic actors to make the case for slum clearance and urban renewal (Rowan, "Settlement Narratives").

48. The history of developments in the social science of poverty is outlined, with much greater detail than permitted in this brief introduction, in O'Connor's *Poverty Knowledge*.

49. Richard Cloward and Lloyd Ohlin, *Delinquency and Opportunity: A Theory of Delinquent Gangs* (New York: Free Press, 1966).

50. Arnove, *Philanthropy and Cultural Imperialism*; G. William Domhoff, "The Ford Foundation in the Inner City: Forging an Alliance with Neighborhood Activists," *Who Rules America?* (blog), September 2005 (http://www2.ucsc.edu/whorulesamerica/local/ford_foundation .html); Parmar, *Foundations and the American Century*; Roelofs, *Foundations and Public Policy*.

51. The history of poverty programs during this era is described with much greater detail in Peter Marris and Martin Rein, *Dilemmas of Social Reform: Poverty and Community Action in the United States* (Chicago, IL: Aldine, 1973); and in Katz, *Undeserving Poor*.

52. Goldstein, *Poverty in Common*; Marris and Rein, *Dilemmas of Social Reform*; John H. Mollenkopf, *The Contested City* (Princeton, NJ: Princeton University Press, 1983); Alice O'Connor, "Swimming against the Tide: A Brief History of Federal Policy in Poor Communities," in *Urban Problems and Community Development*, eds. Ronald F. Ferguson and William T. Dickens (Washington, DC: Brookings Institution, 1999), 77–137; Ananya Roy, Stuart Schrader, and Emma Shaw Crane, "Gray Areas: the War on Poverty at Home and Abroad," in *Territories of Poverty*, ed. Ananya Roy and Emma Shaw Crane (Athens: University of Georgia Press, forthcoming).

53. Domhoff, "The Ford Foundation in the Inner City"; Alice O'Connor, "The Ford Foundation and Philanthropic Activism in the 1960s," in *Philanthropic Foundations: New Scholarship, New Possibilities*, ed. E. Lagemann (Bloomington: Indiana University Press, 1999), 169–94.

54. Paul Ylvisaker, *Oral History* (New York: Ford Foundation Archives, 1973), 20.

55. Roy, Schrader, and Crane, "Gray Areas."

56. For a detailed historical account of the intersections between racial uplift ideology and Black nationalist thought, see Kevin K. Gains, *Uplifting the Race: Black Leadership, Politics, and Culture in the Twentieth Century* (Chapel Hill: University of North Carolina Press, 1996).

57. Roy, Schrader, and Crane, "Gray Areas," 13.

58. Karen Ferguson, *Top Down: The Ford Foundation, Black Power, and the Reinvention of Racial Liberalism* (Philadelphia: University of Pennsylvania Press, 2013).

59. Alan Gilbert and Peter Ward, "Community Action by the Urban Poor: Democratic Involvement, Community Self-Help or a Means of Social Control?" *World Development* 12, no. 8 (1984): 769–82.

60. Nick Cullather, "'Stretching the Surface of the Earth': The Foundations, Neo-Malthusianism and the Modernizing Agenda," *Global Society* 28, no. 1 (2014): 104–12; Nick Cullather, 'The Target is the People': Representations of the Village in Modernization and US National Security Doctrine," *Cultural Politics* 2, no. 1 (2006), 29–48.

61. Gilbert and Ward, "Community Action," 769; Goldstein, *Poverty in Common.*

62. Lewis, *Five Families*; Harrington, *The Other America*; Cloward and Ohlin, *Delinquency and Opportunity.*

63. For a recent historical study on the ways in which the War on Poverty mobilized poor people and energized grass-roots action across the country, see Annelise Orleck and Lisa Gayle Hazirjiam, *The War on Poverty: A New Grassroots History 1964–1980* (Athens: University of Georgia Press, 2011).

64. Goldstein, *Poverty in Common*; Marris and Rein, *Dilemmas of Social Reform*; Katz, *Undeserving Poor*; O'Connor, "Swimming against the Tide."

65. Charles Murray, *Losing Ground: American Social Policy, 1950–1980* (New York: Basic Books, 1984).

66. Ruth Wilson Gilmore, "In the Shadow of the Shadow State," in *The Revolution Will Not Be Funded*, ed. INCITE! Women of Color Against Violence, 41–52; Jennifer R. Wolch, *The Shadow State: Government and Voluntary Sector in Transition* (New York: Foundation Center, 1990).

67. INCITE!, *The Revolution Will Not Be Funded.*

68. Choudry and Kapoor, *NGO-ization.*

69. INCITE!, *The Revolution Will Not Be Funded.*

70. Suzan Ilcan and Lynne Phillips, "Developmentalities and Calculative Practices: The Millennium Development Goals," *Antipode* 42 (2010): 844–74; Karim, "Demystifying Micro-Credit"; Ananya Roy, *Poverty Capital: Microfinance and the Making of Development* (New York: Routledge, 2010).

71. Horace Coon, *Money to Burn* (New Brunswick, NJ: Transaction, 1938); O'Connor, *Poverty Knowledge*; Kevin C. Robbins, "The Nonprofit Sector in Historical Perspective: Traditions of Philanthropy in the West," in *The Non-Profit Sector: A Research Handbook,* 2nd ed., ed. Walter W. Powell and Richard Steinberg (New Haven, CT: Yale University Press, 2006), 13–29.

72. Nancy Fraser and Linda Gordon, "A Genealogy of 'Dependency': Tracing a Keyword of the US Welfare State," *Signs* 19 (1994): 309–36; O'Connor, *Poverty Knowledge.*

73. Picketty, *Capital in the Twenty-First Century.*

74. For example, see the 2013 film *Inequality for All* (http://inequalityforall.com), produced, directed, and popularly marketed by Robert Reich.

75. Joseph Stiglitz, *The Price of Inequality: How Today's Divided Society Endangers Our Future* (New York: W. W. Norton, 2012); Joseph Stiglitz, *Freefall: America, Free Markets, and the Sinking of the World Economy* (New York: W. W. Norton, 2012).

76. Darrick Hamilton and Ngina Chiteji, "Wealth," in *Encyclopedia of Race and Racism*, ed. Patrick Mason, 2nd ed. Detroit: Macmillan Reference USA, 2013.

77. David Graeber, *The Democracy Project: A History, a Crisis, a Movement* (New York: Spiegel and Grau, 2013). Occupy Wall Street organizers continue to self-publish books such as *The Debt Resisters' Operations Manual* through their website (http://occupywallstreet.net).

78. Italian cultural theorist Antonio Gramsci used the term "common sense," a central component of his theory of cultural hegemony, to represent the values and norms propagated by the dominant bourgeois culture that serve as the commonly held values of all—even though they only serve the interests of a few. Successful members of the working class identify their own good with the good of the bourgeoisie, which helps maintain the status quo rather than catalyze revolution. Similar to Pierre Bourdieu's theory of *habitus,* cultural hegemony is wielded through popular "commonsense" ideas, or for Bourdieu *doxa,* which appear self-evident and go without saying as truth—where the social world, even when unjust or disadvantageous, is perceived as natural or as a taken-for-granted unchangeable state.

79. Grace Lee Boggs, *The Next American Revolution: Sustainable Activism for the Twenty-First Century* (Berkeley: University of California Press, 2012).

80. Berube, "Enduring Challenge"; Great Valley Center, *Indicators Report: Economy and Quality of Life, Benchmark Statistical "Indicators" of Great Central Valley's Social, Economic, & Environmental Conditions* (Modesto, CA: Great Valley Center, 1999).

81. California Institute for Rural Studies and California Endowment, "Suffering in Silence: A Report on the Health of California's Agricultural Workers," November 2000 (www.calendow.org/uploadedFiles /suffering_in_silence.pdf); National Center for Farmworker Health, "Facts about Farmworkers," www.ncfh.org/docs/fs-Facts%20about%20 Farmworkers.pdf.

82. The term *forgotten places* is taken from Ted Bradshaw's analysis of uneven development in rural America, "In the Shadow of Urban Growth: Bifurcation in Rural California Communities," in *Forgotten Places: Uneven Development in Rural America,* ed. Thomas A. Lyson and William W. Falk (Lawrence: University Press of Kansas, 1993), 218–56. Ruth Wilson Gilmore describes the Central Valley and the region's geography of prisons in "Forgotten Places and the Seeds of Grassroots Planning," in *Engaging Contradictions: Theory, Politics, and Methods of Activist Scholarship,* ed. Charles Hale (Berkeley: University of California Press, 2008), 32.

83. Phillip Martin, *Promise Unfulfilled: Unions, Immigration, and the Farm Workers* (Ithaca, NY: Cornell University Press, 2003).

84. Richard Marosi, "Hardship on Mexico's Farms, a Bounty for U.S. Tables," *Los Angeles Times,* December 7, 2014.

85. For a history of the material and ideological struggles over the California landscape, including the role of migrant workers, see Don Mitchel, *The Lie of the Land* (Minneapolis: University of Minnesota Press, 1996); Richard Walker, *The Conquest of Bread: 150 Years of Agribusiness in California* (New York: New Press, 2004). For recent histories of the California farmworker movement, see Bardacke, *Trampling Out the Vintage*; Garcia, *Jaws of Victory*; Pawel, *Union of Their Dreams.*

86. Martin, *Promise Unfulfilled.*

87. Judith Butler, *Gender Trouble: Feminism and the Subversion of Identity* (New York: Routledge, 1990).

88. Paolo Freire with Donald Macedo and Henry Giroux, *The Politics of Education: Culture, Power, and Liberation* (New York: Continuum, 1985), page 122.

89. See e.g. Ken Light and Melanie Light, *Valley of Shadows and Dreams* (Berkeley, CA: Heyday Books, 2012); David Bacon, *Communities without Borders: Images and Voices from the World of Migration* (Ithaca, NY: ILR Press, 2006); Deborah Barndt, *Tangled Routes: Women, Work, and Globalization on the Tomato Trail* (Lanham, MD: Rowman and Littlefield, 2008); Ernesto Galarza, *Merchants of Labor: The Mexican Bracero Story* (San Francisco, CA: Rosicrucian Press, 1964); Daniel Rothenberg, *With These Hands: The Hidden World of Migrant Farm Workers Today* (San Diego, CA: Harcourt Brace, 1998); John Steinbeck, *The Harvest Gypsies: On the Road to the Grapes of Wrath* (Berkeley, CA: Heyday Books, 1988); Frances Esquibel Tywoniak and Mario T. Garcia, *Migrant Daughter: Coming of Age as a Mexican American Woman* (Berkeley: University of California Press, 2000).

90. Following the Human Subjects Protocol, individual and organizational names are disguised in this project to protect the identity of those guaranteed anonymity. Reports cited are also disguised to avoid identifying the institutional affiliations of foundation staff and grantees.

91. Arnove, *Philanthropy and Cultural Imperialism*; Coon, *Money to Burn*; Sally Covington, *Moving a Public Policy Agenda: The Strategic Philanthropy of Conservative Foundations* (Washington, DC: National Committee for Responsive Philanthropy, 1997); Mark Dowie, *American Foundations: An Investigative History* (Boston, MA: MIT Press, 2001); INCITE!, *The Revolution Will Not Be Funded*; Craig Jenkins, "Channeling Social Protest: Foundation Patronage of Contemporary Social Movements," Chapter 14 in *Private Action and the Public Good*, ed. Walter W. Powell and Elisabeth S. Clemens (New Haven, CT: Yale University Press, 1998); Roelofs, *Foundations and Public Policy*.

CHAPTER 2

1. Bardacke, Frank. *Trampling Out the Vintage: Cesar Chavez and the Two Souls of the United Farm Workers.* New York: Verso, 2011.

2. Matt Garcia, *From the Jaws of Victory: The Triumph and Tragedy of Cesar Chavez and the Farm Worker Movement* (Berkeley, CA: University of California Press, 2012).

3. Miriam Pawel, *The Crusades of Cesar Chavez: A Biography* (New York: Bloomsbury, 2014). See also Miriam Pawel, *The Union of Their Dreams: Power, Hope, and Struggle in Cesar Chavez's Farm Worker Movement* (New York: Bloomsbury, 2009).

4. An example of similar sentiments about the limits of unionization as a social movement strategy can be found in the ideas of Jimmy Boggs and Grace Lee Boggs. See e.g. Grace Lee Boggs, *The Next American Revolution: Sustainable Activism for the Twenty-First Century* (Berkeley: University of California Press, 2012), 65–66.

5. Meeting minutes of National Farm Worker Service Center, 1969, Field Foundation Archives, Center for American History, University of Texas at Austin, box 2T143, National Farmworkers Service Center folder.

6. Data gathered on Max L. Rosenberg Foundation funding priorities and grants includes: interview with past president Kirke Wilson (April 2009); archived annual reports of the foundation; interviews with past grantees; the United Farm Workers of America archives at the Walter P. Reuther Library at Wayne State University; and the oral history of past president (1947–1976) Ruth Chance in "Bay Area Foundation History, Volume II, Ruth Clouse Chance," at the Regional Oral History Office, Bancroft Library, University of California, Berkeley.

7. "Brief History," Rosenberg Foundation, www.rosenbergfound.org/about/history, accessed May–July 2008.

8. Kirke Wilson, interview with the author, April 2008.

9. Ruth Chance oral history.

10. This story was confirmed in separate author interviews with former Rosenberg Foundation president Kirke Wilson (April 2009), and Isao Fujimoto (March 2007 and April 2008), a Central Valley farmworker organizer and professor emeritus at the University of California, Davis. Mention of Bard McCallister's role in SCICON (mentioned in the next paragraph) can also be found in the Quaker archives, http://visaliaquakers.org/wp-content/uploads/2013/08/BardMemorialMinute.pdf.

11. Pablo Espinoza, interview with the author, September 2008.

12. Rosenberg Foundation, *1965 Annual Report* (San Francisco: Rosenberg Foundation, 1965), www.rosenbergfound.org/sites/default /files/1965.pdf.

13. Carey McWilliams, *Factories in the Field: The Story of Migratory Farm Labor in California* (Berkeley: University of California Press, 2000 reprint [1939]).

14. Rosenberg Foundation, *1965 Annual Report.*

15. Bardacke, *Trampling Out the Vintage,* 68–70; Garcia, *Jaws of Victory,* 24–25. For more information on Saul Alinsky, see P. David Finks, *The Radical Vision of Saul Alinsky* (New York: Paulist Press, 1984).

16. Garcia, *Jaws of Victory,* 29–30.

17. Dolores Huerta, interview with the author, October 2007.

18. Don Villarejo, interview with the author, November 2007.

19. Interview with Jim Drake in Bardacke's *Trampling Out the Vintage,* 110.

20. Bardacke, *Trampling Out the Vintage,* 110–11.

21. Bardacke, *Trampling Out the Vintage,* 253–54.

22. For a specific focus on the unique combination of leadership and organizational strategies of the farmworker movement, see Marshall Ganz, *Five Smooth Stones: Strategic Capacity in the Unionization of California Agriculture,* PhD dissertation, Harvard University, 2008.

23. Ganz, "Five Smooth Stones."

24. Ganz, "Five Smooth Stones," 280.

25. Isao Fujimoto, interview with the author, March 2007; Kirke Wilson, interview with the author, April 2008.

26. James Lorenz, letter to Cesar Chavez, February 1967, United Farm Workers of America Archives, Walter P. Reuther Library, Wayne State University, box 60 UFW Office of the President, California Rural Legal Assistance folder 12.

27. Pablo Espinoza, interview with author, April 2008.

28. Cesar Chavez, letter to Robert F. Kennedy, July 1967, United Farm Workers of America Archives, Walter P. Reuther Library at Wayne State University, box 39 UFW Office of the President, Kennedy, Robert 1967–68 folder 11.

29. Cesar Chavez, letter to Don Waite, September 27, 1967, United Farm Workers of America Archives, Walter P. Reuther Library at

Wayne State University, box 63 UFW Office of the President, Central California Action Associates folder 11.

30. Joan Casey, ed., "Crusade on Poverty Starting Training Program," *National Civic Review* 55 (1966): 598–601.

31. Robert Walters, "Poverty War Shift to Job Programs Stirs 'Politics' Cry," *Evening Star,* January 25, 1968, in Field Foundation Archives, Center for American History, University of Texas at Austin.

32. Field Foundation Archives, Center for American History, University of Texas at Austin, box 2T41, Citizens Crusade Against Poverty folder.

33. United Farm Workers, letter to Board, 1967, Field Foundation Archives, Center for American History, University of Texas at Austin, box 2S413 National Farmworkers Service Center folder.

34. Field Foundation Archives, Center for American History, University of Texas at Austin, box 2T41 Citizens Crusade Against Poverty folder.

35. Bardacke, *Trampling Out the Vintage*; Garcia, *Jaws of Victory*; Pawel, *Union of Their Dreams*.

36. Philip Martin, *Promise Unfulfilled: Unions, Immigration, and the Farm Workers* (Ithaca, NY: Cornell University Press, 2003); Miriam Wells and Don Villarejo, "State Structures and Social Movement Strategies: The Shaping of Farm Labor Protections in California," *Politics & Society* 32 (2004): 291–326; John Zerzan, "Cesar Chavez and the Farm Workers: The New American Revolution–What Went Wrong?" *Politics & Society* 3, no. 1 (1972): 117–28.

37. The Field Foundation was founded in 1940 in New York City by Marshall Field III, grandson of a major merchant who came to Chicago in the 1800s. Field eventually went into the bond business and during the Great Depression decided to use his wealth to assist people struggling in poverty. Throughout the 1950s and 1960s the Field Foundation funded many social movement organizations, focusing specifically on youth, families, and racial and social justice. By 1989 the Field Foundation of New York had fully spent its assets and closed, ending funding commitments to long-time grantees including the NFWSC. Between 1967 and 1969 the Field Foundation granted the NFWSC $85,000, and between 1972 and 1976, over $200,000—a great deal for a movement organization at this time.

38. In the letter, Cahn is referring to Marion Wright Edelman, legal advocate for the Child Development Group of Mississippi and a future founder of the Children's Defense Fund. Cahn is wishing for a similarly catalytic legal advocate for Cesar Chavez's growing movement. Source: Edgar Cahn, letter to Leslie Dunbar, December 10, 1966, Field Foundation Archives, Center for American History, University of Texas at Austin, box 2T143, National Farmworker Service Center folder.

39. Leslie Dunbar, letter to Cesar Chavez, January 30, 1967, Field Foundation Archives, Center for American History, University of Texas at Austin, box 2T143 National Farmworker Service Center folder.

40. Cesar Chavez, letter to Leslie Dunbar, January 30, 1967, Field Foundation Archives, Center for American History, University of Texas at Austin, box 2T143 National Farmworker Service Center folder.

41. Leslie Dunbar, letter to Cesar Chavez, March 14, 1967, Field Foundation Archives, Center for American History, University of Texas at Austin, box 2T143 National Farmworker Service Center folder.

42. Cesar Chavez, letter to Leslie Dunbar, March 17, 1967, Field Foundation Archives, Center for American History, University of Texas at Austin, box 2T143 National Farmworker Service Center folder.

43. The grant budget included an attorney salary of $12,000, a legal secretary at $550 a month, a community worker at $250 a month, a small law library, supplies, telephone costs, rent and utilities, and $200 a month for litigation costs.

44. Martin Garbus, letter to Leslie Dunbar, March 21, 1968, Field Foundation Archives, Center for American History, University of Texas at Austin, box 2T143 National Farmworker Service Center folder.

45. Jerry Cohen, letter to Leslie Dunbar, July 5, 1969, Field Foundation Archives, Center for American History, University of Texas at Austin, box 2T143 National Farmworker Service Center folder.

46. Leslie Dunbar, letter to Jerry Cohen, July 22, 1969, Field Foundation Archives, Center for American History, University of Texas at Austin, box 2T143 National Farmworker Service Center folder.

47. Leslie Dunbar, letter to Cesar Chavez, August 6, 1967, Field Foundation Archives, Center for American History, University of Texas at Austin, box 2T143 National Farmworker Service Center folder.

48. Leslie Dunbar, letter to Cesar Chavez, October 20, 1969, Field Foundation Archives, Center for American History, University of Texas at Austin, box 2T143 National Farmworker Service Center folder.

49. The grants included one from the Norman Foundation for $8,000 to the NFWSC and one from the Rockefeller Brothers for $12,000 for non-violence training sessions. In 1970 the Ford Foundation granted $225,000 for further administrative development of the NFWSC and additional service center operations; the Rockefeller Brothers re-granted $12,000 for the non-violence training; the Abelard Foundation granted $5,000 for the founding of a Cesar Chavez community school; and the Dubinsky Foundation donated $12,000 to develop a clinic in Delano. Funding data for the NFWSC and other UFW movement organizations were collected from UFW memos, grant agreements, and correspondence in the Field Foundation Archives, Center for American History, University of Texas at Austin and the United Farm Workers of America Archives at the Walter P. Reuther Library at Wayne State University.

50. By the late 1970s the UFW had founded eight affiliated "movement organizations," including the Cesar E. Chavez Foundation, the Cesar E. Chavez Community Development Fund, the Juan De La Cruz Pension Fund, the Robert F. Kennedy Medical Plan, and the Farmworker Institute for Education and Leadership Development, which are beyond the scope of this study.

51. For a more detailed accounting of the "purges" and of Chavez's use of The Game, a psychotherapy technique developed through a drug rehabilitation retreat called Synannon, to target members he suspected of disloyalty, see Bardacke, *Trampling Out the Vintage*, 541–65; Garcia, *Jaws of Victory*, 256–91.

52. According to my interviews, archival documentation, and the recent studies of Pawel, Bardacke, and Garcia, Chavez and Chris Hartmeyer of Migrant Ministries conducted the "purge" of board members, volunteer organizers, and legal staff through a process called The Game. Originally used by a drug and alcohol treatment program called Synanon in the Tehachapi Mountains near La Paz, participants in The Game were asked to share their inner fears,

angers, and frustrations. Participants who were comfortable or honest enough to express dissatisfaction with Chavez's leadership were then told to leave the movement. Those loyal to the union claim that the legal team left of their own free will because of their growing demands to be paid as more than volunteers, breaking with the volunteer-based community-union model.

53. Meeting minutes, NFWSC files, Walter P. Reuther Library, Wayne State University, box 6 UFW Administrative Files folder; Meeting minutes, box 27 UFW Information and Research Department Files folder; Meeting minutes, box 2T143 National Farmworker Service Center folder, box 2S450 Citizen Committee for Immigration Reform folder, box 2T10 National Farmworker Service Center folder.

54. In 1975 Chavez's assistant Ann Pluharich said that the movement was in such turmoil that her stress level created health problems that prevented her from sending scheduled reports to the Field Foundation or getting additional grant proposals out. Chavez was also ailing, which included lingering back problems, which were the result of multiple fasts and stress. Letters in minutes in NFWSC files, Walter P. Reuther Library, Wayne State University, box 6 UFW Administrative Files folder.

55. Assorted letters, Field Foundation Archives, Center for American History, University of Texas at Austin, box 2T143 NFWSC folder, box 2S450 Citizen Committee for Immigration Reform folder; Assorted letters, United Farm Workers of America Archives, Walter P. Reuther Library, Wayne State University, box 52 UFW Information and Research Department Files folder.

56. Handwritten memo, "Foundations – Stern Fund," United Farm Workers of America Archives, Walter P. Reuther Library, Wayne State University, box 51 UFW Information and Research Department Files folder.

57. Foundation notes, NFWSC files, Walter P. Reuther Library, Wayne State University, box 51 UFW Information and Research Department Files, Foundation Files folder.

58. ALRB regulations included the Access Rule (the union has the right to go on farm property and talk to workers); the Make Whole Law (if workers are let go early in the season, the grower must pay for the whole season); and Certification (legal union representation and

requirements of good faith bargaining). Chavez spent the next year educating workers on these matters.

59. Garcia, *Jaws of Victory*, 181–82.

60. Meeting minutes, NFWSC files, Walter P. Reuther Library, Wayne State University, box 27 UFW Information and Research Department Files, Service Center 1977 folder.

61. Bardacke, *Trampling Out the Vintage*, 696–98.

62. Bardacke, *Trampling Out the Vintage*, 578–79, footnote 42 in chapter 27.

63. Jennifer Medina, "Family Quarrel Imperils a Labor Leader's Legacy," *New York Times*, May 14, 2011; Miriam Pawel, "UFW: A Broken Contract; Former Chavez Ally Took His Own Path; Where Eliseo Medina Has Gone, Unions Have Grown," *Los Angeles Times*, January 11, 2006; Miriam Pawel, "UFW: A Broken Contract; Decisions of Long Ago Shape the Union Today; In the Late 1970s Cesar Chavez Grew Intent on Keeping Control," *Los Angeles Times*, January 10, 2006; Miriam Pawel, "UFW: A Broken Contract; Linked Charities Bank on the Chavez Name; the Union-Related Philanthropies Enrich One Another, Operating Like a Family Business," *Los Angeles Times*, January 9, 2006; Miriam Pawel, "UFW: A Broken Contract; Farmworkers Reap Little as Union Strays from Its Roots," *Los Angeles Times*, January 8, 2006; Pawel, *Union of Their Dreams*.

64. Robert L. Allen, *Black Awakening in Capitalist America: An Analytic History* (New York: Doubleday, 1969).

65. David J. Garrow, "Philanthropy and the Civil Rights Movement," working paper, Center for the Study of Philanthropy, City University of New York, 1987.

66. 1981 meeting with Peter Drucker, debrief transcript, United Farm Workers of America Archives, Walter P. Reuther Library, Wayne State University, box 52 UFW Information and Research Department Files folder; David Villarino, interview with the author, 2008.

CHAPTER 3

1. To protect the individuals involved in the study, per the Human Subjects Review Board at the University of California, Berkeley,

pseudonyms and contextual changes are used for the case studies featured in chapters 3 and 4. Reports cited are also disguised so as not to reveal the institutional affiliations of foundation staff and grantees.

2. For studies on the rise of participatory poverty programming in the United States, see Barbara Cruikshank, *The Will to Empower: Democratic Citizens and Other Subjects* (Ithaca, NY: Cornell University Press, 1999); Susan Brin Hyatt, "From Citizen to Volunteer: Neoliberal Governance and the Erasure of Poverty," in *The New Poverty Studies: The Ethnography of Power, Politics and Impoverished People in the United States,* ed. Jeff Maskovsky and Judith Goode (New York: NYU Press, 2001), 201–35. For the international development context, see Bill Cook and Uma Kothari, eds., *Participation: The New Tyranny?* (London: Zed Books, 2001).

3. Mary Ellen Boyle and Ira Silver, "Poverty, Partnerships, and Privilege: Elite Institutions and Community Empowerment," *City and Community* 4 (2007): 233–53; Uma Kothari, "Authority and Expertise: The Professionalisation of International Development and the Ordering of Dissent," *Antipode* 37, no. 3 (2005): 425–46; James Petras, "NGOs: In the Service of Imperialism," *Journal of Contemporary Asia* 29 (1999): 429–40.

4. Petras, "NGOs: In the Service of Imperialism."

5. For critical reviews of this trend, see Jennifer Wolch, *The Shadow State: Government and Voluntary Sector in Transition* (New York: Foundation Center, 1990); Andrea Smith, "Introduction: The Revolution Will Not Be Funded," in *The Revolution Will Not Be Funded,* ed. INCITE! Women of Color Against Violence (Cambridge, MA: South End Press, 2007), 41–52.

6. For a review of the partnership approach, see Wendy Larner and David Craig, "After Neoliberalism? Community Activism and Local Partnerships in Aotearoa New Zealand," *Antipode* 37 (2005): 403–24.

7. For a discussion on comprehensive community initiatives, see Larry Parachini and Andrew Mott, *Strengthening Community Voices in Policy Reform: Community-based Monitoring, Learning and Action Strategies for an Era of Devolution and Change: A Special Report Developed for the Annie E. Casey Foundation* (Washington, DC: Center for Community Change, 1997). Also see Ira Silver, "Living Up to the Promise of Collaboration: Foundations and Community Organizations as Partners in the Revitalization of Poor Neighborhoods," in *Foundations for Social Change:*

Critical Perspectives on Philanthropy and Popular Movements (New York: Rowman and Littlefield, 2005).

8. The term "collaborative" was commonly used in the cases I studied which are featured in this and the following chapter.

9. For professional analysis of the failures of multi-partner foundation initiatives, see the reports from Annie E. Casey Foundation, *The Path of Most Resistance: Reflections on Lessons Learned from New Futures* (1995) and *The Eye of the Storm: Ten Years on the Front Lines of New Futures* (undated); both can be found on the website of the LISC Institute for Comprehensive Community Development (www.instituteccd.org).

10. For reports on the Hewlett Foundation initiative, see Prudence Brown and Leila Fiester, *Hard Lessons about Philanthropy & Community Change from the Neighborhood Improvement Initiative* (Menlo Park, CA: Hewlett Foundation, 2007), http://hewlett_prod.acesfconsulting.com /uploads/files/HewlettNIIReport.pdf. For the James Irvine Foundation reports, see Gary Walker, *Midcourse Corrections to a Major Initiative: A Report on the James Irvine Foundation's CORAL Experience* (Philadelphia, PA: Public/Private Ventures and San Francisco, CA: James Irvine Foundation, 2007), http://irvine.org/assets/pdf/pubs/evaluation /Midcourse_Corrections.pdf. And for a general report on the trend of foundations admitting failures, see Stephanie Strom, "Foundations Find Benefits in Facing Up to Failures," *New York Times,* July 26, 2007 (www.nytimes.com/2007/07/26/us/26foundation.html).

11. For a discussion on how relationships with funders and with contracted partners change accountability structures, see Petras, "NGOs: In the Service of Imperialism."

12. Robert Reich, *Supercapitalism: The Transformation of Business, Democracy, and Everyday Life* (New York: Vintage, 2007); Robert Reich, "Why the Rich are Getting Richer, and the Poor, Poorer," in *The Way Class Works: Readings on School, Family, and the Economy,* ed. Lois Weis (New York: Routledge, 2007).

13. Ruth Wilson Gilmore, "In the Shadow of the Shadow State," in *The Revolution Will Not Be Funded,* ed. INCITE! Women of Color Against Violence (Cambridge, MA: South End Press, 2007), 41–52. Also see Dylan Rodriguez, "The Political Logic of the Non-Profit Industrial Complex," in the same volume, 22–40.

14. For a history of how the poor have been regarded as lazy, immoral or otherwise undeserving of public support, a useful reference is Michael Katz, *The Undeserving Poor: America's Enduring Confrontation with Poverty* (Oxford: Oxford University Press, 2013)—see chapter 4, "Interpretations of Poverty in the Conservative Ascendance." Also see Nancy Fraser and Linda Gordon, "A Genealogy of 'Dependency': Tracing a Keyword of the US Welfare State," *Signs* 19 (1994): 309–36.

15. For a summary of statistics on the growth of the nonprofit sector in the first decade of the twenty-first century, see Peter Kim and Jeffrey Bradach, "Why More Nonprofits are Getting Bigger," *Stanford Social Innovation Review,* spring 2012,
www.ssireview.org/articles/entry/why_more_nonprofits_are_
getting_bigger; Lester M. Salamon, ed., *The State of Nonprofit America,* 2nd ed. (Washington, DC: Brookings Institution Press, 2012); Amy S. Blackwood, Katie L. Roeger, and Sarah L. Pettijohn, *The Nonprofit Sector in Brief: Public Charities, Giving and Volunteering, 2012* (Washington, DC: Urban Institute, 2012), www.urban.org/UploadedPDF/412674-The-Nonprofit-Sector-in-Brief.pdf; Chuck McLean and Carol Brouwer, "The Effect of the Economy on the Nonprofit Sector: An October 2012 Survey," *Guidestar,* 2012 (www.guidestar.org/ViewCmsFile.aspx?ContentID=4781).

For data on foundation giving and poverty, see the Foundation Center report *Focus on Poverty* (2007), http://foundationcenter.org/focus/gpf/poverty/.

16. See INCITE!, *The Revolution Will Not Be Funded.*

17. For a collection of studies of "NGO-ization" in the context of global social movements and development, see Aziz Choudry and Dip Kapoor, eds., *NGO-ization: Complicity, Contradictions and Prospects* (London: Zed Books, 2013).

18. For comprehensive studies of California philanthropic trends, see James M. Ferris and Elizabeth Graddy, *Philanthropic Activity in California's Central Valley* (San Francisco, CA: James Irvine Foundation, August 2004); James M. Ferris and Martha K. Sharp, *California Foundations: Trends & Patterns* (Los Angeles, CA: USC Center on Philanthropy and Public Policy, 2002), http://cppp.usc.edu/media-resources/california-foundations/.

19. Rosenberg Foundation, *1978 Annual Report* (San Francisco, CA: Rosenberg Foundation, 1978), www.cybergrants.com/rosenberg/reports /1978.pdf.

20. Grant data were collected from the United Farm Workers of America Archives, Walter P. Reuther Library, Wayne State University, United Farm Workers Administrative files, UFW Information and Research Department files.

21. J. Edward Taylor and Philip L. Martin, "The New Rural Poverty: Central Valley Evolving into Patchwork of Poverty and Prosperity," *California Agriculture* 54, (2000): 26–32.

22. For an in-depth study of both the "push" and the "pull" factors contributing to Mexican migration to the United States, and the daily experiences of migrants, see Judith Adler Hellman, *The World of Mexican Migrants: The Rock and the Hard Place* (New York: New Press, 2008).

23. Seth Holmes, *Fresh Fruit, Broken Bodies: Migrant Farmworkers in the United States* (Berkeley: University of California Press, 2013).

24. For a detailed history of the relationship between the farmworker movement and the immigrant rights movement of the 1990s and early-to-mid 2000s, see Randy Shaw, *Beyond the Fields: Cesar Chavez, the UFW, and the Struggle for Justice in the 21st Century* (Berkeley: University of California Press, 2008).

25. Daranee Petsod, ed., *Investing in Our Communities: Strategies for Immigrant Integration—A Toolkit for Grantmakers* (Sebastopol, CA: Grantmakers Concerned with Immigrants and Refugees, 2007), www.gcir .org/publications/toolkit.

26. Julie Preston, "The Big Funders behind the Push for an Immigration Overhaul," *New York Times,* November 14, 2014.

27. Michael Goldman, *Imperial Nature* (New Haven, CT: Yale University Press, 2005).

28. Michael Woolcock, "Social Capital and Economic Development: Toward a Theoretical Synthesis and Policy Framework," *Theory and Society* 27 (1998): 151–208.

29. Mark Granovetter, "Economic Action and Social Structure: The Problem of Embeddedness," *American Journal of Sociology* 91 (1985): 481–510.

30. Heloise Weber, "The Imposition of a Global Development Architecture: The Example of Microcredit," *Review of International Studies* 28 (2002): 537–55.

31. For an example of the social capital "trust" theory popularized during this time, see Francis Fukiyama, *Trust: The Social Virtues and the Creation of Prosperity* (Washington, DC: Free Press, 1995).

32. Robert Putnam, "The Prosperous Community: Social Capital and Public Life," *The American Prospect* 13 (spring 1993): 35–42.

33. Robert Putnam, *Bowling Alone: the Collapse and Revival of American Community* (New York: Simon and Schuster, 2000).

34. For a complete listing of Urban Institute publications about immigrants and immigration by Jeffrey Passel and Michael Fix, go to www.urban.org/expert.cfm?ID=JeffreySPassel.

35. Ferris and Sharp, *California Foundations*.

36. Alan Berube, *The Enduring Challenge of Concentrated Poverty across America: Case Studies from across the U.S.* (Washington, DC: Brookings Institution, 2008), www.brookings.edu/~/media/Files/rc/reports/2008/1024_concentrated_poverty/1024_concentrated_poverty.pdf; US Census Bureau, "Small Area Income and Poverty Estimates, 2010 Estimates State and County Maps, State and County Maps, Data Tables & Highlights," www.census.gov/did/www/saipe/, accessed December 8, 2011. While beyond the time frame of the IPC, today financial crisis and drought have together created sheer panic for both farmers struggling to maintain profit and farm labor communities struggling to survive. An unprecedented alliance of farmers and workers is now organizing for new guest-worker programs and in protest against environmentalists and legislators who have enacted water conservation policies. United Farm Workers, "UFW Foundation, Community Leaders Join National Immigration Reform Effort" (press release, Keene, CA, June 1, 2009); Donald Munro, "From the Arts to Activism, 'Esperanza and Luz' Tells a Tale of Hope for Mexican Farmworkers," *Fresno Bee*, April 17, 2009, 8.

37. Great Valley Center, *Indicators Report: Economy and Quality of Life, Benchmark Statistical 'Indicators' of Great Central Valley's Social, Economic, & Environmental Conditions* (Modesto, CA: Great Valley Center, July 1999); Ferris and Graddy, *Philanthropic Activity*.

38. Putnam, *Bowling Alone.*

39. These reports are not cited in an effort to protect the identities of the foundation staff interviewed.

40. Discussed in more detail in the previous chapter.

41. Pierre Bourdieu, "The Forms of Capital," in *Social Capital: Critical Perspectives,* ed. Stephen Baron, John Field, and Tom Schuller (Oxford: Oxford University Press, 1986).

42. See chapter 1 of this book for a discussion of Gramscian understandings of philanthropy and control. Also see Joan Roelofs, *Foundations and Public Policy: The Mask of Pluralism* (Albany: State University of New York Press, 2003).

43. Interviews with ICP partners were conducted in 2006 and 2007.

44. In keeping with the fictionalized names throughout the chapter, these project names are not actual names but approximate the general ideas expressed.

45. Patricia Hill Collins, *Black Feminist Thought: Knowledge, Consciousness, and the Politics of Empowerment* (New York: Routledge, 2000).

46. For more information on the field of cultural organizing, see the Arts and Democracy Project, http://artsanddemocracy.org.

47. For a summary of trends in nonprofit organizations adopting business practices, see Bill E. Landsberg, "The Nonprofit Paradox: For-Profit Business Models in the Third Sector," *International Journal for Nonprofit Law* 6, no. 2 (2004), www.icnl.org/research/journal /vol6iss2/special_7.htmhttp://www.icnl.org/research/journal/vol6iss2 /special_7.htm.

48. Goldman, *Imperial Nature.*

49. Of course, as shown in chapters 1 and 2, institutional conflicts and competition were not completely absent during periods of the farmworker movement.

50. This was not an easy task, given the diversity of approaches and constituents as described.

51. Manuel Castells, "The Other Face of the Earth: Social Movements against the New Global Order," chapter 2 in *The Power of Identity* (Cambridge: Blackwell, 1997).

52. Castells, "Other Face of the Earth."

53. Frances Fox Piven and Richard Cloward, *Poor People's Movements: Why They Succeed, How They Fail* (New York: Vintage Books, 1978).

54. Gordon MacLeod and Mark Goodwin, "Space, Scale and State Strategy: Rethinking Urban and Regional Governance," *Progress in Human Geography* 23 (1999): 503–27.

55. INCITE!, *The Revolution Will Not Be Funded.*

56. The IPC eventually incorporated as a 501(c)(3) organization, with a board of directors and very limited funds. Of the partners I interviewed, two are still involved in the limited activities of the IPC.

CHAPTER 4

1. As in the previous chapter, all individual and organizational names for this study are disguised per the Human Subjects Protocol of the University of California, Berkeley. Interviewed about the broader context of farmworker organizing, "public stakeholders" from the United Farm Workers, the affiliated Farmworker Institute for Education and Leadership Development, and Roots of Change agreed to be named.

2. See chapter 3 for more detail on the relationship between NAFTA and agricultural poverty in Mexico and the United States. For ethnographic studies of the impact of neoliberal trade policies on Mexican migrants, see also Judith Adler Hellman, *The World of Mexican Migrants: The Rock and the Hard Place* (New York: New Press, 2008); Seth Holmes, *Fresh Fruit, Broken Bodies: Migrant Farmworkers in the United States* (Berkeley: University of California Press, 2013).

3. For a summary of AgJOBS, see www.immigrationpolicy.org /issues/AgJOBS, from which the following is taken:

> AgJOBS, the Agricultural Job Opportunities, Benefits and Security Act, is a proposed immigration law that would provide agricultural employers with a stable, legal labor force while protecting farmworkers from exploitative working conditions. The AgJOBS compromise was reached in 2000 after years of Congressional and labor-management conflict resulting in tough negotiations between the United Farm Workers (UFW), major agricultural employers, and key federal legislators. On January 10, 2007, Senators Kennedy

(D.-Mass.), Feinstein (D-Cali.), and Craig (R.-Idaho) and Reps. Cannon (R.-Utah) and Berman (D.-Cal.) introduced AgJOBS in the 110th Congress.

4. Michael Edwards, *Just Another Emperor: The Myths and Realities of Philanthrocapitalism* (London: Demos, 2008).

5. Bill Clinton, *Giving: How Each of Us Can Change the World* (New York: Knopf, 2007); Michael Kinsley, ed., *Creative Capitalism: A Conversation with Bill Gates, Warren Buffet, and Other Economic Leaders* (New York: Simon and Schuster, 2008).

6. For a theorization and examples of the "bottom billion" approach, see C.K. Prahaland, *The Fortune at the Bottom of the Pyramid* (Upper Saddle River, NJ: Wharton School Publishing, 2005).

7. For critical development studies about micro-credit programs in the global South, see Ananya Roy, *Poverty Capital: Microfinance and the Making of Development* (New York: Routledge, 2010); Lamia Karim, "Demystifying Micro-Credit: The Grameen Bank, NGOs, and Neoliberalism in Bangladesh," *Cultural Dynamics* 20 (2008), 5–29.

8. Additional structural changes to the farm labor system throughout the 1980s and 1990s were covered in chapter 3.

9. For a nuanced understanding of neoliberalism and relationships of power through the wielding of popular "common sense" framings, see Stuart Hall's discussion of the rise of Thatcherism in the 1980s, *The Hard Road to Renewal: Thatcherism and the Crisis of the Left* (New York: Verso, 1988).

10. All report titles are disguised to protect the identity of research subjects who were guaranteed anonymity per the Human Subjects Protocol of this project. Passages cited from reports are rephrased, retaining all original meaning, to protect the authors.

11. My research findings indicate that it is not just a few "bad actor" farmers that break worker health, safety, and wage laws but rather a majority of large growers. Farmworker advocates revealed that current worker rights and safety legislation does not work because it is easier and more cost-effective for growers to pay fines for violating the law (when caught) than it is to make the required changes to farming practice. In this regard, the task force's recommendation to target "bad actors" failed to address widespread enforcement problems.

12. For a conversation about the ownership of data and local knowledge in poverty and development research, see James Petras, "NGOs: In the Service of Imperialism," *Journal of Contemporary Asia* 29 (1999): 439. Also see Giles Mohan, "Beyond Participation: Strategies for Deeper Empowerment," in *Participation: The New Tyranny?* ed. Bill Cooke and Uma Kothari (London: Zed Books, 2001).

13. As is obvious and has been shown throughout this chapter, private foundations created from corporate wealth simply do not take on corporate or industrial structural arrangements. Also discussed earlier, while many foundations fund immigrant communities and education around immigration reform, they usually do not directly engage with legislative reform in this area.

14. For discussion of how union leadership and worker field reps received Cesar Chavez's ideas around management theory and how this contributed to serious rifts within the movement, see Miriam Pawel, *The Crusades of Cesar Chavez: A Biography* (New York: Bloomsbury Press, 2014), 416–47.

15. David Villarino, interview with the author, 2008. Mr. Villarino agreed to be identified by his real name in this study.

16. According to an article in *Rural Migration News* 6, no. 4 (2000):

The UFW says that its agreement with Bear Creek (Jackson & Perkins Rose) Production Company in Wasco, California is an example of how the "new UFW" is willing and able to cooperate with farm employers to enhance employer profitability while increasing wages and benefits for workers.... The UFW won an election to represent Bear Creek workers December 16, 1994, and signed a three-year contract on March 17, 1995 that increased wages and benefits 22 percent over the life of the contract .... The UFW-Bear Creek relationship got off to a rocky start, with 136 grievances filed in the contract's first 18 months. In July 1996, Bear Creek contacted the UFW about the troublesome relationship, and a two-day session was held in September 1996 to resolve outstanding grievances; it resulted in a pledge to work together as the UFW-Bear Creek partnership. Under the partnership, supervisors and union representatives were retrained to enable them to resolve disputes before they escalated into grievances. Bear Creek workers were asked to make productivity increasing suggestions without fear of layoffs. As a result, the quality of the bare-root roses produced at Bear Creek increased markedly, from 40 percent premium in 1996 to 54 percent premium in 1999.... According to the UFW, average hourly earnings rose from $7.62 in 1997 to $8.02 in 1999, the number of foremen was reduced, and the number of workers' compensation claims reduced by half.

17. David Villarino, interview with the author, 2007.

18. David Villarino, interview with the author, 2007.

19. FIELD planning document, 2000.

20. David Villarino, interview with the author, 2007.

21. While not discussed by FIELD staff, using undocumented immigrants who earn below-minimum wages is one way that farmers with large labor-intensive crops keep costs down and maintain their competitive edge. The union–grower alliance on immigration reform contributes to the "win-win" model by ensuring a secure future of low-wage (temporarily legal) immigrant labor through guest-worker programs. Archival FIELD documents were found in the United Farm Workers of America Archives, Walter P. Reuther Library, Wayne State University, box 28 UFW Office of the President Organizational Structure folder, box 27 UFW Office of the President Farmworker Institute for Education and Leadership Development folder.

22. In keeping with the commitment to protect the identify of research subjects and projects, the name of the site is not used and generalized statistics are given to describe the area.

23. California Institute for Rural Studies, *In Their Own Words: Farmworker Access to Health Care in Four California Regions* (Los Angeles: California Endowment and California Program on Access Care, May 2004).

24. Most prominently cited are the Aspen Institute Roundtable's *Voices from the Field: Learning from the Early Work of Comprehensive Community Initiatives* (Washington, DC: Aspen Institute 1997) and the social capital theories of Cornelia Butler Flora (2003).

25. M. Emery, S. Fey, and C. B. Flora, "Using Community Capitals to Build Assets for Positive Community Change," *CD Practice* 13 (2006); M. Emery and C. B. Flora, "Spiraling-Up: Mapping Community Transformation with Community Capitals Framework," *Community Development* 37 (2006): 19–35; Cornelia Butler Flora, *Rural Community Economic*

Development Case Review (Pittsburgh, PA: Claude Worthington Benedum Foundation, 2003–2004); Cornelia Butler Flora, *Developing Indicators to Refine and Test a Theory of Equitable Change for Rural Communities of Interest and of Place* (Dallas, TX: National Rural Funders Collaborative, 2003–2004); Robert Putnam, *Bowling Alone: The Collapse and Revival of American Community* (New York: Simon and Schuster, 2000).

26. Some of these organizations were founded during the farmworker movement of the 1960s, and some were partners in the Immigrant Participation Collaborative described in chapter 3.

27. For studies that analyze gendered professionalism in the context of development and poverty alleviation programs, see Wendy Larner and David Craig, "After Neoliberalism? Community Activism and Local Partnerships in Aotearoa New Zealand," *Antipode* 37, no. 3 (2005): 403–24; Kathryn Moeller, "Proving 'The Girl Effect': Corporate Knowledge Production and Educational Intervention," *International Journal of International Development* 33 (2013): 612–21; Karim, "Demystifying Micro-Credit."

28. Uma Kothari, "Authority and Expertise: The Professionalization of International Development and the Ordering of Dissent," *Antipode* 37 (2005): 442.

29. Dee Hock is a management and leadership scholar, whose book *Birth of the Chaordic Age* (San Francisco, CA: Berrett-Koehler, 1999) was frequently cited by Michael Dimock.

30. Michael Dimock, director of Roots of Change, interview with the author, 2007. Mr. Dimock agreed to be identified by his real name in this study.

31. For reporting on the implications of recent immigration reform policy on California farmworkers, see Carolyn Lochhead, "Immigration Reform: Farmworkers, Agribusiness Feel Left Out," *San Francisco Chronicle*, November 21, 2014.

CHAPTER 5

1. Grace Lee Boggs, *The Next American Revolution: Sustainable Activism for the Twenty-First Century* (Berkeley: University of California Press, 2012), 60.

2. As quoted in Richard Griswold del Castillo and Richard A. Garcia, *Cesar Chavez: A Triumph of Spirit* (Norman: University of Oklahoma Press, 1997), 116.

3. For a visual tour of agricultural abandonment, the real estate bust, and farmworker poverty, see Ken and Melanie Light's photo documentary, *Valley of Shadows and Dreams* (Berkeley, CA: Heyday, 2012).

4. The South Bronx has the highest unemployment rate in New York City. In June 2012 the rate in Bronx County was 14 percent, while Manhattan was only at 8.8 percent. In Stockton, CA, the unemployment rate was 17.9 percent in June, 2012 (Bureau of Labor Statistics, US Department of Labor, www.bls.gov/lau).

5. Joseph E. Stiglitz, *The Price of Inequality: How Today's Divided Society Endangers Our Future* (New York: W. W. Norton, 2012); Jeffrey D. Sachs, *The Price of Civilization: Reawakening American Virtue and Prosperity* (New York: Random House, 2011); Jacob Kornbluth, director, *Inequality for All* (2013)—a film produced Robert Reich, author and former secretary of labor in the Clinton administration (http://inequalityforall.com); Matt Taibbi, *The Divide: American Injustice in the Age of the Wealth Gap* (New York: Speigel and Grau, 2014).

6. Antonio Gramsci, *Selections from the Prison Notebooks of Antonio Gramsci,* ed. Quintin Hoare and Geoffrey Nowell Smith (New York: International, 1971).

7. Carmel Borg, Joseph Buttigieg, and Peter Mayo, eds., *Gramsci and Education* (Oxford, UK: Rowman & Littlefield: 2002), 147–78.

8. For a discussion about the conflicted identities of poverty professionals, see Ananya Roy's analysis of "double agents" in *Poverty Capital: Microfinance and the Making of Development* (New York: Routledge, 2010), 191–208. Also see my preliminary analysis of the negotiations of the foundation program officer: Erica Kohl, *The Program Officer: Negotiating the Politics of Philanthropy* (working paper, Institute for the Study of Social Change, University of California, Berkeley, 2007).

9. Ananya Roy, "Praxis in the Time of Empire," *Planning Theory* 5, no. 1 (2005): 13.

10. Erving Goffman, *The Presentation of Self in Everyday Life* (New York: Anchor Books, 1959).

11. For a detailed ethnographic case study of farm labor in Imokalee, Florida, and the work of the Coalition of Immokalee Workers, see Sylvia Giagnoni, *Fields of Resistance: The Struggle of Florida's Farmworkers for Justice* (Chicago, IL: Haymarket Books, 2011).

12. Coalition of Immokalee Workers website (www.ciw-online .org), accessed September 2, 2011.

13. Michael Pollan, *The Omnivore's Dilemma: A Natural History of Four Meals* (New York: Penguin, 2006); Michael Pollan, *In Defense of Food: An Eater's Manifesto* (New York: Penguin, 2009).

14. David Villarino, interview with the author, 2007.

15. Slow food resources include Slow Food International (www .slowfood.com); Slow Food USA (www.slowfoodusa.org); Michael Pollan's website (www.michaelpollan.com); Food Routes (www .foodroutes.org), which documents the distance food travels; and the many local chapters of slow food groups.

16. Michael Dimock, interview with the author, 2007.

17. David Bacon, *Communities without Borders: Images and Voices from the World of Migration* (Ithaca, NY: ILR Press, 2007).

18. Julie Guthman, "Thinking Inside the Neoliberal Box: The Micro-Politics of Agro-Food Philanthropy," *Geoforum* 39 (2008): 1241–53.

19. Since 2010, food justice organizing has rapidly expanded across the country. The new groups are too numerous to mention. For a start, see Eric Holt-Gimenez, ed., *Food Movements Unite! Strategies to Transform Our Food System* (Oakland, CA: Food First Books, 2011). For a 2013 map, produced by Colorlines, of some projects that self-identify as food justice organizing, see http://colorlines.com/archives/2013/10 /the_color_of_food_justice.html. Also see Sherry Linkon, "Why the Food Justice Movement Matters," *Working-Class Perspectives* (blog), July 25, 2011 (http://workingclassstudies.wordpress.com/2011/07/25/why-the-food-justice-movement-matters/).

20. Remark made at the 2013 Council on Foundations Conference.

BIBLIOGRAPHY

Adams, Vincanne. *Markets of Sorrow, Labors of Faith: New Orleans in the Wake of Katrina.* Durham, NC: Duke University Press, 2013.

Addams, Jane. *Philanthropy and Social Progress.* Freeport, NY: Books for Libraries Press, 1893.

Allen, Robert L. *Black Awakening in Capitalist America: An Analytic History.* New York: Doubleday, 1969.

Annie E. Casey Foundation. *The Eye of the Storm: Ten Years on the Front Lines of New Futures.* Report, Baltimore, MD, undated. www.instituteccd.org.

————. *The Path of Most Resistance: Reflections on Lessons Learned from New Futures.* Report, Baltimore, MD, 1995. www.instituteccd.org.

Arena, John. *Driven from New Orleans: How Nonprofits Betray Public Housing and Promote Privatization.* Minneapolis: University of Minnesota Press, 2012.

Arnove, Robert, ed. *Philanthropy and Cultural Imperialism.* Boston: G. K. Hall, 1980.

Aspen Institute Roundtable on Comprehensive Community Initiatives for Children and Families, *Voices from the Field: Learning from the Early Work of Comprehensive Community Initiatives.* Washington, DC: Aspen Institute, 1997.

Bacon, David. *Communities without Borders: Images and Voices from the World of Migration*. Ithaca, NY: ILR Press, 2007.

Bardacke, Frank. *Trampling Out the Vintage: Cesar Chavez and the Two Souls of the United Farm Workers*. New York: Verso, 2011.

Barkan, Joanne. "Got Dough?" *Dissent* 58, no. 1 (2011): 49–57.

———. "Hired Guns on Astroturf: How to Buy and Sell School Reform." *Dissent* 59, no. 2 (2012): 49–57.

Barndt, Deborah. *Tangled Routes: Women, Work, and Globalization on the Tomato Trail*. Lanham, MD: Rowman and Littlefield, 2008.

Bennis, Warren. *Organizing Genius*. Reading, MA: Addison-Wesley, 1997.

Berman, Edward H. *The Ideology of Philanthropy: The Influence of the Carnegie, Ford, and Rockefeller Foundations on American Foreign Policy*. Albany: State University of New York Press, 1983.

Berube, Alan. *The Enduring Challenge of Concentrated Poverty Across America: Case Studies from Across the U.S.* Washington, DC: Brookings Institution, 2008.

Bishop, Mathew, and Michael Green. *Philanthrocapitalism: How the Rich Can Save the World*. New York: Bloomsbury, 2008.

Blackwood, Amy S., Katie L. Roeger, and Sarah L. Pettijohn. *The Nonprofit Sector in Brief: Public Charities, Giving and Volunteering, 2012*. Washington, DC: Urban Institute, 2012. www.urban.org/UploadedPDF /412674-The-Nonprofit-Sector-in-Brief.pdf.

Boggs, Grace Lee. *The Next American Revolution: Sustainable Activism for the Twenty-First Century*. Berkeley: University of California Press, 2012.

Borg, Carmel, Joseph Buttigieg, and Peter Mayo, eds. *Gramsci and Education*. Oxford: Rowman & Littlefield, 2002.

Bourdieu, Pierre. "The Forms of Capital." In *Social Capital: Critical Perspectives,* edited by Stephen Baron, John Field, and Tom Schuller. Oxford: Oxford University Press, 1986.

Boyle, Mary Ellen, and Ira Silver. "Poverty, Partnerships, and Privilege: Elite Institutions and Community Empowerment." *City and Community* 4 (2007): 233–53.

Bradshaw, Ted K. "In the Shadow of Urban Growth: Bifurcation in Rural California Communities." In *Forgotten Places: Uneven Development in Rural America,* edited by Thomas A. Lyson and William W. Falk, 218–56. Lawrence: University Press of Kansas, 1993.

Brown, Prudence, and Leila Fiester. *Hard Lessons about Philanthropy & Community Change from the Neighborhood Improvement Initiative.* Menlo Park, CA: Hewlett Foundation: 2007. http://hewlett_prod .acesfconsulting.com/uploads/files/HewlettNIIReport.pdf

Butler, Judith. *Gender Trouble: Feminism and the Subversion of Identity.* New York: Routledge, 1990.

California Institute for Rural Studies. *In Their Own Words: Farmworker Access to Health Care in Four California Regions.* Los Angeles: California Endowment and California Program on Access Care, May 2004.

California Institute for Rural Studies and California Endowment. *Suffering in Silence: A Report on the Health of California's Agricultural Workers.* November 2000. www.cirsinc.org/publications/category /8-rural-health.

Carnegie, Andrew. *The Gospel of Wealth.* New York: Century Press, 1889.

Casey, Joan, ed. "Crusade on Poverty Starting Training Program." *National Civic Review* 55 (1966): 598–601.

Castells, Manuel. *The Power of Identity.* Cambridge: Blackwell, 1997.

Chance, Ruth. "Bay Area Foundation History, Volume II, Ruth Clouse Chance." Bancroft Library, Regional Oral History Office, University of California, Berkeley.

Choudry, Aziz, and Dip Kapoor, eds. *NGO-ization: Complicity, Contradictions and Prospects.* London: Zed Books, 2013.

Clinton, Bill. *Giving: How Each of Us Can Change the World.* New York: Knopf, 2007.

Cloward, Richard, and Lloyd Ohlin. *Delinquency and Opportunity: A Theory of Delinquent Gangs.* New York: Free Press, 1966.

Collins, Patricia Hill. *Black Feminist Thought: Knowledge, Consciousness, and the Politics of Empowerment.* New York: Routledge, 2000.

Cook, Bill, and Uma Kothari, eds. *Participation: The New Tyranny?* London: Zed Books, 2001.

Coon, Horace. *Money to Burn.* New Brunswick, NJ: Transaction, 1938.

Covington, Sally. *Moving a Public Policy Agenda: The Strategic Philanthropy of Conservative Foundations.* Washington, DC: National Committee for Responsive Philanthropy, 1997.

Cruikshank, Barbara. *The Will to Empower: Democratic Citizens and Other Subjects.* Ithaca, NY: Cornell University Press, 1999.

Cullather, Nick. "'Stretching the Surface of the Earth': The Foundations, Neo-Malthusianism and the Modernizing Agenda," *Global Society* 28, no. 1 (2014): 104–12.

———. "'The Target is the People': Representations of the Village in Modernization and US National Security Doctrine," *Cultural Politics* 2, no. 1 (2006), 29–48.

Deegan, Mary Jo. *Jane Addams and the Men of the Chicago School, 1892–1918.* Chicago, IL: Transaction Press, 1988.

Domhoff, G. William. "The Ford Foundation in the Inner City: Forging an Alliance with Neighborhood Activists." *Who Rules America?* September, 2005. http://www2.ucsc.edu/whorulesamerica/local /ford_foundation.html.

Dowie, Mark. *American Foundations: An Investigative History.* Boston, MA: MIT Press, 2001.

Edwards, Michael. *Just Another Emperor: The Myths and Realities of Philanthrocapitalism.* London: Demos, 2008.

Emery, M., S. Fey, and C. B. Flora. "Using Community Capitals to Build Assets for Positive Community Change." *CD Practice* 13 (2006).

Emery, M., and C.B. Flora. "Spiraling-Up: Mapping Community Transformation with Community Capitals Framework." *Community Development* 37 (2006): 19–35.

Faber, Daniel R., and Deborah McCarthy, eds. *Foundations for Social Change: Critical Perspectives on Philanthropy and Popular Movements.* Lanham, MD: Rowman & Littlefield, 2005.

Ferguson, Karen. *Top Down: The Ford Foundation, Black Power, and the Reinvention of Racial Liberalism.* Philadelphia: University of Pennsylvania Press, 2013.

Ferris, James M., and Elizabeth Graddy. *Philanthropic Activity in California's Central Valley.* San Francisco, CA: James Irvine Foundation, 2004.

Ferris, James M., and Martha K. Sharp. *California Foundations: Trends & Patterns.* Los Angeles, CA: USC Center on Philanthropy and Public Policy, 2002. http://cppp.usc.edu/research/research-reports-papers/.

Finks, David P. *The Radical Vision of Saul Alinsky.* New York: Paulist Press, 1984.

Flora, Cornelia Butler. "Democracy: Balancing Market, State and Civil Society." *Research in Rural Sociology and Development* 9 (2003): 89–102.

———. *Developing Indicators to Refine and Test a Theory of Equitable Change for Rural Communities of Interest and of Place.* Dallas, TX: National Rural Funders Collaborative, 2003–2004.

———. *Rural Community Economic Development Case Review.* Pittsburgh, CA: Claude Worthington Benedum Foundation, 2003–2004.

Foundation Center. *Focus on Poverty.* Report, New York, 2007. http://foundationcenter.org/focus/gpf/poverty/.

Fraser, Nancy, and Linda Gordon. "A Genealogy of 'Dependency': Tracing a Keyword of the US Welfare State." *Signs* 19 (1994): 309–36.

Freire, Paolo, Donald Macedo, and Henry Giroux. *The Politics of Education: Culture, Power, and Liberation.* New York: Continuum, 1985.

Frontline. *Rape in the Fields.* (Film.) 2013. www.pbs.org/wgbh/pages/frontline/rape-in-the-fields/.

Fukiyama, Francis. *Trust: The Social Virtues and the Creation of Prosperity.* Washington, DC: Free Press, 1995.

Gaines, Kevin K. *Uplifting the Race: Black Leadership, Politics, and Culture in the Twentieth Century.* Chapel Hill: University of North Carolina Press, 1996.

Galarza, Ernesto. *Merchants of Labor: The Mexican Bracero Story.* San Francisco, CA: Rosicrucian Press, 1964.

Ganz, Marshall. *Five Smooth Stones: Strategic Capacity in the Unionization of California Agriculture.* PhD dissertation, Harvard University, 2008.

Garcia, Matt. *From the Jaws of Victory: The Triumph and Tragedy of Cesar Chavez and the Farm Worker Movement.* Berkeley: University of California Press, 2012.

Garrow, David J. "Philanthropy and the Civil Rights Movement." Working paper, Center for the Study of Philanthropy, City University of New York, 1987.

Giagnoni, Sylvia. *Fields of Resistance: The Struggle of Florida's Farmworkers for Justice.* Chicago, IL: Haymarket Books, 2011.

Gilbert, Alan, and Peter Ward. "Community Action by the Urban Poor: Democratic Involvement, Community Self-Help or a Means of Social Control?" *World Development* 12 (1984): 769–82.

Gilmore, Ruth Wilson. "Forgotten Places and the Seeds of Grassroots Planning." In *Engaging Contradictions: Theory, Politics, and Methods of Activist Scholarship*, edited by Charles Hale, 31–61. Berkeley: University of California Press, 2008.

———. "In the Shadow of the Shadow State." In *The Revolution Will Not Be Funded*, edited by INCITE! Women of Color Against Violence, 41–52. Cambridge, MA: South End Press, 2007.

Goffman, Erving. *The Presentation of Self in Everyday Life*. New York: Anchor Books, 1959.

Goldman, Michael. *Imperial Nature*. New Haven, CT: Yale University Press, 2005.

Goldstein, Alyosha. *Poverty in Common*. Durham, NC: Duke University Press, 2012.

Graeber, David. *The Democracy Project: A History, a Crisis, a Movement*. New York: Spiegel and Grau, 2013.

Gramsci, Antonio. *Selections from the Prison Notebooks of Antonio Gramsci*. Edited by Quintin Hoare and Geoffrey Nowell Smith. New York: International, 1971.

Granovetter, Mark. "Economic Action and Social Structure: The Problem of Embeddedness." *American Journal of Sociology* 91 (1985): 481–510.

Great Valley Center. *Indicators Report: Economy and Quality of Life, Benchmark Statistical 'Indicators' of Great Central Valley's Social, Economic, & Environmental Conditions*. Modesto, CA: Great Valley Center, July 1999.

Griswold del Castillo, Richard, and Richard A. Garcia. *Cesar Chavez: A Triumph of Spirit*. Norman: University of Oklahoma Press. 1997.

Guthman, Julie. "Thinking Inside the Neoliberal Box: The Micro-Politics of Agro-Food Philanthropy." *Geoforum* 39 (2008): 1241–53.

Hall, Stuart. *The Hard Road to Renewal: Thatcherism and the Crisis of the Left*. New York: Verso, 1988.

Hall, Stuart. "Race, Articulation and Societies Structured in Dominance," in *Sociological Theories: Race and Colonialism* (Paris: UNESCO, 1980; reproduction, Oxford: Blackwell, 2001), 305–45.

Hamilton, Darrick, and Ngina Chiteji. "Wealth." In *Encyclopedia of Race and Racism*, 2nd ed., edited by Patrick Mason. New York: Macmillan Reference USA, 2013.

Harrington, Michael. *The Other America: Poverty in the United States.* New York: McMillan, 1964.

Helliwell, John F., and Robert D. Putnam. "Economic Growth and Social Capital in Italy." *Eastern Economic Journal* 21 (1995): 295–307.

Hellman, Judith Adler. *The World of Mexican Migrants: The Rock and the Hard Place.* New York: New Press, 2008.

Henton, Douglas. *Grassroots Leaders for a New Economy.* San Francisco, CA: Jossey-Bass, 1997.

Hock, Dee. *Birth of the Chaordic Age.* San Francisco, CA: Berrett-Koehler, 1999.

Holmes, Seth. *Fresh Fruit, Broken Bodies: Migrant Farmworkers in the United States.* Berkeley: University of California Press, 2013.

Holt-Gimenez, Eric, ed. *Food Movements Unite! Strategies to Transform Our Food System.* Oakland, CA: Food First Books, 2011.

Horton, Myles, Judith Kohl, and Herbert Kohl. *The Long Haul.* New York: Teachers College Press, 1997.

Hyatt, Susan Brin. "From Citizen to Volunteer: Neoliberal Governance and the Erasure of Poverty." In *The New Poverty Studies: The Ethnography of Power, Politics and Impoverished People in the United States,* edited by Judith Goode and Jeff Maskovsky, 201–35. New York: New York University Press, 2001.

Ilcan, Suzan, and Lynne Phillips. "Developmentalities and Calculative Practices: The Millennium Development Goals." *Antipode* 42 (2010): 844–74.

INCITE! Women of Color Against Violence, eds. *The Revolution Will Not Be Funded: Beyond the Non-Profit Industrial Complex.* Cambridge, MA: South End Press, 2007.

Jenkins, Craig. "Channeling Social Protest: Foundation Patronage of Contemporary Social Movements." In *Private Action and the Public Good,* edited by Walter W. Powell and Elisabeth S. Clemens, 202–16. New Haven, CT: Yale University Press, 1998.

Karim, Lamia. "Demystifying Micro-Credit: The Grameen Bank, NGOs, and Neoliberalism in Bangladesh." *Cultural Dynamics* 20 (2008): 5–29.

Katz, Michael. *The Undeserving Poor: America's Enduring Confrontation with Poverty.* Oxford: Oxford University Press, 2013.

Katz, Stanley N. "Assessment and General Education." *Liberal Education* 94, no. 3 (2008): 30–37.

———. "Reshaping US Public Education Policy." *Stanford Social Innovation Review,* Spring 2013. www.ssireview.org/articles/entry /reshaping_u.s._public_education_policy.

Kim, Peter, and Jeffrey Bradach. "Why More Nonprofits are Getting Bigger." *Stanford Social Innovation Review,* Spring 2012. www.ssireview .org/articles/entry/why_more_nonprofits_are_getting_bigger.

Kinsley, Michael ed. *Creative Capitalism: A Conversation with Bill Gates, Warren Buffet, and Other Economic Leaders.* New York: Simon and Schuster, 2008.

Klein, Naomi. *The Shock Doctrine: The Rise of Disaster Capitalism.* London: Picador, 2008.

Knight, Louise. *Citizen: Jane Addams and the Struggle for Democracy.* Chicago, IL: Chicago University Press, 2005.

Kohl, Erica. *The Program Officer: Negotiating the Politics of Philanthropy.* Working paper, Institute for the Study of Social Change, University of California, Berkeley, 2007.

Kornbluth, Jacob, director. *Inequality for All.* Film. Produced by Robert Reich. 2013.

Kothari, Uma. "Authority and Expertise: The Professionalisation of International Development and the Ordering of Dissent." *Antipode* 37 (2005): 425–46.

Kouzes, James M., and Barry Z. Posner. *The Leadership Challenge.* New York: Jossey-Bass, 1995.

LaClau, Ernesto. *Politics and Ideology in Marxist Theory: Capitalism, Fascism, Populism.* London: NLB, 1977.

Lagemann, Ellen Condliffe, ed. *Philanthropic Foundations: New Scholarship, New Possibilities.* Bloomington: Indiana University Press, 1999.

Landsberg, Bill E. "The Nonprofit Paradox: For-Profit Business Models in the Third Sector." *International Journal for Nonprofit Law* 6, no. 2 (2004).

Larner, Wendy, and David Craig. "After Neoliberalism? Community Activism and Local Partnerships in Aotearoa New Zealand." *Antipode* 37 (2005): 403–24.

La Via Campesina. "La Via Campesina Denounces Gates Foundation Purchase of Monsanto Company Shares." September 13, 2010. http://viacampesina.org/en/index.php/actions-and-events-mainmenu-26/stop-transnational-corporations-mainmenu-76/917-la-via-campesina-denounces-gates-foundation-purchase-of-monsanto-company-shares.

Lewis, Oscar. *Five Families: Mexican Case Studies in the Culture of Poverty.* New York: Basic Books, 1975 [1959].

Li, Tania. "Articulating Indigenous Identity in Indonesia: Resource Politics and the Tribal Slot," *Comparative Studies in Society and History,* 42 (2000): 149–79.

———. *The Will to Improve: Governmentality, Development, and the Practice of Politics.* Durham, NC: Duke University Press, 2007.

Light, Ken, and Melanie Light. *Valley of Shadows and Dreams.* Berkeley, CA: Heyday, 2012.

Linkon, Sherry. "Why the Food Justice Movement Matters." *Working-Class Perspectives,* July 25, 2011. http://workingclassstudies.wordpress.com/2011/07/25/why-the-food-justice-movement-matters/.

MacLeod, Gordon, and Mark Goodwin. "Space, Scale and State Strategy: Rethinking Urban and Regional Governance." *Progress in Human Geography* 23 (1999): 503–27.

Marris, Peter, and Martin Rein. *Dilemmas of Social Reform: Poverty and Community Action in the United States.* Chicago, IL: Aldine, 1973.

Martin, Phillip. *Promise Unfulfilled: Unions, Immigration, and the Farm Workers.* Ithaca, NY: Cornell University Press, 2003.

McLean, Chuck, and Carol Brouwer. *The Effect of the Economy on the Nonprofit Sector: An October 2012 Survey.* Guidestar, 2012. www.guidestar.org/ViewCmsFile.aspx?ContentID=4781.

McWilliams, Carey. *Factories in the Field: The Story of Migratory Farm Labor in California.* Berkeley: University of California Press, 2000 reprint (1939).

Medina, Jennifer. "Family Quarrel Imperils a Labor Leader's Legacy." *New York Times,* May 14, 2011.

Mitchel, Don. *The Lie of the Land.* Minneapolis: University of Minnesota Press, 1996.

Moeller, Kathryn. "Proving 'The Girl Effect': Corporate Knowledge Production and Educational Intervention." *International Journal of International Development* 33 (2013): 612–21.

Mohan, Giles. "Beyond Participation: Strategies for Deeper Empowerment." In *Participation: The New Tyranny?* edited by Bill Cooke and Uma Kothari. London: Zed Books, 2001.

Mollenkopf, John H. *The Contested City.* Princeton, NJ: Princeton University Press, 1983.

Morris, Aldon. *The Origins of the Civil Rights Movement.* New York: Free Press, 1986.

Morvaridi, Behrooz. "Capitalist Philanthropy and Hegemonic Partnerships." *Third World Quarterly* 33 (2012): 1191–1210.

Munro, Donald. "From the Arts to Activism, 'Esperanza and Luz' Tells a Tale of Hope for Mexican Farmworkers." *Fresno Bee,* April 17, 2009, 8.

Murray, Charles. *Losing Ground: American Social Policy, 1950–1980.* New York: Basic Books, 1984.

National Center for Farmworker Health. *Facts about Farmworkers.* www .ncfarmworkers.org/2012/06/united-states-farmworker-factsheet/.

O'Connor, Alice. "The Ford Foundation and Philanthropic Activism in the 1960s." In *Philanthropic Foundations: New Scholarship, New Possibilities,* edited by E. Lagemann, 169–94. Bloomington: Indiana University Press, 1999.

———. *Poverty Knowledge: Social Science, Social Policy, and the Poor in Twentieth-Century U.S. History.* Princeton, NJ: Princeton University Press, 2002.

———. "Swimming against the Tide: A Brief History of Federal Policy in Poor Communities." In *Urban Problems and Community Development,* edited by Ronald F. Ferguson and William T. Dickens, 77–137. Washington, DC: Brookings Institution, 1999.

Orleck, Annelise, and Lisa Gayle Hazirjiam. *The War on Poverty: A New Grassroots History 1964–1980*. Athens: University of Georgia Press, 2011.

Parachini, Larry, and Andrew Mott. *Strengthening Community Voices in Policy Reform: Community-based Monitoring, Learning and Action Strategies for an Era of Devolution and Change: A Special Report Developed for the Annie E. Casey Foundation*. Washington, DC: Center for Community Change, 1997.

Parmar, Inderjeet. *Foundations and the American Century: The Ford, Carnegie, and Rockefeller Foundations in the Rise of American Power*. New York: Columbia University Press, 2012.

Pawel, Miriam. *The Crusades of Cesar Chavez: A Biography*. New York: Bloomsbury Press. 2014.

———. "UFW: A Broken Contract; Decisions of Long Ago Shape the Union Today; In the late 1970s Cesar Chavez Grew Intent on Keeping Control." *Los Angeles Times*, January 10, 2006.

———. "UFW: A Broken Contract; Farmworkers Reap Little as Union Strays from Its Roots." *Los Angeles Times*, January 8, 2006.

———. "UFW: A Broken Contract; Former Chavez Ally Took His Own Path; Where Eliseo Medina Has Gone, Unions Have Grown." *Los Angeles Times*, January 11, 2006.

———. "UFW: A Broken Contract; Linked Charities Bank on the Chavez Name; The Union-Related Philanthropies Enrich One Another, Operating Like a Family Business." *Los Angeles Times*, January 9, 2006.

———. *The Union of Their Dreams: Power, Hope, and Struggle in Cesar Chavez's Farm Worker Movement*. New York: Bloomsbury, 2009.

Peet, Richard. *The Unholy Trinity: The IMF, World Bank, and WTO*. Bloomington, IN: Zed Press, 2003.

Petras, James. "NGOs: In the Service of Imperialism." *Journal of Contemporary Asia* 29 (1999): 429–40.

Petsod, Daranee, ed. *Investing in Our Communities: Strategies for Immigrant Integration—A Toolkit for Grantmakers*. Sebastapol, CA: Grantmakers Concerned with Immigrants and Refugees, 2007. www.gcir.org /publications/toolkit.

Picketty, Thomas. *Capital in the Twentieth Century*. New York: Harvard University Press, 2014.

Piven, Frances Fox, and Richard Cloward. *Poor People's Movements: Why They Succeed, How They Fail.* New York: Vintage Books, 1978.

Pollan, Michael. *In Defense of Food: An Eater's Manifesto.* New York: Penguin, 2009.

———. *The Omnivore's Dilemma: A Natural History of Four Meals.* New York: Penguin, 2006.

Prahaland, C. K. *The Fortune at the Bottom of the Pyramid.* Upper Saddle River, NJ: Wharton School Publishing, 2005.

Putnam, Robert. *Bowling Alone: The Collapse and Revival of American Community.* New York: Simon and Schuster, 2000.

———. "The Prosperous Community: Social Capital and Public Life." *American Prospect* 13, (1993, spring): 35–42.

Reckhow, Sarah. *Follow the Money: How Foundation Dollars Change Public School Politics.* New York: Oxford University Press, 2012.

———. *Supercapitalism: The Transformation of Business, Democracy, and Everyday Life.* New York: Vintage Books/Random House, 2007.

———. "Why the Rich are Getting Richer, and the Poor, Poorer." In *The Way Class Works: Readings on School, Family, and the Economy,* edited by Lois Weis, 13–24. New York: Routledge, 2007.

Robbins, Kevin C. "The Nonprofit Sector in Historical Perspective: Traditions of Philanthropy in the West." In *The Non-Profit Sector: A Research Handbook,* 2nd ed., edited by Walter W. Powell and Richard Steinberg, 13–29. New Haven, CT: Yale University Press, 2006.

Rodriguez, Dylan. "The Political Logic of the Non-Profit Industrial Complex." In *The Revolution Will Not Be Funded: Beyond the Non-Profit Industrial Complex,* edited by INCITE!, Women of Color Against Violence Cambridge, 21–40. Cambridge, MA: South End Press, 2007.

Roelofs, Joan. *Foundations and Public Policy: The Mask of Pluralism.* Albany: State University of New York Press, 2003.

Rosenberg Foundation. *1965 Annual Report.* San Francisco, CA: Rosenberg Foundation, 1965. www.rosenbergfound.org/sites/default /files/1965.pdf.

———. *1978 Annual Report.* San Francisco, CA: Rosenberg Foundation, 1978. www.cybergrants.com/rosenberg/reports/1978.pdf.

Rothenberg, Daniel. *With These Hands: The Hidden World of Migrant Farm Workers Today.* San Diego, CA: Harcourt Brace, 1998.

Rowan, Jamin Creed. "Sidewalk Narratives, Tenement Narratives: Seeing Urban Renewal through the Settlement Movement." *Journal of Urban History* 39 (2013): 392–410.

———. *Poverty Capital: Microfinance and the Making of Development.* New York: Routledge, 2010.

———. "Praxis in the Time of Empire." *Planning Theory* 5 (2005): 7–29.

Roy, Ananya, and Emma Shaw Crane. *Territories of Poverty.* Athens: University of Georgia Press, forthcoming.

Rural Migration News. "UFW: Gallo, Bear Creek." *Rural Migration News* 6, no. 4 (2000). https://migration.ucdavis.edu/rmn/more.php?id=470_0_3_0.

Sachs, Jeffrey D. *The Price of Civilization: Reawakening American Virtue and Prosperity.* New York: Random House, 2011.

Salamon, Lester M., ed. *The State of Nonprofit America.* 2nd ed. Washington, DC: Brookings Institution Press, 2012.

Saltman, K. *The Gift of Education: Public Education and Venture Philanthropy.* New York: Palgrave Macmillan, 2010.

Scott, Janelle. "The Politics of Venture Philanthropy in Charter School Policy and Advocacy." *Educational Policy* 23, no. 1 (2009): 106–36.

Shaw, Randy. *Beyond the Fields: Cesar Chavez, the UFW, and the Struggle for Justice in the 21st Century.* Berkeley: University of California Press, 2008.

Silver, Ira. "Living Up to the Promise of Collaboration: Foundations and Community Organizations as Partners in the Revitalization of Poor Neighborhoods." In *Foundations for Social Change: Critical Perspectives on Philanthropy and Popular Movements,* 225–44. New York: Rowman and Littlefield, 2005.

Smith, Andrea. "Introduction: The Revolution Will Not Be Funded." In *The Revolution Will Not Be Funded,* edited by INCITE! Women of Color Against Violence, 41–52. Cambridge, MA: South End Press, 2007.

Srinivas, Nidhi. "The Possibilities of the Past: Two Routes to a Past and What They Tell Us." *Management and Organizational History* 7, no. 3 (2012): 237–49.

Steinbeck, John. *The Harvest Gypsies: On the Road to the Grapes of Wrath.* Berkeley, CA: Heyday Books, 1988.

Stiglitz, Joseph E. *The Price of Inequality: How Today's Divided Society Endangers Our Future.* New York: W. W. Norton, 2012.

Strike Debt. *The Debt Resisters' Operations Manual.* New York: Occupy Wall Street, 2012. http://strikedebt.org/The-Debt-Resistors-Operations-Manual.pdf.

Strom, Stephanie. "Foundations Find Benefits in Facing Up to Failures." *New York Times,* July 26, 2007. www.nytimes.com/2007/07/26 /us/26foundation.html.

Taibbi, Matt. *The Divide: American Injustice in the Age of the Wealth Gap.* New York: Speigel and Grau, 2014.

Taylor, J. Edward, and Philip L. Martin. "The New Rural Poverty: Central Valley Evolving into Patchwork of Poverty and Prosperity." *California Agriculture* 54 (2000): 26–32.

Tywoniak, Frances Esquibel, and Mario T. Garcia. *Migrant Daughter: Coming of Age as a Mexican American Woman.* Berkeley: University of California Press, 2000.

Umoja, Akinyele Omowale. *We Will Shoot Back: Armed Resistance in the Mississippi Freedom Movement.* New York: New York University Press, 2013.

United Farm Workers. "UFW Foundation, Community Leaders Join National Immigration Reform Effort." Press release, Keene, CA, June 1, 2009.

U.S. Census Bureau. "Small Area Income and Poverty Estimates, 2010 Estimates, State and County Maps, State and County Maps, Data Tables & Highlights." www.census.gov/did/www/saipe/index.html.

Walker, Gary. *Midcourse Corrections to a Major Initiative: A Report on the James Irvine Foundations CORAL Experience.* San Francisco, CA: James Irvine Foundation, 2007. www.ccitoolsforfeds.org/doc /Midcourse_Corrections.pdf.

Walker, Richard. *The Conquest of Bread: 150 Years of Agribusiness in California.* New York: New Press, 2004.

Weber, Heloise. "The Imposition of a Global Development Architecture: The Example of Microcredit." *Review of International Studies* 28 (2002): 537–55.

Wells, Miriam, and Don Villarejo. "State Structures and Social Movement Strategies: The Shaping of Farm Labor Protections in California." *Politics & Society* 32 (2004): 291–326.

Williams, Raymond. *Marxism and Literature.* Oxford: Oxford University Press, 1977.

Wolch, Jennifer. *The Shadow State: Government and Voluntary Sector in Transition.* New York: Foundation Center, 1990.

Woolcock, Michael. "Social Capital and Economic Development: Toward a Theoretical Synthesis and Policy Framework." *Theory and Society* 27, no. 2 (1998): 151–208.

X, Malcolm, and Alex Haley. *The Autobiography of Malcolm X.* New York: Ballantine Books, 1992.

Ylvisaker, Paul. *Oral History.* New York: Ford Foundation Archives, 1973.

Zerzan, John. "Cesar Chavez and the Farm Workers: The New American Revolution – What Went Wrong?" *Politics & Society* 3, no. 1 (1972): 117–28.

Zunz, Oliver. *Philanthropy in America: A History.* Princeton, NJ: Princeton University Press, 2012.

INDEX